Fred Perry
An Autobiography

I would like to thank my friend Ron Atkin, the *Observer*'s tennis correspondent and Sports Journalist of the Year 1984, for all his encouragement and invaluable assistance in putting together this book when I needed it most.

Fred Perry

An Autobiography

Hutchinson

London Melbourne Sydney Auckland Johannesburg

Stanley Paul & Co. Ltd

An imprint of the Hutchinson Publishing Group

17–21 Conway Street, London W1P 6JD

Hutchinson Publishing Group (Australia) Pty Ltd
PO Box 496, 16–22 Church Street, Hawthorne, Melbourne, Victoria 3122

Hutchinson Group (NZ) Ltd
32–34 View Road, PO Box 40–086, Glenfield, Auckland 10

Hutchinson Group (SA) Pty Ltd
PO Box 337, Bergvlei 2012, South Africa

First published 1984

© Fred Perry 1984

Set in Linotron Baskerville

Printed and bound in Great Britain by Anchor Brendon Ltd,
Tiptree, Essex
Phototypeset by Tradespools Ltd, Frome, Somerset

ISBN 0 09 155300 8

*This book is dedicated to players and spectators alike,
and to the game of tennis, which has done so much for me*

Contents

Acknowledgements

For permission to reproduce copyright photographs, the publisher would like to thank Le-Roye Productions Ltd, Wide World Photos Inc., Sport & General Press Agency Ltd, *Tennis World*, United Press International (UK) and Keystone Press Agency Ltd.

The author and publisher would also particularly like to thank Arthur Cole and Angela Patmore for their tireless work during the production of this book.

A Little Bit of Luck

When the American magazine *Time* ran a cover picture of me back in 1934 it carried the caption, 'Fred Perry – a bloke needs a little bit of luck.' How right they were. That little bit of luck was what always seemed to give me a shove in the right direction at the start of my career.

Three strokes of good fortune helped to launch me as a tennis player. The first occurred at Wimbledon in 1930 when, as a twenty-one-year-old who was better known for table tennis achievements than lawn tennis skills, I happened to knock out the number four seed, an Italian count called Umberto de Morpurgo, right under the noses of a Lawn Tennis Association selection committee, just as they were meeting to fill the only remaining place in a British team to visit the Americas, North and South. I was chosen.

My second piece of luck was to be a member of the British Davis Cup team which in 1931 overcame years of indifferent performances to reach the Challenge Round – in those days the final – against France in Paris. We lost a gripping tie 3–2, but what I did against France brought me international recognition and was the key, especially in the United States, which opened many doors.

The third lucky stroke was winning the Davis Cup itself in 1933. That was when my career really took off, and by the time I paused for breath, looked around and decided to turn professional in 1936, I had won three Wimbledons, three US Championships, one French and one Australian title. No Englishman has ever won any of these titles since.

I must admit I never thought I'd live to see the day when a statue was put up to the son of a Labour MP inside the manicured grounds of Wimbledon. There will be few former members of the All England Club and the LTA revolving in their graves at the thought of such a tribute paid to the man they regarded as a rebel from the wrong side of the tennis tramlines.

I am, of course, bowled over by the All England Club's decision to commemorate the 50th anniversary of my first Wimbledon win in 1934 by renaming the Somerset Road entrance to the ground the Fred Perry Gates, and honouring me still further by erecting the statue, commissioned from the famous sculptor David Wynne. I can only compare it to the Football Association putting one up for Stanley Matthews at Wembley Stadium, and I'm thrilled to bits.

It shows how we have all mellowed over those fifty years from the days when some elements in the All England Club and the LTA looked down on me as a hot-headed, outspoken, tearaway rebel, not quite the class of chap they *really* wanted to see winning Wimbledon, even if he *was* English. I've mellowed, too. I think I'm very much a leopard who has changed his spots. Looking back fifty years later, I have to concede that I was sometimes a little brash and aggressive about what I regarded as the class-ridden set-up there. But at the time, a young man with my background was bound to feel that snobbery very keenly, and I still get angry about the shabby way I was treated when I won Wimbledon in 1934 – the first Englishman to do it for twenty-five years.

In those days there was no formal presentation of the championship trophy on court. You simply shook hands with your opponent, picked up your gear and walked back to the dressing room. I had beaten the Australian Jack Crawford, and I went for a long soak in the bath to ease my muscles and let the significance of it all sink in with the bathwater. I was the proudest bloke in a bathtub anywhere in England.

Suddenly, out in the dressing room, I overheard the distinctive voice of Brame Hillyard, Club committee man, talking to Crawford. 'Congratulations,' said Hillyard. 'This was one day when the best man didn't win.' I couldn't believe my ears. What about the two previous times I'd beaten him, in the finals of the US and Australian Championships?

Hillyard had brought a bottle of champagne into the dressing room and given it to Jack, whom I so clearly remember having beaten in straight sets not half an hour before. I leapt from the tub, rushed out and, sure enough, found Crawford holding the bottle. True, I hadn't been quite forgotten: there, draped over the back of my seat, was the official acknowledgement of my championship, an honorary All England Club member's tie.

10

Nobody said, 'Here's your tie, Fred. Welcome to the Club.' Nobody even said, 'Congratulations.' The tie was just dropped there for me to find when I came out of the bath. Instead of Fred J. Perry the champ, I felt like Fred J. Muggs the chimp. The Perry balloon was certainly deflated.

I don't think I've ever been so angry in my life. That stuck-up attitude hurt, it really did. All my paranoia about the old-school-tie brigade surfaced with a vengeance.

Still, apart from the time in 1936 when my membership was automatically rescinded when I turned professional, I never had another dispute with the Wimbledon authorities. And even then, I was quite prepared to abide by their decision because that was the rule in those days, when the word 'professional' sent a shiver through their portals.

All those hatchets have been buried now. To its great credit, Wimbledon has been a leader in bringing about change and improvement in the sport.

To me, Wimbledon is the greatest place in the world and Centre Court is the finest arena. There's a certain air of serenity about the place; quite matronly, in a way. It just sits there quietly, not making a fuss.

I have had a love affair with Wimbledon since the time I first stood on Centre Court in 1928 as a paying spectator. Whenever I walk through those gates with the insignia 'AELTC' I still get the sort of thrill I don't experience anywhere else in the tennis world.

When the All England Club moved to their present site from their old Worple Road ground in 1922 everybody told them the place would be a white elephant; they would never fill it. But Wimbledon is not just concrete and seats like Flushing Meadow, the home of the US Open and to my mind the worst by far of the Grand Slam tournament venues. Wimbledon is steeped in a special atmosphere. Wherever I appear, on radio or TV or giving lectures, I am always asked, particularly in America, 'Why is Wimbledon the best?'

This is what I tell them: tennis fans and players alike say they are going to the US Open or the French Open, the Australian Open or the US Indoor, the Chinese Open or whatever, but in Britain they simply say they're going to Wimbledon.

When you think of Wimbledon you don't think of it as a place on the map where the tournament happens to be played. You think of the tournament first and *then* you realize that Wimbledon happens to be a suburb of London! Wimbledon must be the only London suburb

11

known all over the world. Even the Americans, who possess most of the things that are biggest and best, are in awe of Wimbledon, which is why they call it, 'The Big W'.

In America there are always announcements in the sporting magazines from tennis players who have set up as coaches. How do they advertise themselves? Not as 'Former US Open player' or 'Former French Open competitor'; no – 'Former *Wimbledon* player'. That is an acknowledgement of its special place in tennis. There is an aura about Wimbledon, a touch of class. The Virginia creeper on the walls keeps the place looking so traditional, yet the way Wimbledon has expanded over the years, while still retaining that historic showpiece of a Centre Court, has given the greatest championship the best of both worlds.

Wimbledon has been the scene of my greatest triumphs. Yet it was the Wimbledon fortnight in 1983 that almost finished me off, were it not for a large dose of that luck I mentioned earlier.

Thanks to my fanaticism over fitness in my playing days and the fact that I have taken care of myself physically since then, I have spent remarkably little time out of commission. A fall at Madison Square Garden which shattered my elbow in 1942 and a back problem in 1978 were just about the only things that put me into hospital.

Apart from that, I had never been sick in my life, unless one counts the usual crop of tennis injuries. I was a gung-ho keep-going sort of fellow. Nothing bothered me, though I'd noticed in recent years that if I overexerted myself while giving a tennis demonstration I'd get a little out of breath.

So I thought nothing of it when I twisted my knee just before Christmas 1982 in Jamaica – I'd done that lots of times when I was playing. Except that this time I got a funny feeling below the joint and the bump turned red. The mark disappeared after a few days, but in January it showed up again, this time above the knee, as an angry blotch.

In May 1983 I went to Paris for the French Open and developed a dry cough, which persisted when I travelled over to England to cover Wimbledon for BBC radio. I didn't feel at all like driving up from my home in Rottingdean on the south coast to attend the annual dinner of the International Club in London on the Saturday before Wimbledon, but I felt I had to go because I had only missed one since 1936.

Then the following day my wife Bobby and I drove up to London again because some of the big boys from the Fred Perry Sportswear company in America were over in England and wanted to go to the

12

traditional pre-Wimbledon garden party at Hurlingham. On the way home I drove over a couple of traffic islands, but put it down to tiredness. It certainly wasn't because of drink, since I'm a virtual teetotaller.

On Monday I still felt lousy. I had a pain in my left side and thought I had suffered a cough fracture of a rib, or something like that. But I went to the first day of Wimbledon anyway – I love Wimbledon – though I was very uncomfortable sitting in the commentary box. I was late leaving that night because the fourth seed, Guillermo Vilas, had gone out in a long five-setter and we had to wait for interviews. I must have blacked out on the drive home to Rottingdean because I hit the kerb, burst a tyre on my car, and had to get my wife to pick me up.

After a sleepless night I had to send for the doctor. I still planned to be at Wimbledon for the start of the second day's play, but he ordered me to go for X-rays, and two hours later I was tucked up in a hospital bed. When I asked the radiologist, 'Which rib did I break?' he told me, 'You didn't break anything. It's like a foggy day in London in there.' They diagnosed pleurisy, but by the weekend I felt fine again and the doctors agreed to let me go home. I rang the BBC and told them I'd be back at work on Monday, 27 June.

That morning Bobby came to pick me up at about 10.30 a.m. and I thought I'd better take a bath before I left the hospital. The nurses had prepared a tub for me and I stepped into it. Suddenly I couldn't breathe. I felt as if I had a steel band clamped around my chest, and my only thought was to get the heck out of that bathroom as fast as I could. I crashed through the door, the nurses heard the commotion, grabbed me, and had me on oxygen inside a minute.

It seemed that a blood clot had formed from that bump on the knee in Jamaica the previous winter and it had been working its way up my body all this time before suddenly lodging in my lung. When it hit me I knew for some reason that I had to keep everything going; I didn't want to give in. I was talking like crazy and fluttering my fingers to prove I could still move them. I remember thinking at the time that I must have looked a bit like Liberace at the keyboard.

They told me later that doctors were treating me inside five minutes only because the attack happened on the hospital premises, and that's where I had my biggest slice of luck. If it had happened fifteen minutes later I would have been going home in a car. A few hours later I would have been in the commentary box at Wimbledon – in which case, I wouldn't be around to tell this, the story of my life.

13

I first saw the light of day on 18 May 1909 in Stockport, at 98 Carrington Road. My father Sam Perry was at that time a cotton spinner, though he held ambitions of a life in politics. My mother's name was Hannah, and I had – and still have – a sister, Edith, who is six years older than I am.

Stockport has been good to me. When I won Wimbledon in 1934 the borough honoured me by holding a public collection. The people gave so generously that I was presented by the Mayor of Stockport with a silver tea service, a replica of the Louis XIV gold service in Windsor Castle. They would have liked to copy the set in gold, but they couldn't get permission, so they did it in silver instead.

Because of my father's political activity with the Cooperative Party we stayed at Carrington Road only until I was two or three years old before moving to Bolton for an equally brief period. Then we moved on again to Wallasey, for my father had become secretary of the Cooperative Party, headquartered in Liverpool, where he had an office in the Liver Building.

My first memory of life in Wallasey was the burial of my maternal grandfather Birch, because my parents sent me out of the house while the arrangements were being made. Grandad Birch was the first older member of the family I was close to. We used to play draughts all the time and he was always pulling my leg about being a cheat!

I went to Wallasey Grammar School and was in a class of forty-five boys, all bright-eyed and well polished. A Scottish lady, Miss Byers, was our teacher. As a child in Wallasey I remembered living in a big house with a wide alleyway alongside it, deep front and back gardens, and a sweet shop which was a long walk away.

A few years back I was driving up to Hoylake to do a radio commentary for the BBC at a tournament there, so I thought I would make a pilgrimage along the way to have a look at our old home. Eventually I pulled up outside a tiny house, with a front garden about

14

four feet deep. The back garden was not much bigger, the broad alleyway of my childhood was just an entry, and the distant sweet shop was in fact right around the corner – and still in operation.

I knocked at the door of the house and, putting on my American accent, told the lady who answered that I had once lived there and would like to look around for old times' sake. She invited me in, and I was really surprised by how tiny it all was. How wise people are when they say, 'Never go back,' because it had once looked pretty grand to me. She asked me my name and when I told her she said, 'Oh, we know about you. Look here.' And as she pushed the front door closed, there, inside the doorway, was a plaque saying 'Fred Perry lived here'. Don't ask me why they put it *inside* the house!

The years I lived in Wallasey coincided roughly with the First World War and my outstanding recollection of the war, necessarily remote to a small schoolboy, was being given the day off school to go and welcome home the Mersey ferry boats *Royal Iris* and *Royal Daffodil*, which had taken part in the famous Zeebrugge Raid. Although it was great to be given the day off, the catch was that we were all handed Union Jacks and had to congregate on Merseyside and wave them furiously.

When my father was transferred to the Cooperative Party's London office we moved from Liverpool only a few days before it was bombed, setting up home at the new garden village of Brentham, at Ealing, West London. Although the war was by now in its latter stages, we suffered a couple of air raids in the area and once, on a Saturday morning, I was sent into a field with all the other children to lie beside a large Red Cross flag in case the 'dreaded Hun' should come chasing us.

For a year or so, until I was old enough to go to Ealing County School, I attended Drayton Green elementary school, and it was here that I met and made friends with Bernard Sunley, who was to become a very wealthy and important man and have a profound influence on my life.

Living at Brentham was paradise after the bleak streets of the North because everybody in the garden village had the use of the Brentham Institute and its cricket field, football pitch, tennis courts, bowling green and – an important thing for me – table tennis facilities. It was there that I first became interested in watching and playing sport, because it was all on the doorstep. It was a great place for a kid from the North.

I tried my hand at all the sports and found I was pretty useful at

15

most of them; I played inside-left for the Ealing County School football team. One of our masters was a fellow called Brooker, who used to play for Dulwich Hamlet, a great amateur team in those days. He was a hero of mine, or at least he was until one day our scheduled match was cancelled and it was decided that the school team should play the masters instead. I happened to get in the way of one of Mr Brooker's boots and went further than the ball. After that, I soon became disenchanted with football.

I used to play for the school cricket team, too, as wicket-keeper. I appreciated the big gloves you were allowed to wear for the job, since that hard ball didn't appeal to me. The thought of something like that coming for your legs at top speed didn't interest me all that much either, and I soon gave up cricket to concentrate on what I really preferred – individual sport as opposed to team effort.

Table tennis was what I enjoyed most. I hated homework and used to drive everybody in the house crazy because in the evenings I would push the kitchen table up against the wall, put up a net, and for hours on end hit the ball over the net and back off the wall. It was marvellous practice. Because the ball always came back I soon developed a good sense of rhythm and feeling for the game, and ever since those days I have been a firm believer that to succeed in all moving ball games, acquiring a sense of rhythm is half the battle. This 'home' table tennis stood me in good stead in my lawn tennis career because in both games the spins and the counterspins are the same, the flight of the ball is similar and so is the parabola of that flight. So table tennis was a good springboard.

Being self-taught, I learned to play table tennis in my own peculiar way. From the very first day I picked up a bat, I held it with the old hatchet grip rather than the approved penholder style. Later on, when I took up lawn tennis, I just transferred the grip to my new sport and never ever changed it.

After joining the local YMCA my table tennis improved no end and I didn't take much interest in the table-less variety until I was fifteen. That year, 1924, my father, who stood (on that occasion unsuccessfully) for Parliament in Stockport, took us all on holiday to Eastbourne yet again. Like many English families in those days, we used to go paddling down at the same resort year after year, though on reflection I suppose we were lucky to be able to afford a holiday at all.

One day I was late back for lunch and got a severe ticking off from my father, who wanted to know where the hell I had been. I told him I had wandered down to a big place in the middle of Eastbourne called

Devonshire Park, where there were people running around in smart white togs playing tennis. I liked the look of that set-up and in my precocious way said to my father, 'There are a lot of expensive cars at the tennis courts – do they belong to the people watching or the people playing?' When he told me, 'Most of them belong to the people playing,' Perry Junior formed a most promising impression of the game.

To help get me started on this new sporting craze my father gave me an old racket he had bought for five shillings. 'After all,' as he put it in an article in the *Sunday Chronicle* some years later, 'I was not a rich man.'

As soon as we got home from Eastbourne I was in action with my 'new' racket at the Brentham Institute, where there were plenty of courts, both hard and grass. If they were occupied I used to practise on the bowling greens until I was chased off. I also spent hours practising at home because our house had a big wall facing south and a greenhouse in front of it. I specialized in learning to volley over the greenhouse and on to the wall. My volley prospered better than the greenhouse, but this lone practice was invaluable in helping me to develop rhythm, feel and movement, just as it had done for table tennis.

I used to do the long walk to and from school four times a day, coming home for lunch, if I didn't get lost in those thick yellow fogs we used to have before London was made a smokeless zone. Occasionally, when the walking, the fog and the homework ganged up on me, I would play truant in the company of Bernard Sunley and Dudley Pope, a useful cricketer who became opening bat for Essex, so that I could get in some more work on my tennis.

We had a sort of syndicate. The other two used to throw or hit balls to me for a while, and when it was Dudley's turn we would bowl to him. Bernard wasn't too interested in sport and when it was his turn for a favour we used to load a wheelbarrow with horse manure, take it to the local residents and sell it for their gardens for half a crown. All the money went to Bernard. Eventually he saved up enough to buy a handcart and later, after he left school, a horse and cart. He went into the landscaping business and became one of Britain's best-known property developers and home builders.

In May 1926 came the General Strike. In those days the double-decker buses had stairs up the outside of the vehicle and the driver used to sit up-front in the open, with a tarpaulin tucked under his chin when it rained. In order to keep public transport running, police and

17

soldiers guarded the buses, standing alongside the drivers and enmeshed in chicken wire so they wouldn't get hurt when protesters threw stones at them. My father was heavily involved, of course, in his political role, but by then tennis was of much more importance to me than a strike.

My big ambitions were helped by a Brentham member called Jenkins, who was the dressing-room supervisor at Queens Club. He taught me a great deal about the amateur tennis set-up and advised me strongly to join a better-class club where the members looked as if they were going places. So I joined the Herga Club in Harrow, of which I am still a life member.

During my school holidays the following summer, I arrived with my tatty old racket and my do-it-yourself hatchet grip at the Middlesex Junior Championships, where I caused a small sensation by reaching the singles final and winning the doubles.

Encouraged by this progress, I entered the Wimbledon Junior Championships, again with my one racket. I think the occasion proved too much for the racket, which collapsed. So did I, beaten in the fourth round. But Cyril Eames, a Davis Cup player who had been watching my matches, was sufficiently interested in what he'd seen to give me a brand new racket.

Around this time I was generally a competent quarter-finalist in junior tournaments, until at the Herga Club I met the man who was to influence my tennis more than anyone else. His name was A. R. Summers, but his fatherly attitude earned him the nickname 'Pops'. A representative for the Slazenger sporting goods company, Pops wasn't a great player himself, but he certainly understood kids, and he was a master of court psychology.

Pops was one of the people behind the success of Betty Nuthall, the young 'find' of British tennis at that time. For some reason he took a liking to me, and that proved to be the turning point. From then on I didn't have to worry about rackets and equipment: Pops got me on the free list with his company, and subsequently I never played a big match without consulting him first.

He suggested I enter the annual schoolboys' tournament at Queens Club, and though I had always believed the competition was restricted to boys from public schools, my father and I read in a London evening paper an article by the Queens Club secretary denying this. So I entered.

As I arrived at Queens I was asked for my name and school. I told the commissionaire, 'Perry of Ealing.' 'I beg your pardon?' he said, so

I told him, 'Ealing County School.' 'Oh. We don't seem to have any assigned position for you.' So I said, 'Never mind, I'll change on the floor.' I didn't win that tournament either, but I did what I set out to do, which was to get into something I wasn't supposed to get into.

At Queens Club I saw the dressing-room supervisor, Mr Jenkins, the Brentham club member who had helped me join Herga. When I greeted him as 'Mr Jenkins' I was told by a rather pompous official that 'We don't address attendants like that here.' I replied that I had known Mr Jenkins much longer than I had known Queens and proposed to address him as I thought fit. I was a determined young cuss even then and was very conscious that I was regarded as being from the wrong side of the tracks.

I made up my mind early on that I wasn't going to let people tell me what to do or order me about. If they said, 'We would rather you didn't do that,' there was no problem; but if they gave me an outright prohibition then I would deliberately find a way round it. Bloody-mindedness was one of my specialities, and revenge was never against my principles either.

Another was that I never could abide coming second. If I lost a table tennis match I was very upset for a couple of days and was so embarrassed that I would stay away from my friends. If I lost a tennis match it was the end of the world.

There were excellent table tennis facilities at the Herga Club so my skills flourished in both sports. It was at table tennis, however, that I made the first breakthrough. I was chosen to play for England in the home internationals against Scotland, Wales and Ireland. I was only nineteen and played in the team with Adrian Haydon (Ann Haydon Jones's father) and a fellow called Charlie Bull, who later became a spin bowler for Kent.

I still hadn't won anything big in table tennis, so I was surprised to be chosen again by England for the world championship in Stockholm in 1928. This was the first time I had travelled abroad and it was a memorable trip because we nearly won the Swaythling Cup, the team championship. The following year I was nominated for the world championships again, to be held in Budapest, and this time I won the singles title.

I was world champion at twenty, so I decided to retire while I was still at the top. Tennis was becoming more important to me, though I still have the bat with which I won the world table tennis title. I only ever played the game seriously once after becoming world champion – in 1932 just after I had returned from a tennis trip to South Africa.

England had a match against Hungary at the Farringdon Hall in London and they wanted me to play. So I practised for three days beforehand and got a bad case of wrist tendon inflammation from working on my flick shot. After that I devoted myself to tennis.

I was much influenced by the comments of my father, who considered that table tennis was not only bad for my tennis but bad for my health, too: 'You play at night, under lights in a smoke-filled atmosphere and on Sunday mornings you look like death warmed up. You've won the world championship; what else is there to win? Why not concentrate on tennis? If you're going to be Jack of all trades, you can be master of none.' So I concentrated on tennis.

By now I had left school and was earning my living. My first job, thanks to my father, was with the tea department of the English and Scottish Joint Cooperative Wholesale Society in the Aldwych in London, opposite Bush House. I was a clerk, sitting on a high seat and working on ledgers, though I couldn't add up for all the tea in China.

The object was to undergo training there for a year or so before being sent to India or Ceylon to work on the tea plantations. But I decided a career as a planter was not for me; I didn't want to go abroad! Yet I've lived out of a suitcase ever since. I handed in my notice and went to work for Spaldings, the sporting goods company, an environment which was much closer to tennis, where I wanted to be.

My tennis quickly improved at the Herga Club and there I teamed up with Frank Wilde, who later toured Australia with me and became a Davis Cup player. I also joined Chiswick Park, a great club. The first time I walked into the clubhouse I noticed at the entrance a picture of the Doherty brothers, Laurie and Reggie, who won Wimbledon nine times between them. I remember admiring the portrait and thinking that it would be nice if one day I could get my picture up there alongside theirs, and when it eventually happened I was delighted. Even when I was champion, I never played a Queens Club tournament before Wimbledon because on the preceding Saturday I always represented Chiswick Park in the Middlesex Club competition.

It was at around this time that I first played for Middlesex and met another fine man who was to help me enormously. F. T. 'Skipper' Stowe was captain of the county side, which was full of promising youngsters. In fact, Harold Lee was the oldest – at the age of twenty-two.

Skipper Stowe, from the Cumberland Club, was probably the only man who could give me a friendly clip over the ear to emphasize a point and get away with it. I wouldn't appreciate it, but I would take it. He was a strict disciplinarian and made sure you knew you would be awarded your county colours only when *he* decided you deserved them. In fact, I had made my first overseas tour with the Lawn Tennis Association before Stowe decided to award me my Middlesex colours!

In 1929 I qualified for Wimbledon for the first time and got through two rounds before being beaten in four sets by John Olliff, one of my contemporaries from the other side of the fence – public school.

I was happy enough with my performance, but Pops Summers knew there was a long way to go yet before I could hope to reach my goal – being the best player in the country. He decided that my forehand, unorthodox and already clearly my best stroke, needed to be made more potent by taking the ball early in its bounce to give me a better chance of getting to the net and dominating the point from there.

Among present-day players, Jimmy Connors is expert at taking the ball early to put added pressure on his opponent. John McEnroe can do it, too – in fact, McEnroe can do just about anything he wants to with the ball; he has such uncanny control.

But in those days the only player who consistently hit an early ball was the Frenchman, Henri Cochet, one of the famous Four Musketeers. So I really modelled my game on his, with the eventual difference that, because I was bigger, stronger and faster, I hit the ball harder. I watched Cochet whenever I could and read everything I could about his style and his approach to the game. Of course, I didn't get all that many opportunities to see him as we were seldom in the same place, but I was able nevertheless to carry his methods a stage further than Cochet himself, for I studied him carefully and asked other players questions about his game.

I spent five and a half months in the autumn and winter of 1929–30 working at perfecting the early ball and I confess that sometimes I thought I would never manage to master it. At Herga and Chiswick Park there were relays of people just serving to my forehand and I would take a God-awful swipe at the ball as it came off the ground, almost on the half-volley. I think I broke more tennis club windows and was guilty of more air shots than anybody in Britain.

For hours and days and weeks I worked at it. It took me quite a while before I actually realized what I was trying to do, and to twig that you don't use the shot all the time but keep it up your sleeve for a special occasion – like a fast bowler in cricket – while employing the same racket motion as for a normal stroke.

Every time I tried to make the shot I would rush to the net as if I were trying to catch a bus, and for a long time I had trouble adjusting my balance once I got there. Then one magical Sunday morning we were playing a doubles at the Herga Club and my opponent served to my forehand. I just leaned into it and everything jelled. I almost decapitated the guy at the net and the shot dropped a couple of inches inside the baseline, a completely natural shot, perfection. 'My God, I've got it!' I said, and then Pops told me, 'Right, stop now. Go away for a week and don't even look at a tennis ball. But just keep telling yourself that you know how to take the early ball now, then come back here next Sunday.' He took this precaution so that, having finally learned how to hit the shot, I wouldn't get frustrated by missing a few. I went back to Herga the next Sunday – and I still had it.

That shot, executed with a short swing so that less can go wrong before you make contact, was to stand me in good stead many times, particularly at places like Forest Hills in New York, home of the US Championships, where the grass is tougher than at Wimbledon and the bounce less predictable. Taking the ball only six or seven inches after it had bounced didn't leave it as much time to deviate.

My exuberance at the progress I was making in tennis was shattered in January 1930 by the death of my mother through a nervous disease, which the doctors seemed to think had been brought on by the strain of being associated with my father's political life. It wasn't a long illness, but her death upset me very badly. Throughout my career I would never play on the anniversary of her death.

By the spring I had recovered enough to want to test my early-ball skills in the British Hard Courts Championship at Bournemouth, but in order to do so I had to obtain time off from my job at the Spaldings sports shop in Cheapside, where I was earning £4 a week and spending about £3 of it on tennis equipment. The head of the tennis department was E. T. Lamb, and because he wanted to go to Bournemouth himself to watch the tennis, I was refused leave of absence to play.

That was where my father stepped in. He had been brought up the hard way – a half-timer at the age of ten in a Stockport cotton mill on a salary of 1s. 6d. a week – and as he was to write later, 'I wanted my son, as do all parents, to have a better life than mine.' My father and Pops talked to me about what I wanted to do with my life and I reiterated that what I wanted to do most was play tennis. So my father told me to resign my job with Spaldings and that he would support me financially for a year, unless, of course, I made the grade sooner than that.

At Bournemouth I reached the final against the British number one, Bunny Austin. I had a match point against him, but eventually lost in five sets, which was particularly annoying. Losing hurt me anyway, but to lose after having held a match point was even more of a blow: something I just couldn't stomach. I mulled over the match for a long time, trying to figure out where I'd gone wrong and swearing to myself that it would never happen again. Unfortunately it did once or twice, but by and large you learn from your mistakes – that's what Pops Summers always taught me. Everybody was surprised that I had done as well as I had, but I felt I'd missed a great opportunity. If I had beaten Austin, I would have been there: I'd have made it. That would have been my breakthrough.

Pops Summers knew how I hated to lose, and he observed all this as we drove back to London in his car. Pops was a chain pipe-smoker. He had a tree of filled pipes in a chamois leather folder which lay beside him on the front seat, and from time to time he would replace a spent pipe in his pouch and put a fresh one in his mouth, smoking continuously. He looked at his downcast passenger, puffed thoughtfully on his pipe, and said, 'I'm glad you lost that match. It would have come too early for you. The public would have been expecting something brilliant every time you came on court. It will also keep the press off your back. I think you'll be ready by the end of the year.' For once, Pops was wrong. My breakthrough was to come less than three months later.

3   My First Big Break

In addition to being an MP, my father was an ardent temperance worker and a Wesleyan preacher, and to recruit me to his principles he offered me £100 if I didn't drink before I was twenty-one and another £100 if I didn't smoke. I lost the £100 offer on smoking because I took to a pipe, though I used to carry it around and fiddle with it more often than I smoked it. But I easily cashed in on the other policy. I had had an uncle who, years previously in one of his inebriated moments, had hung me upside down from a clothesline, which struck him as a huge joke. He eventually died of drink and that taught me a lasting lesson.

So in May 1930, on my twenty-first birthday, I was able to claim my £100. After that, despite the pressures and the parties, I very rarely drank – maybe a beer or a glass of white wine occasionally. I sipped champagne twice: after Britain beat France to win the Davis Cup in Paris in 1933, and when I won Wimbledon for the first time the following year. In Paris I was nicknamed Monsieur Limonade, because that was what I always used to call for when I was playing there. At parties I would drink ginger ale or lemonade because my ambition was to be the fittest man in my sport, which I eventually became, and you can't be that if you are burning the candle at both ends.

When I was playing Wimbledon I would never be found at a party until the tournament was over. I was always in bed at my father's home in Ealing by ten o'clock, with the phone off the hook so that I wouldn't be disturbed. My father was never given any cause to think he was wasting his investment in me.

In 1930, needing to qualify for Wimbledon again, I had to play the British circuit through the early summer, and my father was laying out at least £10 a week for my entrance fees, fares and hotel expenses, for which I am eternally grateful to him. I had a deep affection for him and a great respect for the way he had overcome poverty and lack of education to become a much-admired man, a union president at twenty-one and a JP before he was thirty, the youngest on the Stockport bench.

He was an excellent speaker, though a quietly spoken person. But if he said, 'I don't think you should do so-and-so,' I wouldn't argue. He would let me have my head up to a certain point, but was insistent that I shouldn't let anybody down. From the time I was old enough to answer the door I remember him saying that whoever called should be made to feel they were the very people I wanted to see, and treated accordingly. If anybody came into the house I was to stand up, hold out my hand and say, 'How do you do, pleased to meet you.' Father told me, 'If you do those two things, you and I will never get into a fight. But if we do get into a fight there is no possible way you can win.' So we never got into a fight.

I learned very quickly that if your father is a politician, the whole family is involved at election time, like it or not. The first election my father contested was in 1923 when Baldwin's Conservative government found itself in a minority and was replaced briefly the following year by the first-ever Labour government under Ramsay MacDonald.

My father, however, wasn't among the new MPs. He stood, along with another Labour candidate with the most un-Labour name of Sir Leo Chiozza-Money, for the two seats in the Stockport constituency. They came third behind the Liberals and the Conservatives – but ahead of another candidate, an Irishman who was in prison at the time and had fought the election from his cell.

In the 1929 election, however, Sam Perry got into MacDonald's second Labour government when he won Kettering, Northants, from the Conservative, Sir Mervyn Manningham-Buller. At that election I was actively involved in helping my father. We had a tough time of it because in that part of the country the hunting set flourished and Labour was a dirty word. Troublemakers would show up at meetings in dinner jackets, determined to have some fun from the back of the hall and shouting things like, 'Which flag do you stand for, Perry, the Red Flag or the Union Jack?'

It was a spread-out constituency, containing ninety-eight towns and villages, so we had to plan six or seven meetings a night. The dinner-jacketed hecklers and our other opponents would attempt to jostle and delay us at each one in the hope that by the time we got to the last – and biggest – meeting our supporters would have got fed up and gone home. So we decided to hire a few 'minders' to protect us, in the shape of chauffeurs provided by Joe Starmer, who ran a car-hire firm and garage in Kettering. His regulation was that all his drivers had to be useful with their fists, and on many a night they were obliged to use them in our defence as we battled our way between meetings.

There was one bodyguard, a Welshman called Jennings, who incidentally was a good amateur boxer, who used to take particular care of my mother and sister at these meetings. He would sit at the front of the hall and if anybody took it into his head to advance on the speakers, he would confront them, turn them around and politely suggest they return to their seats.

Joe Starmer, a former middleweight champion and Lonsdale belt-holder, was always there, too, and sometimes one of our hunt-set assailants would tell this ex-boxing champion, 'I've a jolly good mind to take you outside,' to which Joe would reply with a wistful expression, 'Oh, God, please do.' If anybody gave persistent trouble he would find himself dumped into a dustbin outside the hall.

By the time my father stood for re-election I had become fairly well known in the sporting world and his advisers wanted me to help with his campaign. So I came home a few days early from a tour of South Africa to find that my job was to go round the factories and kiss all the girls – not a bad assignment, and based on the assumption that we should go after the so-called 'Flapper' voters, newly enfranchised!

Father's constituency of Kettering was next to Northampton, which was held by Lord Burleigh, the former Olympic hurdler. I read in the paper one day that at a meeting he had run down the aisle and leapt on to the platform, in the words of the report, 'as only an athlete could'. As an athlete myself, I wasn't going to be outdone by this show of flamboyance. At my father's next meeting I sprinted down the aisle, only to find myself approaching an unusually high platform. I misjudged it and fell flat on my face.

After those experiences on the campaign trail – the politicians, the hecklers, kissing the babies and looking for the vote – I decided to steer clear of anything remotely political in the future. And I have never voted since.

It was only in later years, after my father had lost his parliamentary seat following his refusal to join Ramsay MacDonald in a national government, that I learned just how respected he was in the Labour movement. He was one of half a dozen prominent Socialists who chose to tour the country lecturing, preferring this to the seat he was offered in the House of Lords or to a job, at £5000 a year, as a member of the newly formed Transport Commission.

A few years ago Bobby and I rented an apartment at Marble Arch during Wimbledon. We used to keep our car at a garage across the street, and when I went to collect it one day there stood Lord George-Brown, complaining at the top of his voice that he had put only 500 miles on his new Jaguar and already it wasn't working. So, facetiously, I went over to him and said, 'At least you won't have to worry about the battery running flat. You don't need to use the hooter with all the noise you're making.' He looked at me and said, 'I know you. You're Sam Perry's son.' And he continued, 'He was a great man. You know, those six people who stomped around the country in the thirties did more for the Labour movement than anybody. Yet they begged him to go to the Lords.'

'That's right,' I said. 'But they didn't believe in that then, did they? Times have changed since then.'

He looked at me, grinned, and said, 'They certainly have.' Then he added, 'By the way, have you read my book? It's outselling Harold Wilson's by three to one.'

As I mentioned earlier, my first big break in tennis came at the 1930 Wimbledon Championships when, in the third round, I was drawn against an Italian baron and First World War air ace, Umberto de Morpurgo. That year Baron de Morpurgo was ranked fourth in the world behind Bill Tilden, Henri Cochet and Jean Borotra, and was also seeded fourth at the championships. He was a fiery competitor with a good forehand and although he wasn't a particularly good volleyer, nobody reckoned I had much of a chance. It seemed they were right when Morpurgo led 5–1 in the first set. But, driving the ball to the corners and charging the net, I saved a set point and eventually took the set 10–8.

By this time the Wimbledon 'bush telegraph' was at work and every inch of space around Court Three was filled. Most important for me, a committee of the Lawn Tennis Association was holding a selection meeting in a room at Wimbledon overlooking that court. They were choosing a four-man team to tour the United States that autumn and a mixed team to go to South America after that, and there was a place for one man still open.

The meeting was temporarily suspended as Morpurgo and I battled it out. He won the second set 6–4 to level the match, but my fitness and speed took me through the next two sets 6–1, 6–2 and, amid much excitement from the spectators, I pulled off a big upset.

That one vacant place on the touring team was promptly awarded to me, so I date the beginning of my tennis career from that day at Wimbledon in 1930.

My father was among the many people who came to the dressing room to congratulate me, and he recalled hearing an official tell me, 'Don't be surprised if you play terribly badly in the next match. You are bound to suffer a reaction.' As my father put it, 'It seemed to me undesirable to dampen confidence thus.'

That third-round win meant that on the first Saturday of Wimbledon I was to face Dr Colin Gregory, a Davis Cup player and later chairman of the All England Club, in the fourth round.

The tournament referee was F. R. Burrow, a little man who smoked cigars all the time and wore pince-nez. In those days nobody ever dreamed of sending for the referee to resolve on-court disputes, and if any trouble was ever reported to him, Burrow would send back a message: 'Complete the match and then come and see me.' He was a tough character and it would have been interesting to see how he would have handled today's outbursts at Wimbledon.

Burrow summoned me to his office on the Friday and when I arrived, wondering what the devil I'd done now, he told me he planned to put me on Centre Court for the first time in my match with Gregory. He knew I would be nervous about such an honour, so he told me, 'Come early tomorrow and I'll take you out there,' which was a very considerate gesture. So at about noon the following day we walked on to a deserted Centre Court and he told me to stroll around, throw a ball or two up in the air and generally get used to the atmosphere.

Nothing in the world can prepare you for the Centre Court. It is completely surrounded by a covered stand and once the ball goes up in the air you see it like a football because of the dark background. You think you've got all the time in the world to hit it, but this is one of the greatest pitfalls for anybody playing his first match there. The debutants are usually all over the place for a set and a half because their timing is wrong. You see, all tennis courts are 78 feet long, so when the server stands on the baseline and you're waiting to receive serve, on the other baseline or just behind it, you have 78 feet in which to see the ball and prepare to hit it. Now, on most of the courts on which we played there would be about 21 feet behind the court and about 17–18 feet on either side, at which points the stands would begin. At Wimbledon on the Centre Court, however, there is a runback of something like 30 feet to the wooden barrier where the

28

linesman sits; and behind that barrier is another space, about 20–25 feet, before you reach the covered stand. Even then, the sea of faces is not in direct sunlight, but subdued light. So when the ball is tossed up by the server above the level of the backstop, you can see it clearly enough, but it seems to be about a hundred miles away. In reality, of course, it is *still* only 78 feet away, but you think you have more time than you actually do. This is why so many inexperienced players on Centre Court suffer from so-called 'Centre Courtitis' and can't hit their hats until their eyes get used to the puzzling conditions.

Their problems are compounded by the fact that inexperienced players are often pitted on Centre Court against name players, and have a different approach to the ball. In general, a lesser player runs to a ball and then swings and hits it. The class player doesn't do that; he brings his racket back as he moves. The trick is not to run to a ball and hit it, but to run to a place from which you can conveniently reach out for an anticipated return. There's a hell of a difference.

It's for these reasons that you see so many qualifiers or players who have just managed to make the draw facing a seeded player on Centre Court and being made to look terrible. They simply cannot get their timing right.

One recent example of this came in the famous 'boycott year' of 1973 when Sandy Mayer, having knocked out the favourite Ilie Nastase in the quarter-finals, was put on Centre Court for his semi-final; he didn't manage to hit a decent ball for about a set and a half.

To me the Centre Court is the greatest place in the world and from the word 'play' it suited me right down to the ground. On the day of that fourth-round match in 1930 I was confident, I was poised, I was playing well against Gregory – and then the King turned up.

King George V made one of his rare visits to Wimbledon that day, so the match was stopped while we bowed to him. And after that my game was up and down like a fiddler's elbow. I had been winning until the King's arrival, but then I started to do badly. When the royal party got up to go for tea I began to do better, but when they came back again that was curtains for Perry. I lost in five sets. I suppose you could put it down to nervousness and inexperience. I hadn't been around long enough to be able to handle that sort of thing. So that was the end of my Wimbledon ambitions for 1930, but by no means the end of an exciting fortnight or what was to be a memorable year.

Bill Tilden, who won the championship that year, as he had done in 1920 and 1921, came over to me in the dressing room later and said,

'My name's Tilden, William Taten Tilden the Second. Call me Bill. They tell me you're going to be a very good tennis player. I shall watch you with interest.' What a wonderful thing! I was so proud that I went home and told my father all about it.

The match with Baron de Morpurgo and my subsequent selection to the touring teams relieved my father of the need for any further financial sacrifice on my behalf and he was a happy man when he called on the Lawn Tennis Association's secretary, Anthony Sabelli, to discuss arrangements for the tour. When my father handed over my passport Sabelli expressed astonishment that when it was first issued in 1928 for my table tennis trip to Sweden my height was given as 5 feet 3 inches. In the two years since then I had shot up another nine inches. My father had told me that swimming would extend my capacities!

We boarded the *Mauretania* at Southampton for our journey to the United States, and I was so proud of my white team blazer with the Union Jack crest and crossed rackets that I almost wore it to bed. The captain of our team, which included John Olliff and Harold Lee, was Leslie Godfree, husband of Kitty Godfree who, as Kitty McKane, had won the Wimbledon women's singles in 1924. I had early cause to be thankful to Leslie Godfree for his no-nonsense and common sense approach to my inclusion in the squad at the age of twenty-one, considered tender years for a British overseas team player in those days.

After our first lunch on board, Godfree told me to unpack and then join him in his cabin for tea. There he reminded me that we would be playing in half a dozen tournaments during our American tour and gave me the following advice:

We don't expect you to win one round even. You're here to learn and the others are here to help you.

You are part of a family, not a loner [he was wrong there, because a loner was exactly what I was]. If you get knocked out in the first round, as we anticipate, I want to see you watching our matches and practising every day, otherwise you *will* be in trouble.

As captain of this team I represent the LTA, and while you're on tour you will respect and adhere to the regulations laid down about dress and deportment on and off court.

That last comment worried me because, given half a chance, I was a bit of a firebrand when it came to arguing with linesmen and bashing balls angrily about the court. Godfree continued, 'If you want to have it your own way you'll be on the next boat back to England and you will never play for your country again.' At my age, with a five-and-a-half-month tour ahead of me, that was just the sort of straight talk I needed. Full of cheek, I remember requesting to know when this new ruling started. I was told, 'It just did.' From then on, everything was shipshape and bristol-fashion in the behaviour department.

As a young man going off on my first tour I was glad to have the protection of the team. Today the kids are thrown in at the deep end on their own. They may be making a fortune at eighteen or nineteen, but some of them have no idea what's going on and can make enemies easily.

What a thrill it was to be travelling on one of those floating cities called transatlantic liners. The Age of Speed competition was just under way in 1930, and that year the German liner *Europa* gained the blue riband for the fastest Atlantic crossing. (On a more sinister note, the Germans launched their first pocket battleship *Deutschland* less than a year later.) When I stepped ashore in the United States for the first time, little realizing that only eight years later it would become my home country, I was overwhelmed by the speed and hustle and dash of everything in New York.

I didn't win many matches on that first visit to the States, but I certainly played a lot. I used to run around pleading with Americans to practise with me or, if that didn't register, asking if they wanted to 'hit some'. But that tour changed my game and my attitude. I matured a lot, my game started to jell, and the backhand on which I had been working so hard started to get better.

I managed to get to the last sixteen in the US National Championships and it was also at Forest Hills, in an England *v.* USA match, that I first met Ellsworth Vines, whose career was to run parallel to my own for so long in later years.

After the American tour there were a couple of weeks to spare before Harold Lee and I were due to join up with Eric Peters, Phoebe Watson and Ermintrude Harvey to go to Argentina, Chile and Uruguay, so we were set to play in Brazil, sailing aboard the *Northern Prince*.

The LTA had made arrangements for Lee and I to represent Britain in a match against Brazil at the Fluminense Club in Rio de Janeiro, and after winning that match we set off to spend the second week of our stay in São Paulo. There was a revolution going on in that part of the country at the time, and the rebels weren't very far away from São Paulo. All lines of communication were down and neither the LTA nor our families knew exactly where we were. The rest of the team to tour South America were supposed to meet us in the port of Santos, but we had no way of contacting them either.

The Chief of Police in São Paulo sent for us and told us we were being taken into protective custody for our own safety. The proposed matches were cancelled anyway, but we were told it was all right for us to practise if we wanted to, under a police guard against the possibility of kidnapping. He ended by saying he wanted to give us one little piece of advice. If somebody pointed a gun at us we shouldn't worry because there was no way he would hit us. But if he started shooting at somebody else we should duck quickly!

On the day we were supposed to travel to Santos we were taken to the station by the army and put on an armoured train with a number of other travellers, and eventually we pulled up safely alongside our ship, with Eric Peters peering over the side and thanking God we had made it.

Things were a little quieter after that excitement in Brazil, but not much. We went to Chile first and at Vina del Mar there had been an earthquake shortly before our arrival. There were huge cracks in the court so we spent our time trying to hit the ball into them.

In Argentina I won my first national championship, beating Eric Peters in the final without losing a set on the way. Over the preceding few months I had played, practised, watched senior squad members and asked for advice, and now it was all paying off. I wrote home to my father and told him I had 'put 15' on my game.

But I didn't get away from South America completely unscathed. In Uruguay, after our match, we had a reception to attend. We packed, put on our dinner jackets, and sent on our luggage to the ship as we were due to go straight there from the dinner.

At the reception they served lobster, which I had never had before. As a result they had to carry me out of the dinner and I didn't leave the cabin once on the journey home. After suffering this fearsome lobster attack I was advised to give all shellfish a wide berth in future because I was clearly allergic to it, and I have done my best to comply. I've never had it since, except in Jamaica five years ago. I went to a dinner party where they were serving Hungarian goulash. Nothing fishy about that, I thought. But somebody in the kitchen had decided to pep up the goulash with a few oysters. I took four or five mouthfuls of the stuff and I was rolling on the floor again within half an hour.

4   Meeting the Musketeers

By 1931 public interest in the Davis Cup, the international team championship which dated back to the beginning of the century, was at rock-bottom in Britain. Since winning the trophy in 1912 Britain had achieved little, although we had managed to reach the European Zone final against Germany.

France's Four Musketeers – René Lacoste, Jean Borotra, Henri Cochet and 'Toto' Brugnon – had wrested the Cup so firmly from American domination that the massive, solid-silver punchbowl which was the emblem of the world team championship of tennis had been safely in Paris for the last four years and looked like remaining there for some time to come.

Delighted though I was at being chosen for the 1931 season of Davis Cup campaigning, I never dreamed that I might end up that summer battling against those very Musketeers in the final. But our finest doubles combination, Dr Colin Gregory and Ian Collins, declared themselves unavailable for business reasons, while Harold Lee, my companion on the trip to South America who had spent every evening of his voyage from the United States to Brazil studying for his accountancy exams, was now preparing to take those exams, which in his opinion came before tennis.

Perhaps it was the withdrawal of these three that opened the way for me to join the squad, but I liked to think that my steady improvement as a 'team man' on that recent five-and-a-half-month tour had had something to do with it. Other members of the British team were Bunny Austin, Charles Kingsley and Pat Hughes, who, like me, came from a non-public school background and with whom I got on well both on and off the court. The non-playing captain was H. Roper Barrett, a Wimbledon singles finalist in 1909 and doubles champion there on three occasions just before the First World War.

Roper Barrett was a real character. He used to sit at the courtside with his hands crossed gravely over the handle of his walking stick. He

33

was a strict disciplinarian who was none too highly regarded by the All England Club after he and his 1909 championship partner Arthur Gore had played a first-round doubles match against the Duke of York and the Club chairman, Wg. Cdr. Sir Louis Greig. Perhaps forgetting the distinguished nature of the opposition, Barrett and Gore severely trounced them. It was rumoured the Duke was so angry and upset that he swore he would never come to Wimbledon again – and I don't think he ever did.

The squad got off to a gentle start (with me playing the second singles position), winning 5–0 in Plymouth against Monaco. Next we went to Brussels, where again we marked up a 5–0 win over Belgium, but neither Austin nor I did as well as we had hoped in the French Championships which followed the Brussels tie. Austin injured an ankle and I went out early to the ambidextrous Italian Giorgio de Stefani.

De Stefani beat me several times because his type of game intrigued me. He hit anything on his right-hand side with his right hand and anything down the left-hand side with his left hand. He couldn't volley because of the long swing he took at the ball, but he could keep a rally going for ever and was tough to beat from the baseline.

At that time I still didn't know enough to sit and wait such people out. In Paris I tried to catch him with his racket moving from one hand to the other, but by the time I realized his left hand knew exactly what his right hand was doing, I was two sets down. De Stefani always gave me trouble.

After Paris we switched back from a hard surface to the grass of Eastbourne, where I had first peeped over the wall of Devonshire Park seven years previously, to play South Africa in another Davis Cup tie. Again we won 5–0, and when the Japanese came to Eastbourne the following week we routed them 5–0, too. I delighted myself by beating their number one Jiro Satoh, who was always a menace, even to the world's best players. So Britain was in the European Zone final without having lost a single rubber. It seemed a happy augury for some British successes at Wimbledon.

This was not to be, however. Austin went out in the quarter-finals to the American Frank Shields after holding a match point, while I lost in the semis to Sidney Wood in four sets. If only I had managed to beat Wood I would have been champion at Wimbledon that year without needing to hit another ball, because the other finalist, Shields, defaulted with a sprained ankle.

My Wimbledon that year was spoiled by a senseless succession of malicious practical jokes played on me. Shoes, trousers and suits were mysteriously ordered in my name and delivered to the All England Club. My own things disappeared. One day, without my knowledge or permission, I arrived at Wimbledon to find most of my white flannels had been removed for cleaning, and I allowed all this to prey on my mind and affect my play.

Our next Davis Cup match was against Czechoslovakia, in Prague, which involved changing back again from grass to hard courts, with only a week – including travelling – to get accustomed to the vastly different playing surface.

The Czechs' biggest hope, literally, was the 6 feet 3 inch Roderick Menzel, who possessed a high-kicking service. He hit the ball very hard, but was erratic and also vulnerable because he was liable to go off at the deep end. An aspiring poet and a real personality, Menzel later became a great friend of mine. Once he was playing a tournament in Los Angeles and his match was scheduled for noon, which didn't accord with his eating habits. In the middle of the match he suddenly sent for coffee and a sandwich, and had his lunch where he stood.

Austin got us off to another great start against Czechoslovakia, beating Menzel in five sets. I won both my singles and we took the tie 4–1, so we were through to the Inter-Zone final against the Americans. The tie was being played in Paris, with the winning team earning the right to take on the champion nation, France, in the Challenge Round. On paper it seemed as if we had no chance, especially after those Wimbledon results, but I was confident. The Americans have never been able to master the slow, red clay of the Roland Garros Stadium. Even nowadays, players like McEnroe and Connors, champions elsewhere, can't win the French Open. The rallies are interminable and you have to discipline yourself to stay out there, whereas the Americans are accustomed to cannonball serving and top-speed tennis.

Even so, Britain's chances looked slim by the end of the second day. Austin began by beating Sidney Wood, but I lost to Frank Shields; then Pat Hughes and I were beaten by George Lott and Johnny Van Ryn in the doubles. On that Saturday night, one down and two to play, I don't think many people back in Britain were exactly on tenterhooks.

To keep us alive I *had* to beat Wood, my Wimbledon conqueror and the current champion. He was one of Bill Tilden's protégés, a very gifted player, who had every shot in the book and, strange thing, used to play in plus fours. I don't know why he never made it right to the top, with all that material. Perhaps it was *because* he was one of Tilden's protégés; most of them were great for a little while, then petered out. Looking back over the years on my friendship with Sidney Wood, I think he lacked the necessary drive to be a great champion. He suffered lapses of concentration when he just wasn't hungry enough to punish himself any more – as a champion has to do. I don't think defeat was a big enough disaster for Wood.

After much effort and hard running I managed to take the match against an opponent who, I felt, was still a little demoralized by his loss to Austin two days earlier.

Now it all depended on the Austin-Shields match, and Austin came through in straight sets in that neat, copybook, flawless style of his. We returned to our headquarters, the Crillon Hotel, to be greeted by a deluge of telegrams and messages of congratulation.

Perhaps the Americans paid the price of overconfidence. It certainly seemed that way when we heard they had booked their passage back to the United States on a ship which was due to sail *after* the completion of the Challenge Round. It was understandable, however, because since 1919 they hadn't once failed to reach the final round of the Davis Cup.

Away-ties in the Davis Cup have always been an added strain for the players because of the problems caused by chauvinistic officials and linesmen. Before we played the Americans, Roper Barrett told us the French had come to him and said he should have no worries about the line-calling in the Inter-Zone final. But the Challenge Round against France in Paris? That was different. When we played away in the Davis Cup we always used to say that our side of the court was very wide and theirs narrowed to a point!

The Musketeers had held the Cup for France since 1927, and of that famous four, Lacoste was the only one I never played. Known as 'The Crocodile' (the symbol of his sportswear company), Lacoste was never a well man and retired early. Even today, in the heat of the French Open, René will don a hat, coat and scarf at about four o'clock in the afternoon, when he goes to watch the tennis.

Borotra and Cochet were to be my singles opponents in that Challenge Round and I had made a point of studying both of them. Before I played Borotra for the very first time, in the International Club match between England and France which always used to precede the French Championships, Pat Hughes told me I would have to watch out for a lot of tricks from the 'Bounding Basque', the great crowd-pleaser. He warned me: 'Borotra will take out three or four berets with him and after a couple of games will go over to the umpire's chair, select one and put it on, which always gets the crowd buzzing. Then, early in the match he will put up a very simple lob to you. You smash it one way and he will bound the other way, right over the barrier and in among the spectators, usually on to a woman's lap. He gets big applause and a big laugh for that one!'

So I told Pat I had a few ideas of my own to combat that sort of thing. We knew the owner of an *haute couture* place on the Rue Royale, so I dropped round there and asked him if one of his models could come to the championships with me that afternoon.

The girl's name was Hélène Raillaire, and I remember her well, not just because of this little story, but because, sadly, she was later shot by the Germans during the Second World War as a member of the French Resistance. She was a stunning-looking girl. We decked her out in a big hat and sat her right next to the court, opposite the baseline. In the very first game I put up an easy lob which Borotra smashed into the corner. As he hit it, I took off in the opposite direction, over the wall and on to Hélène's lap. She gave me a big red lipstick kiss and the place was in uproar.

Later, with the score at 2–2 and as I was getting ready to serve, Borotra – really worried by now – said, 'Excuse me a moment,' and went to put on a beret. When he walked back and indicated he was ready to carry on, I said, 'Excuse me,' and went over to the umpire's chair myself. For the occasion I had chosen a particularly natty white tennis cap with a big peak on it.

I got a heck of a rocket from the LTA, but, as I told them, I didn't believe in going out on court to come second, even in the gamesmanship stakes. I think that was a sobering experience for Borotra because he never managed to beat me.

On the first day of that 1931 Challenge Round Cochet was too good for Austin over four sets, but I levelled the tie by beating Borotra in five, literally seconds before a thunderstorm broke over the Roland Garros Stadium.

Since my five sets with Borotra had worn me out, Roper Barrett decided to rest me from the next day's doubles and to partner Charles Kingsley with Pat Hughes instead. Although Kingsley had travelled everywhere with the team that season, he had not played in the Davis Cup since the first-round tie against Monaco, when he deputized for me on the last day after I strained a shoulder. That lack of match tightness was clearly a handicap against such a well-integrated pair as

Cochet and Brugnon, who won in four sets. That meant that on the last day we needed both singles to pull off an upset.

While Austin and Borotra battled it out, Cochet and I sat in the dressing room after massage, listening to the stamping and shouting of the crowd in the stands like another thunderstorm over our heads. I didn't watch a single ball played in that match because I have always believed that it's stupid to watch tennis when you are about to play it – at that level of competition at any rate. If you do watch it, you do so from ground level and from the back of the court, which is the position you're going to play from.

So I sat and sipped tea, trying to estimate how the match was going from the reactions of the French spectators. Twice – once during a break for rain and then at the ten-minute rest period at the end of the third set – the two players and their followers crowded into the dressing room.

Eventually I heard a huge cry and, above the tumult, the name of 'Austin'. He had beaten Borotra in four sets. The tie was now level and it was all down to the final rubber between me and Cochet, the man I admired so much, the man whose early ball I had made part of my game. For me, facing Cochet across a net was almost like looking in a mirror, apart from our physical differences. Our style and strokes were so similar that we each knew well enough what to expect from the other.

My father, who had been brought to Paris by the LTA, was among the packed crowds that day, and though I had been tight and nervous during that interminable wait in the dressing room, my nervousness vanished as soon as I got on to the court as it nearly always did. There was nothing wrong with my determination either, but that day, a rainy day in Paris, Henri Cochet sure as hell outsmarted me.

After leading 4–1, I lost the next five games and the first set. I took an even bigger lead in the second set, going 5–1 up before rain drove us off court for half an hour. When we returned the red clay surface looked like a marsh, and in an attempt to prevent the balls becoming hopelessly waterlogged it was agreed to change them every five games instead of the usual seven.

I quickly levelled the match at set-all, but the conditions were playing havoc with my rackets. I broke the strings on four of them and was down to my last one, while Pops Summers worked frantically down in the dressing room trying to string up a couple of new ones.

The rain returned in the third set, but play was not suspended. Cochet was leading by then, but you learn to expect a home-field advantage in the Davis Cup. I was trailing 7–8, 15–30 and serving to save the set. My first serve was a fault and Cochet hit the ball clean out of the court and into the stands. He refused to restart play until this particular ball was returned and the spectators weren't about to let us have it. Eventually, however, after a lot of shuffling and squabbling, the ball re-emerged from the sea of French faces and I promptly served a double fault. On reflection, I think Cochet conned me, but I'm willing after all these years to give him the benefit of the doubt! I lost that set 7–9 and by then Cochet was not to be stopped. At such moments, with an excited French crowd urging him on, he was twice the antagonist, and I finished well beaten at 3–6 in the fourth set.

At the end of the match Cochet and I stood in the drizzle for the national anthems, then all hell broke loose as Cochet's supporters swarmed on to the court and hoisted him on their shoulders.

When we got back to London the LTA threw a big dinner for us at the Savoy Hotel, almost as if we had won the Cup. Still, we had done well to get to the final: no other British team had managed that for twelve years.

The next day Pat Hughes and I sailed for America again on the *Mauretania*, but this year, though, there was a difference. When I first went to the United States in 1930 I was looked upon as an English kid who might have a future. Now, having beaten the Americans in Paris and done well in the Challenge Round, we were considered people of some importance, and much sought after.

5   Amateur Travels

How things had changed since my last landfall in New York twelve months previously! The towering Chrysler Building was now complete, and we, too, had gone up in the world and were being lionized by the American press and tennis authorities, who bore us no ill will for having beaten their Davis Cup team.

We had had another fabulous crossing on the *Mauretania*, because I had become friendly with a lot of the crew the previous year, and after New York, with all its illuminated skyscrapers, we drove out to Westchester – two golf courses, swimming pools, polo, dance bands. Then on to Newport, with its yachting atmosphere. I thought, this is the life for me.

However, I wasn't so sure the following week when we moved on to Boston. We stayed at the Lennox Hotel, a square, straight up and down building. On the street side were the tramcars and behind the hotel were the railway yards. I thought, maybe this isn't for me after all.

We were in big demand to play tournaments and one of the first offers we received – made through a journalist on behalf of the Southern California Association – was for Hughes and I to travel to Los Angeles and play in the Pacific Southwest tournament immediately after the US National Championships.

Hughes, as captain of the team, said he would have to contact London to obtain the LTA's permission, though we were both anxious to make the trip. When we'd been given the go-ahead, we were told by the journalist that the Southern California Association would take care of our train fares across America and all our expenses.

Then he eyed us warily. 'And what are your personal terms?' he asked. Hughes, who loved a practical joke, said, 'As far as I'm concerned, I will play the tournament if my first date in Los Angeles is with an attractive twenty-one-year-old blonde who has at least a million dollars in her own right.' The man looked a little taken aback, but said he thought it might be arranged. Then he turned to me and asked for my 'terms', not realizing his bargaining advantage in that if Hughes went to Los Angeles I *had* to go with him anyway, as part of the British team. I told him straight: 'I'm not interested unless my first date is with Jean Harlow.'

We didn't hear any more and forgot about the whole thing as we prepared for the American circuit. I struck form right away, winning the Eastern Grass Court Championships at Westchester. My prize was a solid-silver cocktail set – not much use in those days of prohibition, especially to a teetotaller!

On that 1931 tour I beat seven of the top ten Americans without managing to win another tournament, and I lost four times to the man I most wanted to defeat, the tall Californian Ellsworth Vines. After being beaten by him in the final of the Newport Casino Invitation event, I ran into him again at the semi-final stage of the US National Championships, which were celebrating their jubilee. I thought a celebration of my own was on the cards when I won the first two sets, but Vines took the next three, went on to defeat George Lott in the final, and became champion of his country at the age of nineteen. Just as well for us that Vines hadn't been included in America's Davis Cup team that summer.

After that it was 'all aboard' for the train trip to California, the most fascinating part of that 1931 tour. Apart from the friendliness and openness of the people, the vastness of the country was what most impressed me on that transcontinental journey.

We travelled from New York to Chicago on a train called *The Twentieth Century Limited*, one of the many wonderful names they had. Pat Hughes and I sat in the observation car, drinks in hand, being pampered by smartly dressed attendants in white coats, dark trousers and peak caps, admiring the beauty of the Hudson River valley. What a life for a couple of English lads!

We arrived in Chicago the following morning, then had to shuttle across the city in a maelstrom of traffic to change trains, boarding the Sante Fe Railroad's *Super Chief* for a three-day journey to the West Coast.

I really regret the passing of such trains, with all their luxury and comfort. The attendant came in to us one evening and said, 'Tomorrow morning early, we get to La Junta, New Mexico, and there'll be fresh mountain trout coming aboard if you'd like some for breakfast.' We most certainly would, we told him.

Lots of famous people travelled on those trains, especially the movie stars, and at every one of the smaller halts children would swarm aboard and run through the carriages armed with autograph books looking for the famous. Eventually, when I had made the trip a couple of times, they came looking for me, too. After that first journey, of course, the ride inevitably became less exciting, but I never ceased to marvel at the sheer size of America.

My first trip to California in 1931 marked the start of a new era and changed my life for ever. I became an annual visitor to the Pacific Southwest tournament and very much a man-about-Hollywood, where the lively life style suited me down to the ground. I played the Pacific tournament for five years, losing the 1931 final, winning it the next three times and again getting to the final in the following year. As a three-time winner I was awarded the trophy permanently, but I gave it back to the tournament for perpetual competition.

On arrival in Los Angeles that first time Pat Hughes and I were installed at the Hollywood Roosevelt Hotel, and we went off to practise as soon as possible. I had never even seen a concrete court before, but it certainly didn't do my early-ball game any harm. I could swing at the bounce of the ball knowing it would be true: no deviations or wobbles or skids.

Because of the interest and involvement of the Hollywood community with the Pacific Southwest tournament there were exhibition matches, dinners and parties galore during the weekend before the event got under way, and Hughes and I were invited to a dinner at the tennis club on our first night in town. We were told a car would collect us at seven.

When we went to meet the transportation the driver said to me, 'This is Mr Hughes's car, sir; yours will be along in a minute.' With that, Hughes disappeared and in a moment or two my car purred up; I simply assumed this must be some grandiose Californian way of impressing visitors.

After leaving the hotel my driver swung to the left, towards the ocean and away from the tennis club. When I mentioned this he said, 'I know, sir, but we have to pick somebody up first.' On we went to Beverly Hills, stopping in the driveway of a grand colonial mansion. I went to the door, which was opened by a maid, gave her my name and told her we were supposed to be collecting someone for the tennis club dinner. 'Come right in,' she said.

I stepped inside one of the most beautiful vestibules I have ever seen – a circular hall with a staircase on each side and an ornate balcony at the head of the stairs. I heard a voice say, 'Hello,' and looked up. There, in the flesh, stood Jean Harlow, stunning in a black dress and with platinum-blonde hair.

It would be fair to say I was dumbfounded, but I wasn't the type to stay senseless for long. I escorted her to the car and she asked where we were going. 'To the tennis club for dinner,' I told her, at which she wanted to know if I had been to Hollywood before. When I said it was my first visit she wondered, in the nicest way, if I would like her to show me the town.

Only a fool would have said no to that offer, but as I accepted I did manage to point out that I was only an ordinary bloke from England with not much money in my pocket as an amateur tennis player. 'Don't worry about that,' she said. 'Wherever we go I just sign the bill to the Metro Goldwyn Mayer publicity department.' 'You've made a deal,' I told her, and off we went to dinner, followed by a couple of night spots. We never went near the tennis club.

When I got back to the hotel Hughes wanted to know where I had been. I told him, and asked how the tennis dinner had gone. 'The same thing happened to me,' he said. 'Mysterious car journey, big house, butler at the door, a blonde to meet me. She got into the car and said, "Before we go any further, Mr Hughes, I have some credentials to show you." And she pulled out a letter from the bank guaranteeing that she was twenty-one years old and had a million dollars in her own right.'

So Pat and I both got our 'wish', made in New York back in August. That was typical of the crazy things they used to do in Hollywood in those days which endeared you to the place.

After the snobbery and class divisions of the tennis set-up, and life generally, in England, America in 1931 was like a breath of fresh air. I had never seen anything like its hurry-hurry, move-your-ass, don't-write-a-letter-use-the-phone sort of approach, and it all appealed to me because I'm a fast-acting character myself. I played tennis the same way and compare myself a bit with Ilie Nastase – outgoing, quick on the uptake, lots of repartee. His isn't always the right sort, but then neither was mine.

I was dazzled by Hollywood, where I met stars like Mary Pickford and Douglas Fairbanks. Even though we were newly arrived in Hollywood and didn't yet know the movie stars personally, we were invited to Pickfair for lunch: that was 'the thing to do' – Pickfair was a must. It was a beautiful house – they all were – just like walking into fairyland. At that age, about twenty-two, I couldn't have cared less what style of furnishings it had; to me a chair was a chair and I didn't know or care whether it was a Chippendale or a Marks and Spencer's. But I liked what I saw. Everything bright; everything glittering. This was Tinsel Town. Everyone had a magnificent library, usually with a huge gleaming radiogram in one corner, and row upon row of British Club leatherbound editions which often turned out to be mock-ups with nothing behind. It was all fascinating to me, like the movie set façades which weren't even painted at the back but which looked pretty convincing from the front. There you could walk through a splendid 'house', through a door into an impressive living room with doors leading off to adjoining rooms at the side – except that the other rooms didn't exist. But when the time came to *use* that door on the left, there would be something there, and to me this was all most intriguing.

The stars were always in and out of each other's homes, and eventually when we lived there, they were in and out of ours. You soon discovered Randolph Scott in the kitchen, or Marlene Dietrich in the garden, sunning herself; it was open house really. Later on, when Vines and I owned the Beverly Hills Tennis Club, we got to know everybody well. Ben Lyon and Bebe Daniels would invite us over for drinks, or throw a party for us, and we soon became close friends. David Niven and Errol Flynn became familiar faces, and Ben and Bebe would invite me to stay at their Malibu beach home in Santa Monica whenever I had an off-tennis weekend. They also owned a smaller place next door, which eventually became the home of Marlene Dietrich, but which was also the beach retreat of Cary Grant and Randolph Scott before they were well known. That house on the beach was quite a place. The guest room where I always stayed had a bathroom to end all bathrooms. The walls, the ceiling, the floor and even the toilet were all inlaid with little tiny mirrors like crazy paving. I'd have a shave in there, and I could see 600,000 other guys all doing exactly the same thing.

I don't think I ever 'went Hollywood' though. I think I got dragged into it really, because of owning the tennis club later on. But at that stage of my life, it was all pretty impressive. To see these people from the big screen and actually be involved with them, from inside and behind the scenes, was unbelievable. These were the names I'd read about: the originals.

When the Pacific Southwest tournament was on and the tennis players were in town, everybody was tennis nuts. All the stars had private boxes at the championships – Harold Lloyd, Ben Lyon and Bebe Daniels, Marlene Dietrich, Clark Gable, Charlie Chaplin, and the Marx Brothers. Everybody wanted to throw a party. When you played tennis as seriously as we did it was usually a question of six days playing and one party, but in Hollywood there was one every night.

Hughes and I were invited by big movie bosses, like Jack Warner, to visit their studios, another indication that we were of some substance internationally after our Davis Cup run. Warner told me he appreciated that, if I wanted to take any of his starlets out to dinner, I couldn't really afford it, so I should just sign the bill and Warner Brothers publicity would take care of things. If one of their actresses went out with us it got publicity, not only in the United States but all around the world in countries which were interested in our tennis exploits. So everybody benefited: Warner, the stars, and F. J. Perry. I learned very early on in my career that as long as people need you, they take care of everything beautifully. The trick is to know when they don't need you any more just before they realize it themselves.

In those days there was no television, of course, and radio was no more than a crystal set, so people lived on the tales of Hollywood. Another reason I got on well there, I think, was that sporting people tend to gravitate to show business people and vice versa; basically, we're all in the same game.

I was always an entertainer at heart. I was never much of a musical person and still kick myself to this day that, because I couldn't be bothered, I didn't take up my parents' offer of piano lessons when I was a child. In England Jack Hylton and his band were great friends of mine and there was nothing I liked more than to sit at the back of the bandstand and let their music wash over me. I spent as much free time with them as I could and they used to follow my career. Once, when I was in France, I travelled out from Paris to play an exhibition match against Marcel Bernard at a club that had just opened in Roubaix. The same weekend the Hylton band were in Lille, a few kilometres away. All of them came over to watch me, and to liven up the proceedings each brought an instrument. Every time I won a game they'd let out a blast. This not only annoyed poor Marcel, who blew his chances, but upset British-French tennis relations for a while as well.

My Hollywood musical friends were Guy Lombardo and his orchestra, who used to play at *the* night spot in those days, the Coconut Grove. I was probably the world's worst-ever practice player. I preferred to play with my pals, and when Lombardo's boys asked me to hit with them I was happy to oblige. The problem was that all eleven of them turned up and decided they wanted to take me on at the same time. They were lined up like an American football team: four at the back, four in the middle, and three at the net. What they didn't realize was that the more people you play against, the easier it is, because all your opponents get in each other's way. Eventually the joke ended badly because three of them chased a lob, collided with each other, and the drummer fell over and broke his ankle.

Apart from unfortunate things like that, however, sportsmen and show business folk got along well together probably because they couldn't hurt each other professionally. Some tennis stars *are* showbiz folk. Bill Tilden, who came from a theatrical family, was a great showman, and he also nursed the ambition to act. His twin careers were once beautifully summed up by a critic: 'Bill Tilden is the greatest actor who has ever walked a tennis court and the greatest tennis player who ever walked a stage.'

Things don't seem to have changed much since my day, either. In America the show business people all want to sponsor or appear in golf and tennis tournaments, while players like John McEnroe and Vitas Gerulaitus dream of being rock musicians. More than ever now, tennis is showbiz. I suppose even walking out on court, covered from head to foot in trade logos, is part of the razzmatazz.

My travels for the year of 1931 weren't over yet. While we were in Hollywood Pat Hughes got a cable from the LTA asking if we would go to Stockholm for a special match indoors, Britain *v.* Sweden, to help celebrate the engagement of Princess Astrid to Leopold of Belgium.

We played a match against Canada in Montreal on the way home, travelled back to England on the *Empress of Britain*, and immediately set off for Stockholm, a journey which took almost two days then. As soon as we arrived and booked in at the Grand Hotel there was a knock on the door. An equerry presented his compliments and asked us to join the King of Sweden, Gustav V, at a party downstairs. Gustav, you understand, was crazy about tennis and it was a ritual that whenever a visiting tennis personality arrived in Sweden he always played a gentle match or two with the King.

When the party was over that night and we were all saying goodnight in the hotel lobby at about 2 a.m. before wending our way upstairs to bed, the King said, 'Where are you off to, gentlemen? We took the liberty of moving you into the palace.' So we stayed at the palace for the week of the match. We looked out of the window and could see the changing of the guard, and although we were at the back, it was just as good as being at the front. I was always trying to learn something from everything I saw or did, and although I was impressed, I tried never to be taken aback by anything. As far as mansions and palaces were concerned, I never bothered about what other people possessed. I was never envious by nature. I did feel I ought to take a shave every time a palace guard passed me at close quarters, but the only thing I ever coveted was a tennis shot that maybe somebody else had and I didn't.

Gustav was so keen on tennis that they even built a new centre in Stockholm called the King's Club, which had a private changing room with toilet facilities especially for Gustav. After inspecting it, he asked the guide, 'What, no pottie?' So they had to go out and find him a chamberpot, by appointment.

In the years that followed, it was always very pleasant to go to the South of France for a couple of weeks during the winter, if I wasn't away touring, and get in some tennis, and I would always run into King Gustav on the courts there. He used to play under the name of 'Mr G.'.

Later on, when I was Wimbledon champion, the best player around was always paired with Mr G. in the handicap men's doubles competition. Mr G. used to stand at the net while his partner ran miles, and eventually his opponents would put up an easy one for him to hit. One was never allowed to hit the ball hard to him because he was about eighty by then. He preferred to play in the morning because by the time he had had a good lunch he was in the mood to move even less than he normally did.

Yet it was quite a serious business for hard-up amateurs like myself, because the prize money was about 3000 francs for the winning pair, a lot of money in those days.

In one such match a Frenchman called Glasser – a good player who never made the Davis Cup team because of the Musketeers – hit a ball which just missed King Gustav at the net. I apologized and said it was my fault because I had hit a poor shot before that, but Mr G. said, 'It wasn't very nice of him to hit the ball so close.' To smooth things out, I said, 'Just leave the next easy one to me, Your Majesty.'

Eventually we got an easy one and Glasser knew what was coming. He was standing at the junction of the service box and as I moved in for the smash he turned his back on me. I hit him flush on the tailbone

47

and the ball ricocheted a mile. He went down as if poleaxed. The King looked at me, smiled regally, and said, 'I rather enjoyed that.'

We won two tournaments together, worth about 6000 francs in vouchers. The King told me how much he had enjoyed our partnership and said he wanted to get me something really nice to commemorate it. He kept all the winning vouchers, mine as well, so I looked forward to my commemorative gift no end, for it had already cost me 3000 francs. At the next Wimbledon a Swedish official brought me my present. It was an autographed photo of the King – unframed.

6   Match Point in Berlin

One point – just one little point – ruined the 1932 season for me. And it happened in Berlin, right in front of Adolf Hitler.

Yet things had started promisingly, both in the Davis Cup and in my own little world. After a short winter tour of Bermuda and Jamaica, where I won both championships, I came home to win the British Hard Courts title at Bournemouth, as I was to do for the following four years.

We started our Davis Cup campaign with a 5–0 win over Romania in Torquay, and after the French Championships, where I was beaten in five sets by the Czech Roderick Menzel, we travelled on to Warsaw for a Davis Cup tie with Poland, which we won 4–1.

The poor old Poles had been drawn against us five times in eight years, with bleak results every time, so it was heartening to see how they celebrated when Tloczynski, their number one, beat Harold Lee in a 'dead' rubber after we had taken a winning lead. He was the first Pole to win a set, never mind a match, against an Englishman, and the crowd carried him off court on their shoulders, an indication of how Davis Cup excitement used to infect the continental nations.

From Poland we hurried back to London, with only two days' practice on grass before Wimbledon. Here I ran into an inspired Jack Crawford in the quarter-finals and was beaten in four sets. All my ambitions and hopes were deferred for another year.

It was a memorable Wimbledon for Britain, however, because Bunny Austin reached the final and it was on the cards that he would become the first home player since Arthur Gore in 1909 to win it. But in the end the championship went to Ellsworth Vines, who was in irresistible form.

Still, there was the Davis Cup. Our next round was against Germany at the Rot-Weiss Club in Berlin, where we had been beaten three years previously. But with Austin back in the team after a nose operation I don't think even the Germans expected to put our proboscises out of joint. Before the start we were introduced to Hitler, who was such a little man and totally surrounded by tall bodyguards and aides. With all those people around him I don't know how he managed to see a single ball being hit.

The Germans got off to an unexpectedly good start when their number one, Daniel Prenn, beat Austin, who was playing his first match on a hard court since the previous year's Davis Cup Challenge Round. But all appeared well when I beat Gottfried von Cramm for the loss of only six games, and then Pat Hughes and I took the doubles easily: 2–1 up and only one more win needed.

After his great effort at Wimbledon, though, poor old Austin was listless and drained, and Von Cramm beat him comfortably. So there I was again, for the second successive year, lumbered with the match that was going to decide the whole thing.

Prenn, who eventually emigrated to England, was a slow-moving but solid baseline player. He liked to keep the tempo down and be allowed to take his time and, of course, slow courts like the one at the Rot-Weiss Club suited him perfectly. Playing on the sunken court was like playing in a soup bowl. It was about 60 feet down, surrounded by banks and stands which excluded the breeze, and the clubhouse overlooking the whole thing was built at ground level.

At the start of the match the court was very wet and the Germans got quite excited as Prenn took the first two sets. I was in trouble because I hadn't been able to make use of my speed and superior footwork, but by the third set the court had dried out a little and I got back into the match, two sets to one down.

At the end of the third set we went off, up the steps to the clubhouse, for our ten-minute break. When the time came to go back on court the officials told me they would take me down by the back way to avoid the crowds. How kind these Germans are, I thought. When we got down there the back gate was locked, so I had to climb all the way up the steps to the clubhouse again, where I found Herr Prenn still easing his limbs on the massage table. Then on down to the court – the right way this time.

I was good and mad by now. I won the fourth set 6–0 and went 5–2 up in the fifth, with Prenn serving to save the match. All through the match he had been serving solidly and slowly, and had not been foot-faulted once. I had established domination by basing my tactics on the theory that sooner or later, whether it took him five strokes or twenty minutes, he would hit a ball short to my forehand and I would wallop it past him.

Eventually I had him at match point. Although our captain, Roper Barrett, was not there on this occasion, he had always drummed into us the need for extra caution at match point in Davis Cup ties away from home. We were never to hit the ball anywhere near a line, where it might be called out, but always at least two feet over the net.

Prenn served and went the wrong way as I hit a forehand down the line past him. As I moved up to the net to shake hands and to prepare to celebrate Britain's 3–2 victory, I noticed a hell of a row going on at the baseline.

The baseline judge had called a foot-fault on Prenn, his first of the match, so he had one more serve to come. He saved the replayed match point with a volley and I didn't win another game. Prenn took that fifth set 7–5 and Germany was in the European Zone final.

I've often been asked what happened. How could I have lost five games in a row after having had match point? Well, to this day, I still don't know. The pendulum had simply swung in Prenn's direction: I'd had a long run, and he'd won only two games in the fourth and fifth sets up to that particular point. Suddenly the bottom fell out of my game. I can't give anybody an explanation; I wish I could. The gamesmanship and replayed points didn't bother me: you expect this anyway in the circumstances and, if anything, that just made me madder and more determined. The first point of the fifth set I won three times serving with new balls, yet I was down love-15. Still, you take the rough with the smooth, or you should do. It's strange that players always notice the things that went against them in a match. You hear them say they got two bad calls, or the other so-and-so got a couple of let calls; you never hear them say they got a couple of good calls just when they needed them.

If our captain, Roper Barrett, had been there that day and put in a protest about the baseline judge, I doubt that it would have made any difference to the final result. This was a pre-war match and it wasn't done to protest in those days. In fact, it might have started the war early! There were little groups of stormtroopers hanging about – you never saw one on his own – but there again, the politics didn't bother me either. The players never discussed the subject. We were out there playing tennis; we never went looking behind the walls. If we were all together with Prenn or Gottfried von Cramm, we never discussed politics: it never entered our heads. We were eating, sleeping and playing tennis, and that was the be-all and end-all of our existence. I couldn't have cared less which government was where; perhaps I should have done. Still, looking back, perhaps if Roper Barrett *had* been there, he just might have been able to say something to me at the crucial moment to stop the rot. He was particularly adept at pulling in the reins and he somehow knew what to say to make me snap out of whatever train of thought I was in, even though he didn't always say it in a way I liked.

I will never forget the rockets I got for that defeat. There were allegations that I had thrown away the match and let my country down. I really took a roasting, despite having won one singles and the doubles and damn near won my second singles.

I wasn't the only one in Berlin that day who thought the match was over when I led 5–2 at match point. Wallis Myers, the *Daily Telegraph*'s tennis correspondent, had hurried off to file his story on Britain winning the tie, only to find when he made a quick check that we had lost it instead.

When the team got home we ran into more bitterness, and Austin and I were castigated in one paper as 'carthorses'. Austin was then twenty-five and I was twenty-three.

The English team to tour the United States that autumn included Ted Avory, John Olliff, Austin and myself. We were joined aboard our liner at Cherbourg by the American Davis Cup team of Vines, Allison, Van Ryn and Shields, who had just lost to France in the Challenge Round after edging out our conquerors, Germany, in the Inter-Zone final.

All our Davis Cup disappointments were forgotten on a pleasant crossing. Sea voyages provided the ideal opportunity to relax and to meet prominent people in the entertainment business, with which I was fascinated. Once I travelled over on the same ship as Horowitz, the distinguished concert pianist. He had a silent keyboard with him and would play it by the hour, deep in concentration though not a single note came out of it. It was marvellous just to watch his hands.

The United States were even livelier than usual when we sailed into New York, since 1932 was an election year. It was the first time I had been mixed up in the fervour of an American election (which Franklin D. Roosevelt won, becoming President for a record four terms until his death at the end of the Second World War). Roosevelt was a deal more popular than his Republican opponent Herbert Hoover, as I realized when I spotted a car bumper sticker carrying the message, 'Vote For Anybody But Hoover'.

Our reception by the Americans was as warm as ever, especially in Newport, Rhode Island, home of the America's Cup yacht race. The previous year Austin and I had met Stuart Duncan, the Lea & Perrins sauce heir, and he invited us to stay at his mansion, Bonnycrest, which was built on a bluff overlooking the yacht harbour. It was certainly an imposing pile, commanding views all around and out to sea, with the yachts moored underneath. Duncan's favourite joke was that he had made a fortune out of what people left on their plates. He had spent quite a bit of this fortune dismantling Bonnycrest, which had been a castle in Scotland, and re-erecting it stone by numbered stone in Newport.

Bonnycrest had a guest tower with two bedrooms, one overlooking the ocean and the other facing down the imposing driveway. Duncan offered us the use of the guest tower, and since Austin was the British number one that year he got the room looking out on to the water.

There were servants all over the place. Goodness knows what our socialists back in England would have thought. When I woke up on my first morning a butler in striped waistcoat was standing over me with my morning tea. Then he brought my dressing gown and fetched a bowl of water so that I could test the temperature to see if it was to my liking for my bath.

I had a giggle when he had gone, thinking about this common fellow from Ealing sitting up in bed, putting his finger in a bowl of water and saying to the flunkey, 'A little warmer, if you please.'

When I got out of the tub and went to look for my clothes there wasn't a stitch in sight. Eventually my friend the butler came back into the room carrying them and saying, 'I took the liberty of pressing your suit.' On another occasion I wore the same clothes two days running, which didn't please him at all. When I pointed out that I was only going down to the tennis club he said, with a touch of frostiness, 'Begging your pardon, sir, but a slight change of clothes might be preferable.'

Our host Stuart Duncan was preoccupied while we were staying with him because his daughter's coming-out party was scheduled for the following year and he was worried that there was no ballroom big enough in Newport to accommodate it except in the home of his worst enemy, and he was damned if he would ask him. When we got back to Newport the following year (with me in the tower room overlooking the sea this time), Duncan had resolved his problem in typical fashion by having a ballroom built, with matching stones, on to the side of Bonnycrest.

Newport was very, very social: the yachting mecca where Dukes and Vanderbilts alike had huge homes. A million dollars bought a little shack. But somehow Bonnycrest stood apart: medieval, with iron gates, great studded doors, turreted towers and leaded windows, and a musicians' gallery in the dining room. The first year we were there the whole place was abuzz with Barbara Hutton's coming-out party and everybody had a ball. Those were the days of 'cutting in', the American version of the Excuse Me, whereby a fellow was expected to tap a man on the shoulder and request his dancing partner. Some chaps paid substitutes a couple of dollars to do their cutting in because they didn't like the look of the debs involved, but in general it was all very formal.

Even Newport Tennis Week was a social affair. In the casino bandstand there was always an orchestra blasting away, ruining concentration while we sweated our guts out on the court, and Duncan, who was then in his fifties, liked to enter into the spirit of the occasion by wearing a striped blazer, bow tie, white pants and straw boater. He always had a walking cane and very twinkling eyes. I don't know what's happened to Newport these days, since the Americans lost their precious Cup to the Australians; perhaps the whole place is in darkness! I believe Bonnycrest is a retirement home now. I'm still in Newport, of course. I was inducted into the Hall of Fame, the first non-American-born tennis player to be so honoured, and I have another little connection with Newport, too: I knew Emil Mosbacher, whose son Buzz was the skipper of the yacht *Weetamoe*, chosen for the America's Cup. During the Cup trials I happened to notice the *Weetamoe* crew pictured in a magazine all dressed in Fred Perry sportswear – blue shirts and white shorts. I did offer to send Buzz a free consignment, but he said he'd known me for years and they could afford to pay.

After Bonnycrest and Newport, almost anything would have been a let-down except winning the US Championships. For another year – just one more year as it turned out – I was out of luck again, this time losing to Sidney Wood in five sets after having led two sets to love.

In the space of three months I had lost three vital matches in the fifth set, so I made up my mind that when I got back home from America I would set about making myself the fittest tennis player around. It wasn't just a question of fitness: you reassess your situation from time to time and change your strategy to improve your game. If you feel that a particular shot is not working, you go away and practise; and if you lose a couple of matches from two sets to one up or from match point, you worry about it and try to make some adjustment. It's no consolation that you've *won* matches from *losing* positions; it's psychological. Losing five-setters is maddening: you do get a bit fed up with it. I used to mull over a match for two or three *days* if I lost from a winning position; I was impossible for three or four. I wouldn't talk to anybody; I'd go for long walks or get in my little car and drive away to a movie, or to hear a band.

Everything I did was built around my forehand drive: that was the key. Sooner or later my opponent would hit one short to that; I just had to be able to stay out there longer than he could. Then the longer the match lasted, the more the pendulum would swing my way. I was fit already; I knew that. But if I could get fitter still, fitter than anybody, I would have that advantage. In a five-setter I'd have the security of knowing that I would outlast my opponent; that I'd have a tankful of gas left for the finish. I'd know that, and what was more to the purpose, so would the other guy. He'd get the message. That was the reason behind my leaping the net at the end of a match. I wanted to impose my fitness on his mind, for the next time we went out and beat one another to death.

By this time I knew that unless something was dreadfully wrong, nobody was going to take three straight sets from me; I was going to get at least one. And if I got one, then my opponent would have to go four or five. So I changed my strategy. From now on, all my efforts would be concentrated on trying to win the first set – somehow – and get that under my belt so that I had something to play with. Then, if I lost the next two sets, I still had to win the match – because nobody could better me for three straight sets. And if I were the fittest player around, I could keep going. Once I'd made up my mind about this strategy and made the decision to get fit, that was it – I went into training. And the wheels were already greased for me to go to the Arsenal Football Club. Tom Whittaker, trainer of the legendary team, had offered to make arrangements for me to train with the players. I decided to take up that offer.

But first there was the Pacific Southwest tournament and another fling in Hollywood. I won the tournament that year, the first of three successive wins there, beating Austin in four sets. Everyone pointed out at once that I would now win the US title, because for the preceding five years the winner of the tournament in Los Angeles had gone on to capture the championship at Forest Hills the following September. They were right, too!

That was the year I became friendly with the actor Charlie Farrell and a rising young actress, Bette Davis. Farrell invited me down to the Warner Brothers studios to watch a picture he was making. I was taken on to the set and there, tucked up in a nice double bed, was

Bette Davis with a lovely dog perched on the counterpane alongside her.

As I was being introduced I said, 'Hence the expression: lucky dog.' We got on well – she liked smart alecks – and I invited her to come and watch the tennis when she had finished shooting for the day. I left her some tickets for Harold Lloyd's box, and while I was playing I looked up and there she was, wearing a sensational pair of shorts, which was unheard of in those days. Afterwards, as a joke, I went over and said I wasn't going to be seen with her while she was dressed that way. So Bette took it in good part, went home, changed, and came back again.

Bette and I became very good friends over the years, as we seemed to have so much in common. She was a *very* dedicated actress and always seemed to have to battle for the things she wanted in her career, in much the same manner as I had to in mine. We had a lot of fun just spending time together. She was married to a bandleader, Harman Nelson, who was away working in San Francisco and not often around in Hollywood. Bette and I became firm, fast friends: we were both quick on the uptake, and our repartee didn't miss a beat. That first remark I ever made to her, about the dog, struck her as funny, and it seemed as natural for me to say it as it did for her to laugh. We were both a bit on the rebellious side to start with, and Bette was convinced of the things she could do, and she was certainly going to do them. There was nothing formal about her. If we bumped into one another in a New York restaurant, she would say, 'Hi, there!' in that sweet way of hers, and we were so much alike that we were always easy and natural in each other's company. Not exactly family, but almost.

As soon as I got back to London I contacted Tom Whittaker, who was our Davis Cup trainer, too, and arranged to start my training with the Arsenal. They had a great team then, almost every man an international, and were just embarking on their run of three league championships in a row. There was Moss in goal, Male and Hapgood at full back, Crayston, Roberts and Copping at half back, and the forwards were Hulme, Jack, Lambert, James and Bastin.

I was invited to report to Highbury every morning whenever I was free of tennis commitments, to train with them. They started me off by walking me halfway up the terrace steps, then back again, which brought to mind Prenn on the massage table. Then I progressed to running a quarter of the way up and crawling the rest. Finally I got to the stage where I could run all the way up and back down again.

Every Wednesday the Arsenal used to play a practice match and they put me in the forward line for about fifteen minutes facing the great Herbie Roberts at centre half. I used to get knocked all over the place and got a bit fed up bouncing off Roberts, who seemed to have sharp points on his hips and shoulders, like a porcupine. So I decided to get a bit of my own back and waited until he was poised on one leg, about to collect the ball. I took off full pelt and down he went. Tom Whittaker blew his whistle and told me, 'Don't do that, Fred; Herbie's a bloody valuable man.' 'So am I,' I said. From then on I was one of the boys and used to get thrown in the team bath regularly after training.

I am not a gambler by any means, but it was on these training sessions that I got involved in a little wager. The others used to bet me a shilling a time that I couldn't score a penalty against Moss in goal. Eventually, before I got through there, I was putting them away with both feet. I needed the money.

The only other 'gamble' I took, if you can call it that, came when Bill Tilden and I toured together as professionals. Whenever and wherever we played we had a standing bet of one dollar per set, and at the end of the match the dollar bills would change hands.

After that winter of training with the Arsenal I really felt the fittest man in tennis. I worked it out that I had reached the stage where nobody could beat me in straight sets, so by going flat out to win the first set, or even by losing it something like 9–11, I was testing my fitness against my opponent, and I planned to be going just as fast at the end of the fifth set as I had been at the start. It worked, too. I only ever recall losing two five-set matches after that in the four years until I turned professional.

7   A Cup for the Cabhorses

A short winter tour of South Africa, in which a British team made up of Betty Nuthall, Eileen Whittingstall, Mary Heeley, Pat Hughes, Harold Lee and myself lost all three 'Test matches', did not exactly help to dispel the gloom over our Davis Cup defeat by the Germans in 1932, and as we prepared for the 1933 Davis Cup with the same team – Austin, Hughes, Lee and myself – the moaners surfaced again.

Some sections of the media advised the LTA not to send 'the same old cabhorses' (even worse than the earlier 'carthorses') to Barcelona for the first-round tie with Spain. By now we found the whole thing amusing and referred to each other as 'cabhorse'. When I won the US National title later that year Austin sent me a cable which read, 'Well done, old cabhorse', and to this day when he writes to me he refers to me as 'Dear cabhorse' and signs his letters 'The other cabhorse'.

But we were annoyed when it was suggested that the LTA might have saved face – together with half the fares – by sending a junior team to represent Britain instead of those who had supposedly let the nation down in Berlin.

We shut up the critics by beating Spain and then Finland, while I won the Hard Courts title for the second year by defeating Austin. Next we thrashed Italy at Eastbourne, after which I took a week's break (spent with Jack Hylton's band in Brighton), before going back to Eastbourne to help beat Czechoslovakia in the fourth round.

I went into the 1933 Wimbledon quite fancying my chances – only to be knocked out in the second round by Norman Farquharson, a South African and Cambridge blue. He was a pretty good player and an excellent volleyer, though he was better known for his doubles expertise. He decided to attack me at the net and had one of those days at Wimbledon when everything comes off. The new super-fit Perry, I'm sorry to say, was beaten in five sets.

My father used to watch all my Wimbledon matches. During his time as an MP this occasionally proved difficult, since Labour was in

58

power with only a small majority; but a Conservative MP friend of his, Victor Cazalet, used to help by arranging to be paired with him. Cazalet was a tennis buff and quite a useful player himself – in fact, so useful that he was the only person the great Helen Wills Moody would practise with when she was in Britain.

At Wimbledon that year, while my father was sitting in the stands enduring my misfortunes, he had to put up with a loudmouth nearby who was telling everybody it was inconceivable that the British could tolerate somebody as badly behaved as Fred Perry. Why, he had 'seen me only the previous night drinking at a club until 4 a.m.' and 'in a very inebriated state'. My father was not the sort to suffer fools gladly and told the man that, on the contrary, I had been home in bed by ten o'clock. 'Are you calling me a liar?' asked the loudmouth. 'Yes, I am,' said my father, and then explained who he was. Silence reigned.

Being home in bed early every night was part of my meticulous preparation for what eventually became three years of triumph at Wimbledon. A friend of mine, Sandy Thomson, used to help by coming to stay with me at my father's house in Ealing for the duration of the tournament. Sandy wasn't my 'minder' – that title belonged to Pops Summers – but he kept people away from me when the going was tough, and generally looked after my needs. He never got paid for the work; it was simply done out of kindness, while he took time off from his job as a salesman in the soft-drink business. Sandy drove me everywhere during Wimbledon. I avoided driving because it affects the focus of your eyes before tennis matches and I was determined to eliminate all possibilities of error.

Another way in which I used to try to avoid the hurly-burly and lessen the pressure before a match was by going to the golf club across the road from Wimbledon, having a little fun on the putting green and sharing a cup of tea in the golf shop with the pro Bill Cox, until I was called by Dan Maskell half an hour before I was due on court. Then Maskell would give me a warm-up.

I never shook hands with anybody before a match. I wasn't being snooty, but if you greeted fifty or sixty people you could lose some feeling in your hand. This was especially true if you happened to be playing an Australian or an American and one of his husky friends with hands like shovels came along and simply had to wish you good luck. Sandy Thomson was always there to ward them off, as politely as possible, and I used to keep my right hand in my pocket anyway for extra insurance. (This practice was adopted in recent years by Gary Player, who refused to shake hands with anybody before a round of golf.)

I also took great care of those other little essentials – my feet – and went to a lot of trouble over the choice of footwear. If your feet hurt, you can't play tennis; it's as simple as that. So I had my shoes (they were called 'plimsolls' in those days) specially made by a man in Pinner. They were of buckskin, laced to the toe and with a very thin leather sole, under which was stitched a slightly thicker crêpe sole. These plimsolls were extremely light and durable and not only fitted like a glove but could be bent over and popped into my pocket if necessary: say, if somebody tried to shake me by the foot.

Wimbledon was the setting for our next Davis Cup tie in the 1933 competition, against Australia, and it promised to be a toughie, since their number one, Jack Crawford, had just won the singles title at the championships.

Sure enough, Crawford beat Austin in the opening rubber, but I levelled it by defeating Vivian McGrath. Contrary to popular opinion that the double-handed backhand was invented by Jimmy Connors and Chris Evert-Lloyd, the first player to use the shot was the Australian Vivian McGrath in the early thirties. He hit his forehand with his right hand and had a two-handed backhand on the other wing. In fact, he had a quite heavily top-spun forehand drive – not as exaggerated as Borg's, but top-spun nevertheless. Well, then Hughes and I won the doubles. Austin clinched our success on the third day by outplaying McGrath, which was just as well because I had injured my shoulder and Harold Lee took my place for the final 'dead' match with Crawford.

I stayed behind in London for treatment at the skilled hands of a wonderful osteopath, W. F. Hugh Dempster, while the rest of the team set off for Paris, where they were to meet the United States for the right to challenge the champions – France. It was agreed that I should arrive by the boat train on the following Wednesday evening for a work-out with our coach, Dan Maskell, at Roland Garros Stadium before the team was announced the next day.

When I met Dan he told me we could practise as long as we liked because we were not necessarily required, as was usually the case, to join the rest of the team for dinner. The practice revealed no problems, so Dan phoned Roper Barrett to tell him I would be able to play, and then we made our own way to dinner.

We passed a rather posh restaurant called the Café Royal in the Bois de Boulogne, a lovely place near the lake, so I suggested we eat there. Why not? Maskell considered it a bit expensive for the likes of us, but I pointed out that the rest of our team, not to mention their LTA officials, would very likely be in a similar place with wonderful food; I proposed to dine equally well and avoid the shellfish.

So in we walked. The maître d'hôtel, who was one of the owners, welcomed us personally by name, and as the orchestra struck up 'God Save the King' Dan said, 'Do you know these people?' I never even knew the band.

We had a memorable meal and asked for the bill, wondering whether we would be the first Davis Cup players ever to have to wash the dishes. But the owner insisted on taking care of it himself. 'It is my pleasure,' he oiled.

Dan and I got back to the Hotel Crillon at about 10.30 p.m. to all sorts of flak. Nobody would believe we had had a free meal at such a fabulous place, but the fact that we had was yet another indication of the level of interest in the Davis Cup at that time, with France doing so well.

Dan Maskell was a valued member of that Davis Cup squad and went everywhere with us. He was also coach to the All England Club and the LTA, based at Wimbledon. Other non-playing members of the group were the captain Roper Barrett, our trainer Tom Whittaker, of Arsenal fame, and the secretary of the LTA, the likeable Anthony Sabelli, who came along to pay the bills. A lovely story comes to mind about Anthony Sabelli. Some years later we were all at the Grosvenor House in London at one of the LTA balls. It was a rather sumptuous affair with a toastmaster and MC in a red coat, and the LTA President and his wife standing at the top of the stairs to greet the incoming guests. As you came in, you gave your name to a fellow with a loud voice who announced you to the throng below, and then you would be presented to the President and make your way down the staircase with as much dignity as possible. Sabelli entered with his wife in due style and whispered his name to the announcer, who turned towards the ballroom and bellowed, 'Sir and Lady Belly!'

I guess Dan Maskell's role on the squad was 'troubleshooter'. I don't think it was a question of actually teaching us anything because Austin, Lee and I all had our own personal way of playing by now. But if I wanted to practise something Dan would work with me for hours and hours, even days. He helped put the finishing touches to our preparations.

We worked hard on those preparations and studied the opposition a little more carefully than most of the other teams did. In addition to our on-court captain and trainer, we stationed a man at each corner of the court amongst the crowd so that if anything happened – and in Europe it could happen all the time because the Europeans are so nationalistic – we could head for the corner to let off steam without getting into trouble and could find a friendly face instead of someone who was booing us.

The key to our success over the Americans that year was the wonderful form of Bunny Austin. He routed Ellsworth Vines, who had just reached the Wimbledon final and who had beaten him in the previous year's final, in straight sets with some thrilling tennis, and I beat Wilmer Allison almost as easily.

Although we lost the doubles to that redoubtable combination of George Lott and Johnny Van Ryn, Austin clinched our place in the Challenge Round with a four-set win over Allison. The tie might have been decided, but the drama was by no means over. Vines and I got embroiled in an exhausting five-set battle until eventually I stood at 7–6 in the fifth set and 40–15 on Ellie's service.

He threw up the first ball to serve. Fault. As he prepared to throw up the second, I moved over to run around the serve on my forehand, as if to tell him, 'Here it comes, my friend.' As he leaned into the ball to hit it, Vines collapsed face forward on to the court. He had injured an ankle in the fourth set, and the combination of pain, a hot Sunday afternoon in Paris and the stress of being match point down, even in a 'dead' rubber, had been too much. Vines was carried off court and that was the end of the match. I knew then that, despite that second-round setback at Wimbledon against Farquharson, I was now good and ready.

So we moved on to what's known these days as 'the big one'. With the comforting presence of Roper Barrett at our side, whispering sharply to us at every moment of crisis 'HYBT' (Hold Your Bat Tight), we swept the two singles matches on the opening day of the final against France.

Austin brushed aside the French nineteen-year-old André Merlin at a cost of only seven games, but I had the devil of a battle to subdue Henri Cochet 8–10, 6–4, 8–6, 3–6, 6–1. It wasn't until Cochet began to tire noticeably in the fifth set that I knew my superior fitness would again be the crucial factor.

One of my methods of injecting a little gamesmanship into a big match was to vault the net if I had won and congratulate my opponent, thereby giving the crowd the impression that this Perry fellow was fit enough to play another five sets. It's rather like a boxer who has been clobbered senseless, dancing around to make people think he didn't feel a thing.

I had another trick up my sleeve if I was involved in matches with a ten-minute break at the end of the third set. I'd start by wearing off-white gaberdine trousers and an off-white shirt. Then, after the rest period, I would re-emerge in dazzling white duck trousers and a fresh white cotton shirt, my hair neatly parted. The crowd always thought I looked twice as fresh as the other man, but of course it was just window dressing.

Well, there I was in my dazzling white gear at match point against the redoubtable Cochet. In desperation he came to the net and I threw him a lob over his backhand side. He took off after it, but it was obvious he wasn't going to make it. I went to the net and was preparing to spring when Roper Barrett shook his stick at me and shouted, 'Stay where you are; don't you dare move!' The moment the ball hit the ground on Cochet's side of the net he said, 'Now you can go.'

Vaulting the net after such a gruelling match definitely *was* the boxer's shuffle on my part. In the privacy of the dressing room I passed out completely, then came round to find myself on the massage table with Roper Barrett and Maskell fanning me. My condition, due as much to the mental strain as physical exertion, was hushed up for tactical reasons, and as a precaution I was rested from the doubles, in which Pat Hughes, now partnered by Harold Lee, lost to Jean Borotra and Toto Brugnon.

It's hard for anyone who wasn't there at the time to understand the particular strain of playing the Challenge Round of the Davis Cup in Paris. We were trying to take the Cup away from the French on their own territory and Paris was like a seething cauldron. You never knew what was going to happen and everything you did was like another step along a tightrope. The court was purpose-built to suit the Frenchmen and spike the Americans' game, so the French had every advantage to start with, and the 15,000 people who were jammed into Roland Garros Stadium that day were all frenzied Frenchmen, whistling and jeering. If there was a bad call, it took four or five minutes to silence the eruption. It's a very nerve-racking thing to play tennis in that kind of charged atmosphere. And to try to beat Cochet, who, let's face it, was my idol, on his own territory, in the Davis Cup Challenge Round and in such a decisive match, was a staggering responsibility. I think, when I beat him, the bottom dropped out of my act. I think it was the sheer joy and relief of thinking, 'My God, we made it!'

I always went out on the court determined to win, and I never pictured myself losing this match or any other. But don't forget, I'd had a spot of bother two years earlier, playing Cochet in the rain, and if I had been leading, I'm pretty sure that match would have been called. And then there was the incident with the ball in the stand. All these things race through your mind when you're about to clinch a critical set, and I think the whole squad was uptight about the outcome. I think all the boys were nuts for half an hour afterwards, I really do. I don't believe any of them knew what they were doing. I certainly didn't know what I was doing, but I did feel like a wet sock that had been put through a wringer; I was completely and utterly drained.

I had still not fully recovered twenty-four hours later. When the doubles match was over Roper Barrett ordered Austin and I out for a quiet practice session as a loosener for the next day, but within five minutes the captain had decided I was not even up to that and packed me off to bed. After a good night's sleep I felt decidedly better, though still far from 100 per cent.

The final day's play, with the Davis Cup on prominent display, was again hard on the nerves. Cochet, twice a set behind, outlasted Austin in a match that went the distance, and once more it was up to me to win for Britain and deny France a record-equalling seventh consecutive year of Davis Cup possession.

Showing remarkable maturity and coolness, young Merlin passed me time and again at the net in the early stages. I lost the first set and had to save two set points in the second before things began to go my way. On one of the set points I cracked the ball down Merlin's backhand side as he came in and it hit the line, making a clearly discernible mark because in those days the lines were of porcelain. The ball skidded and was called good.

Pandemonium followed, however, as it usually did (and still does) on this sort of occasion involving a Frenchman. Boos, catcalls, whistles. But the point stayed good. Yet as I prepared to receive the next serve, I noticed a fresh official on the line. The poor devil who had called my ball in was *out*.

Eventually I broke serve in the fourth set to lead 5–4 and needed only to hold my service for the match – and the tie and the Cup. I remember some pompous idea I had in mind of showing the French nation how to finish off a tennis match, but I promptly lost the game and needed to work very hard to break Merlin again for a 6–5 lead.

Right: Teenager Perry in Middlesex sweater

Below: The author at a tender age, with sister Edith

'Lloyd George knew my father' – Sam Perry, MP

I was never restricted in my movements because I wore long trousers. Forehand (*top*) and backhand (*bottom*)

Right: Airborne in my featherlight plimsolls

Below: My game was built around my forehand

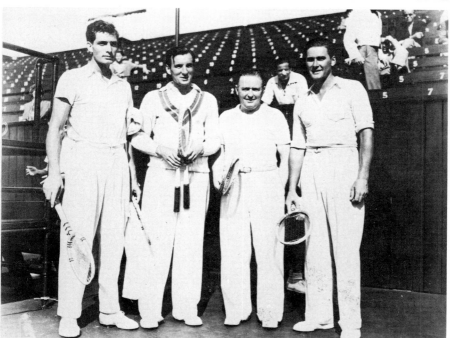

Together with, from left to right, Frank Shields, Elmer Griffin and Errol Flynn

Left: Honoured by Stockport and the Mayor

Below: King Kong wouldn't like it: exchanging glances with Fay Wray

A cast worth thousands. Left to right: Loretta Young, Clark Gable, Elizabeth Allan, Bette Davis, myself, and Rocky and Gary Cooper

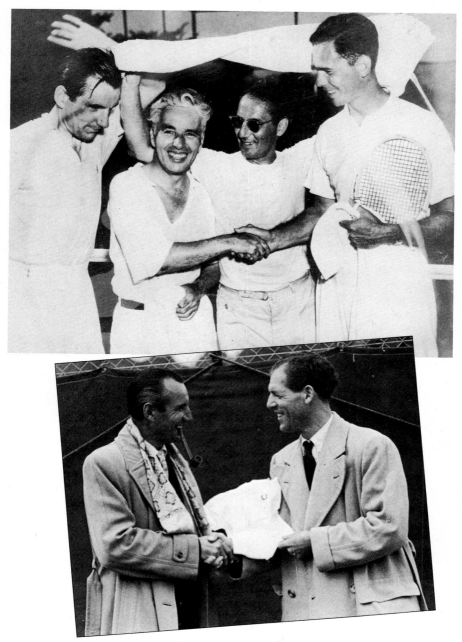

Top: The Beverly Hills Tennis Club inaugural doubles: Messrs Fred Perry and Charles Chaplin, representing Great Britain, and Messrs Groucho Marx and Ellsworth Vines, representing the United States

Above: The clothesline: handing over one of our baby shirts to Tony Mottram – perhaps for baby Buster

Left: Ellie Vines with Bunny Austin
Below: Bill Tilden. The one thing he couldn't stand was being called 'Tillie'

Old friends and foes on board the *Olympic* in 1932. Left to right: Frank Shields, Wilmer Allison, Bernon Prentice, John Van Ryn, L. A. Baker and Ellie Vines

Top: Henri Cochet: I based my game on his

Above: Wimbledon final, 1934, with Jack Crawford and the famous referee F. R. Burrow

Above: Two stills of the MGM film shot at Beverly Hills Tennis Club

Above: More laurels, this time my Lebanon Chevalier of the Order of the Cedar

Left: Entering the Centre Court with Don Budge in the Davis Cup. My blazer pocket insignia includes the laurel wreath emblem which became the Fred Perry sportswear logo

As we were changing ends, with no time allowed for a sit-down in those days, of course, Roper Barrett got up from his chair and said to me, 'Let's go for a walk.' While I was taking a drink, he looked around us and said, 'Nice day ... big crowd.... Look over there in that corner: now, there's a good-looking girl. I'll tell you what, win this game and I'll get you a date with her.' (I think he was just talking to take my mind off the race. It certainly did the trick.)

That changed the whole picture. I wasn't straining any more. I held serve, won the match 4–6, 8–6, 6–2, 7–5, and Britain had possession of the Davis Cup for the first time since 1912. The Associated Press reported that when the Cup was formally presented to Roper Barrett 'he hugged it tightly as though it were a baby, while the fans, with lumps in their throats, bade it godspeed'.

After standing motionless for the national anthems I missed the rest of the post-match ceremonies and celebrations. I was flat on my back in the dressing room again, having passed out for the second time in three days, drained as before.

On the way back to the hotel in our open-topped bus we tastelessly flourished the trophy we had taken away from the French after six years, much to the disgust of the passers-by.

That evening, after the official dinner for both teams, Cochet, swallowing his national sorrow, said to me, 'Let's go out for a night on the town and take the Cup with us.' 'We can't do that,' I said. 'Oh, yes we can,' he insisted, and we did. With a few friends of his we got the trophy out of the hotel and set off on a tour of the Paris night clubs. Everywhere we went the band would strike up the 'Marseillaise', followed by 'God Save the King'. We would fill up the Cup with champagne, everybody would take a drink, and then we'd go off to the next club. Well, the others were drinking: I was sipping.

The celebrations went on all night and it wasn't until about 7 a.m. that we made our way back to the hotel across the Place de la Concorde, carrying the Davis Cup and followed by an orchestra we had picked up along the way and a decidedly mixed gathering of hangers-on.

I don't suppose the tennis authorities would have approved had they known that their precious trophy had been on a grand tour of Parisian night spots, but despite this the LTA found the Cup where it was supposed to be when the time came for them to take it back to London that morning.

On arrival in Dover, where a telegram of congratulation from King George V awaited us, we all looked a bit green because the Channel crossing had been rough. But we soon pulled round. The whole length of the journey up to London on the train people were standing in their back gardens waving to us as we held up the Davis Cup, and at Victoria Station it was chaos. About ten thousand people swamped the police cordon, grabbed Austin and myself, and marched us off on their shoulders. The ringleaders were a few people from my part of Ealing, though I didn't know that at the time. I lost all my baggage and rackets in the turmoil and thought they had disappeared for ever, until two days later Pops Summers called up and told me they were safe in his car.

Such spectacular involvement in Britain's Davis Cup triumph created even more interest in me when I got to the United States that summer, and stirred early speculation that, though I still had to win a major championship, I might be considering turning professional. It wasn't long before the newshounds were after me.

By now I had a group of firm friends in the United States, who had a great bearing on my life. There was Bertram Weal, manager of the Madison Hotel, New York, who always used to come down and meet me off the boat, joining in the press conference by wearing a raincoat, trilby hat and a press badge bearing the title *Zit's Weekly* (zits being American slang for pimples). Other friends were Bill Riordan, father of the man who became Jimmy Connors' manager, George Leisure, the law firm partner of 'Wild Bill' Donovan (the wartime general who commanded the OSS), and Irving Squires, who was in the men's clothing business. Squires was also a sheriff of Queen's County, where the Forest Hills stadium is situated, and he used to ensure that I arrived in spectacular style for my matches by providing me with a police motorcycle escort.

That year, just as they prophesied when I had won the Pacific Southwest tournament the previous autumn, I won the United States national title, coming back from two sets to one down to beat the Australian Jack Crawford 6–3, 11–13, 4–6, 6–0, 6–1.

Crawford and I were great friends. Though we were keen rivals we respected each other's game. When we went out on court we just got down to business and that was that; there was never an argument. Crawford had beaten me several times before, but by now I was faster and fitter than he was, despite the fact that he was a husky man, hit the ball hard and generated a lot of power with comparatively little effort.

You always had to try to out-think Crawford. You could sense he was working you into a certain situation and I always tried to work myself out of it. It was certainly never boring playing him.

He was a perfect opponent for me because, like Von Cramm and Austin, he preferred to stay on the baseline. If I ever got into trouble with any of those three I used to sit back and wait for the opportunity to present itself, playing them shot for shot. I knew they weren't going to hit the ball hard enough to embarrass me on the baseline, so they weren't going to beat me, whereas Americans like Vines, and the Czech Menzel, could hit the ball straight through you.

Like almost every other top player, Crawford had his idiosyncrasies, which Pops Summers and I had studied and discussed. Crawford's trademark was that he used to play with his sleeves rolled down; once in a while with just one sleeve down. When he wanted to wipe the sweat off his hand he would rub it down his trousers, but if he began to get nervous he used to wipe it on his shirt. Well, wiping a wet hand on a wet shirt is not the best thing to do if you're using a leather grip, so when that happened I'd go after him right away.

That match with Crawford was the first all-foreign men's final at Forest Hills for seven years, and at one stage it looked likely that Crawford would add the American championship to those of Wimbledon, France and Australia which he already held.

When Crawford won the third set and we took our ten-minute break, I went off to the changing room to put on my fresh white clothes, but Crawford just sat in a courtside box with his wife, smoking a cigarette. He didn't even change out of his sweaty clothes.

The Associated Press reported: 'Most of the spectators thought Crawford was already "in" and had completed his Grand Slam of tennis.' Perhaps Crawford thought so, too, but in my opinion he was 'all-in' rather than 'in' at the end of that third set. It was a very hot day and I think the plug had been pulled.

On those unpredictable Forest Hills grass courts you had to work awfully hard in difficult conditions, and Crawford had been late finishing his semi-final the previous evening. The same sort of thing had happened to me a couple of times at Forest Hills, where they used to save a good match, the one we called 'the five o'clock match', to attract the people coming home from work.

In the 'five o'clock matches', once the sun dipped below the perimeter of the stand it became quite dark and the dew settled quickly because the courts were six feet or so below ground level. You had to contend with heavy dark-green balls and it was tough. If you won that match you had to go out and play the final the next day at one o'clock, in 90 degrees, bright sunshine, on hard courts and with the balls flying all over the place. This was what happened to Jan Kodes, Wimbledon champion in the 'boycott' year of 1973. He got to the final of the US Championships on his hands and knees and lost to John Newcombe in five sets after having played a semi-final the previous evening against Stan Smith – which didn't finish until about a quarter to nine.

I think the same fate befell Jack Crawford. At any rate, he won only one game in the next two sets and blew his chance of becoming the first Grand Slam holder of the four major championships.

The United Press man, Henry McLemore, reported the occasion as follows:

Perry's arrival at Forest Hills for the final was a thing to make you gasp. He came in a Rolls Royce preceded by four motorcycle policemen, sirens ablast ... Now please don't get the idea that Frederick John Perry is an egotistical sort of guy. Cocky, yes! Sure of himself, immensely. He's got a right to be. He's a sweet tennis player.

His mannerisms are never offensive because he makes you think of the ordinary person's reactions to becoming a hero. In short, he is a man who can strut and make you like it.

His is a game without a flaw. His forehand packs a lethal wallop and with it he can part your hair at twenty paces. Crawford hammered at his backhand through five sets yesterday and not once did it show any signs of faltering. Unlike most English players, Perry has a devastating smash and a service that carries authority.

Now that's what I call reporting!

Bad weather had delayed the US Championships, so Crawford and I were a little late travelling out to Los Angeles for the Pacific Southwest. We finally got off the train on the Sunday, the last day of the exhibitions which traditionally preceded the actual tournament.

Crawford and I, as US Championship finalists, were scheduled to play an exhibition, though neither of us was in the mood after that five-set match and a four-day train ride. The Los Angeles event had a different big-name Hollywood personality as its official hostess every day, and on this particular day it was Marlene Dietrich. She was sitting in a courtside box as Crawford and I changed ends in this rather humdrum exhibition match. Suddenly we heard this beautiful voice say, 'Well, gentlemen, I think you could at least *try*.' From then on we worked a bit harder.

Since I was shortly to make my first tour of Australia and New

Zealand as a member of the British team, I determined just to enjoy myself in Hollywood and concentrate my energies on the coming Australian Championships; but I won the title again, beating Jiro Satoh of Japan in the final.

The tournament secretary, Perry T. Jones, presented me with the trophy and told me that, in accordance with the time-honoured prophetic custom, it had also been decided to 'award me the US Championship of the following year'. Once again, this prophecy was to come true, but by the time that happened I would hold two more of the world's four major titles.

8   The Placards Said 'Fred'

I loved Australia and the Australians – and still do. I like their easy-going attitude, and in the days of our tours theirs was close to the American way of life, except that it retained many of the formalities of England. The difference was that they were a lot less stuffy and would take you as they found you.

Pat Hughes and I ran into a spot of bother early on the tour because of what was regarded as our extravagant dress sense. We had both splashed out on the 'new' white tuxedo dinner jackets while in America and we wore them to a dinner in Melbourne, collecting a broadside from the press and others for 'not conforming'. I guess we must have looked like a couple of real swells to those Aussies, and I don't think I helped the situation either when I made a short speech to our Australian hosts. I said I really loved the place and the people; I said that Australians, in my view, were some of the best folk in the world, and that they should be because, after all, they'd been picked by some of the best judges in England.

On that first trip there was still a lot of bad feeling between the two countries engendered by the 1933 'bodyline' cricket tour and Harold Larwood. In fact, one of the reasons for our tennis team being there was as a placatory gesture. But the cricket controversy still rankled, as we discovered at a dinner in Sydney when the mayor, a no-nonsense man who didn't trouble to sound his aitches, got up to welcome us: 'Last year,' he said, 'we 'ad the cricketers out 'ere. They brought with 'em something we knew nothin' about, bodyline bowlin'. What we want to know, Mr 'Ughes, is what 'ave you brought with you?'

As captain of our team, Pat Hughes rose to reply, stressing every aitch: 'We are very happy to be here. We do not use a hard ball, but it's not really necessary because we have brought with us Fred Perry, who's going to beat the hell out of you all.'

As in America, I rapidly made friends with the affable Aussies. One of my first acquaintances was a big, extrovert sugar baron called

70

Lennie Muir. While we were in Sydney we stayed in the old Australia Hotel on McQuarrie Street, right across the road from the Hotel Usher, where Lennie had a suite. He was always ringing me up to ask what I was doing that day.

Then, one morning at about eight o'clock, two fellows walked into my room and said they had a job to do. They produced a length of wire, a basket and some of those round metal containers that used to be used in department stores to send money and receipts up to the cashier's desk, and proceeded to sling the wire across McQuarrie Street. Lennie Muir had decided we needed a direct line from his room to mine so that he could send me a note without bothering to go to the trouble of phoning up. The line stayed in place and whenever I was in Sydney after that I always booked into the same room, number 301.

Despite 'Mr 'Ughes's' boast to the mayor of Sydney, we didn't fare at all well in the five tennis 'Test matches' between Australia and Britain, winning only the final one in Perth. But I maintained my domination of Crawford, beating him in the final of the Victorian Championships and taking his title away from him, in straight sets, in the 1934 Australian Championships.

Crawford played rather badly in defence of his Australian crown. His concentration always needed to be at its peak and I think he was still tired after spending most of the previous twelve months travelling around the world. I did learn one lesson from Jack Crawford in that final, however. He played with a racket with a flat, rather than rounded, top. It was a unique shape and everybody recognized it as his, which, despite his lost championship, helped its sales in Australia.

My rackets were specially made for me by a man in England called Stanley Barnes on behalf of Slazengers, who also had sales outlets in Australia. The favourite racket in England was the Slazenger Queen's, but 'Queen's' wasn't a word you used in macho Australia. So the rackets I used there were always repainted to look like local models – but they lacked distinction. One night, over dinner with Slazengers' Australian sales manager Jimmy Hines, I suggested we paint my rackets a distinctive colour and we eventually decided they should be white.

Before my final with Crawford I warmed up with an ordinary racket, but when we were ready to start I went to the courtside and unsheathed my dazzling white 'prototype'. I could hear the buzz of conversation.

That final was played on a very hot day and by the third set,

71

because I used to twiddle my racket around in my hands, the paint started to come off. When I rubbed the sweat off my face I was well and truly smeared, prompting Jimmy Hines to send me down a note: 'Hurry up, you're running out of paint!' I obliged him by finishing the match in straight sets, and as Crawford and I walked off court a big box kite was floated over the stadium carrying the message, 'The white racket is a Slazenger.' It should have said, 'The Red Indian is Fred Perry.'

We had lots of inquiries about the racket which had won the Australian Championship, though, and when I got back to England Slazengers decided to produce an all-white racket there, too, with a red stripe for men and a blue one for women. 'Look here, I'm king,' I told them. I wanted a gold stripe for my personal rackets. But they said no, everybody else would want gold, too; so I had red.

During that trip to Australia I joined in the modern craze by making my first flight – and in the most distinguished company. The British and Australian teams for the 'Test matches' travelled around the country in the famous aircraft *The Southern Cross*, piloted by Charles Kingsford Smith.

Kingsford Smith was one of the long-distance aviators setting new solo flying records in those days when people were travelling further and faster. In 1934 Adolf Hitler became Reichsführer of Germany on the death of President Hindenburg and the following year Ramsay MacDonald resigned in Britain, to be succeeded as Prime Minister for the third time by Stanley Baldwin. But, such major events apart, it was people like Kingsford Smith who made the headlines with their bravery.

Donald Campbell set a new land speed record of 301 m.p.h.; Amelia Earhart flew from Honolulu to California in eighteen and a half hours; and in Britain the Silver Jubilee train travelled at 112 m.p.h. The pace of life was quickening all over the world.

Kingsford Smith, who was later lost over the Indian Ocean, was the personification of the expression 'flying by the seat of your pants', and my first flights were memorably bumpy and rather rudimentary, too.

That first flight I made in Australia was quite an experience: the bi-plane was a boneshaker with two wings and a prayer, all held together with wire and chewing gum. We didn't fly very high in it either, so you felt every bump because the weather was hitting from all sides. There was no co-pilot: the pilot didn't seem to need one. He knew exactly where he was going, in cloud or out, without any need of modern technology. He, at least, gave you confidence. But it was rather strange sitting in mid-air in this rattling contraption with your back pressed against the side of the plane to keep your teeth in. There were a few windows, not very many, and room for about a dozen people squashed along benches either side of a wooden table down the centre. For our in-flight comfort there were also a few cold drinks in a box. It was a worse way to get away.

We flew on that occasion to Dubbo, 300 miles from Sydney and way to hell and gone to no place. There was a sheepranch there owned by a fellow called Perry, and that's why they took us there. He had about 500 square miles of ranch land, a little plot in the Outback, and we stayed there for two or three days on this 'jaunt'. We lost a great deal of interest when we had to go outside in the mornings and break the ice in order to shave. This farmer Perry showed us the countryside, and they gave Crawford and myself rifles so that we could all sail after kangaroos in cars, a traditional Australian pastime. When they told me it was my turn I pointed the gun at the kangaroo, and he looked me in the eye. I couldn't shoot it. I let it go. But that trip was fun because we were seeing places we had only ever read about and could never really picture, and here was the vast Australian Outback, looking exactly that, with millions upon millions of rabbits scurrying across the sand, digging under the chainlink fences which had been put there to try to contain them. Seeing these things, you learn what goes to make up a country. There's a Long Bar in Sydney, a tremendous place. They say if you wait there long enough, you will meet everyone you ever knew in Australia.

There were other globetrotting adventures, too. After I won the Australian Championship in 1934, I stopped off in India for a few days to spend some time with my friend the Maharaja of Kutchbeha, who had invited me over for a change of scenery. I was met at the dock and escorted on the train to a sumptuous palace with rows of servants standing out in front. I asked, naturally, if my host was inside, assuming this to be the royal residence. Oh, no, said they, this was my personal accommodation while I was in India. Dinner would be with His Illustriousness at the palace, which turned out to be even bigger and more sumptuous still. The whole set-up was beyond my comprehension. Later we were taken on a tiger hunt and I was relieved to look behind me while I was sitting 'in the blind' and see a couple of fellows in the trees with rifles poised in case I missed.

The Maharaja was a keen tennis player and arranged for us both to perform for a couple of sets for the edification of 'the help', which turned out to be a small crowd of some 2000 people.

73

On another Indian visit I was hit with malaria in Bombay just as I was due to come home. I spent a week in the Taj Mahal hotel all by myself waiting for the next ship back to England, and my only 'visitor' apart from the doctors was the youth (called a busboy) who brought up my meals for me. The world is a very small place. Some forty years later my wife Bobby and I were in South Africa, staying at the Beverly Hills Hotel (which the locals called the Heavily Bills Hotel) at Umschlage Rocks near Durban. We were going in for dinner one evening when we were greeted rather effusively by a big, good-looking and immaculately dressed Indian maître d'hôtel, who said, 'How do you *do*, Mr Perry; what an honour it is to see you again!' As I didn't know either the place or the Indian in question, we spent our dinner trying to figure out who the hell he was, and fishing for information on his identity. Finally he said, 'I do hope you have had no recurrence of your malaria,' and I knew this was the little busboy who had brought me my meals in India all those years ago.

As soon as I got off the train at Victoria Station on my return to London in the spring of 1934, the questions started: 'Are you turning professional?' Henri Cochet and Ellsworth Vines had quit the amateur game and everybody wondered if I would join them. 'I'm not even interested,' I was reported as saying, and at this stage of my career it was true, though by now I held two major titles. The reason was that I was chasing the third – and the greatest – the Wimbledon Championship.

Because Britain had won the Davis Cup and did not need to defend it until the Challenge Round in July, my spring and early summer schedule was easier than usual and I was able to enjoy the London social scene a little more.

At that time I owned a green Austin Seven, with a sliding roof, which had cost me £140, paid for by the articles I had written for the London evening papers. Provided we didn't write about the matches in which we played, we were allowed to become columnists without infringing our amateur status. Bunny Austin used to write, too, for whichever paper I wasn't hired by. One day, coming out of Wimbledon, I saw one newspaper poster saying, 'Bunny Austin – by Fred Perry' and another saying, 'Fred Perry – by Bunny Austin'. After that Austin and I doublechecked who was going to write about what!

The actor Robert Montgomery, who had become a friend of mine

74

during my stays in Hollywood, came over to London at that time and I offered to show him around in my Austin Seven. When I picked him up at his hotel Montgomery was clad in what he fondly imagined was the required clothing for a London gent – dark suit, bowler hat and carrying an umbrella. He was a tall man and couldn't fit inside my tiny car until I opened the roof, so we drove round London with his bowler hat sticking out of the top of the Austin. He went in my car only once, because he claimed the London double-decker buses scared the hell out of him in such a tiny car.

Speaking of Austins, although he was my chief contemporary, I didn't mix much socially with Bunny. He moved in a circle of theatrical friends through his wife, the actress Phyllis Konstam, and was a very quiet man. One evening, however, Austin and I were in London together so we decided to go out for dinner. On the way we met an American friend of mine from the film industry, who offered to buy us a meal. Naturally, we were delighted. He took us to one of the best places in town, Sovrani's Blue Train in Piccadilly, a favourite restaurant of the Prince of Wales. The American even asked for the Prince's table, but was told, 'Sorry, the Prince is dining here tonight, but we'll get you a table nearby.'

This was done and we were enjoying our meal when I felt a hand on my shoulder and a voice saying, 'Don't get up, Mr Perry.' It was Edward, the Prince of Wales. He said, 'I would like to congratulate you on winning the American and Australian Championships. It is very remiss of me, but I can't for the life of me recall the name of the gentleman whom you beat in the two finals.' I said, 'Thank you very much, sir; it was Jack Crawford, the Australian.' The Prince wished me luck at Wimbledon, and returned to his table. I would have stood up like Austin and the other chap, but I'd had my back to the Prince's party and hadn't realized it was him coming over. As I rose from my seat, the Prince pushed me back down again. He was a very gracious man, and he never forgot this encounter in the restaurant. Whenever I saw him afterwards he would greet me cheerily, 'How are you, sir?'

Although I won the British Hard Courts title at Bournemouth later that year for the third successive time, I wondered whether my luck was, in fact, out. Early in the French Championships I damaged an ankle in the second set of my match against the ambidextrous Italian, Giorgio de Stefani.

I didn't want to default so I told Giorgio that if he didn't make me run around too much I was prepared to play the rest of the match and give him an honourable victory. But I don't think he trusted me; he had me stretching and running, which made me really mad.

Eventually I lost comfortably, or in this case uncomfortably. I was so annoyed that as we came off court I said to him, 'Right, Giorgio, next time we play it's going to be 6–0, 6–0, 6–0.'

After that it became a ritual that at every tournament we both entered I would go up and ask him which part of the draw he was in. It took me another couple of years to catch up with him, but it finally happened in Australia, in Melbourne, in a semi-final and on grass, not his favourite surface.

If I won the toss at the start of a match I always used to let my opponent serve first because, particularly when playing the big-serving Americans, this always gave you a chance to break in that opening game while he was still warming up. But in that semi-final I told Giorgio, 'I'll serve.' When he asked, 'But you don't usually do that,' I told him, 'It doesn't make any difference today. I told you, Giorgio, it's going to be love, love and love, anyway.' So I started to serve and promptly went 15–40 down. But I scrambled out of it and, just as I had promised, beat him 6–0, 6–0, 6–0. It had taken two years to get even, but I did it.

That determination was part of my character. If I made up my mind to do something, come hell or high water I was going to do it. As far as I was concerned on court, my opponent was there because he had the honour of playing against me! So I tried to impose my will on him. I let him know, by whatever method I could – even by telling him directly, as I did to poor Giorgio de Stefani – that I wasn't the slightest bit interested in what *he* wanted to do. Of course, it's one thing to have this approach oneself and quite another to put up with it from an opponent. *That* just made me as mad as hell!

The better I got the more I realized that if I did what I was expected to do and the ball went where I aimed it, there was little my opponent could do, unless he played me when I was injured, as De Stefani had done in Paris, or unless he just got lucky.

After Paris I didn't play any more tennis in 1934 until Wimbledon, in a bid to get my ankle fully repaired. Despite the expert attentions of Hugh Dempster, who had treated my shoulder before the 1933 Davis Cup triumphs, I still felt a little awkward as I won my first two matches.

In the third round I had to face the hard-hitting but erratic Czech, Roderick Menzel. In a major two-week championship there is always one day when things aren't quite right, when you have a bad day and the other fellow grabs his chance with both hands. Difficult conditions are great levellers of tennis players and you do need a little bit of luck at the right time.

Menzel had fistfuls of luck that day. Everything he attempted came off. I lost the first set 0–6 and eventually found myself trailing two sets to one. I hadn't been really moving wide on my forehand because I was worried about my ankle giving way again. Dempster had told me to go for the first wide ball because if my ankle was going to give, it would happen then.

Was this to be another disappointment, I wondered, just as Paris had been? Suddenly a note arrived at courtside for me. It was from Dempster and it said, 'Either you go for the wide ones or I'll pull you off court.' I did as he ordered, won the last two sets, and from then on had no more worries about the ankle.

In the quarter-finals I faced George Lott, who had put out De Stefani in the second round and spoiled my chances of early revenge for Paris. Having beaten Lott in both our previous matches, I had no fear of him, though I respected his skills, particularly in doubles. Victory in four sets over him brought me up against another American, Sidney Wood. It was Wood who had beaten me at the same stage of his championship year, 1931, and it took me five hard sets to reverse the result of that match.

So for the first time I was in the Wimbledon final – where my opponent was, once again, Jack Crawford. I had beaten him in five sets for the US National title and in three sets for the Australian one, after which Stanley Doust wrote in the *Daily Mail*: 'Each time they have met Perry has won by a bigger margin and I see no reason why he should not carry on.'

Doust was right. It took me only an hour and ten minutes to beat Crawford 6–3, 6–0, 7–5, and if that seems a remarkably quick time for a three-set match, remember there was no ninety-second sit-down at the change of ends in those days. In fact, of course, there was no sit-down at all.

At one stage I reeled off twelve games in succession and the only time Crawford looked like halting the rot was when he broke my serve to lead 5–4 in the third set. But, as the Associated Press reported, 'Perry just opened the throttle a little wider.'

The final point was an anti-climax. Crawford's first serve, which he thought was an ace, was nullified when he was foot-faulted. He netted the second serve and the championship was mine on a double fault. Crawford gave a scornful little bow to the linesman who had foot-faulted him a split second before I arrived to shake hands with him, having done a cartwheel before vaulting the net.

I was the first Englishman to win Wimbledon for twenty-five years but, as the Associated Press correspondent pointed out, the spectators managed to restrain any excesses of enthusiasm: 'Crawford received far more applause than Perry.'

I have to agree with the comment of John R. Tunis in an article for *Esquire* magazine:

To put things bluntly, Perry is not a popular champion at home. He isn't happy with the Wimbledon galleries. Why? Simply because Wimbledon is the most snobbish centre of sport in the world. The members of that Holy of Holies ... seem to resent the fact that a poor boy without a varsity background should have yanked himself to the front – even though in the process he yanked England back into the tennis picture from which she had been absent since 1909. Extraordinary people!

I'd always been regarded as an upstart who didn't really belong in such exalted company. I was someone who didn't have the right credentials for this noble game. But I don't think the frostiness of the Wimbledon crowds towards my victory was simply a question of snobbery or resentment of the kind that might be felt over a mongrel winning Cruft's. There was more to it than that. You see, they had never really seen an Englishman of this era who didn't like to lose. I freely admit I wasn't a good loser: I didn't go out there to lose and it hurt me very much if I did. I was confident and I was arrogant, because in one-to-one confrontations like boxing and tennis you have to be. Your opponent isn't going to look up to you if you look down on yourself, and you have to try to impose your superiority on him as forcefully as you can. Give him a beating to remember. Well, I don't think this was an approach generally favoured in England at the time. It was un-English. It wasn't done, old bean. Not in tennis, anyway.

It reminded me of that famous story about Sir Jack Hobbs, probably the greatest batsman England ever had, playing against a county side one day and suffering the impertinence of their fast bowlers sending down bumpers. Hobbs got up to the bowler's end and had a word with one of them: 'Look, old boy,' he said, 'if you bowl properly, like a gentleman, I'll get my 100 and get myself out, but if you choose to bowl in this fashion, I'll stay here all day and break your back.' And that's exactly what he did. I believe I was the first to bring this attitude, of breaking an opponent's back, to Wimbledon and to tennis, and I don't think the crowds were quite sure how to take it. When we won the Davis Cup, that was great, because that was winning for Great Britain. But when it came to winning Wimbledon, that was an individual thing, and anyway, what was this Perry fellow doing there in the first place?

Still, there *were* people who appreciated what that win meant to English tennis. As I came off court Dan Maskell greeted me and he was crying. Then they brought my father down to congratulate me and he was crying, too. Then Anthony Sabelli, the LTA secretary, shook my hand and he was in tears. I thought, what the heck's going on? I've just won Wimbledon and everybody is crying!

But I must confess I was almost in tears myself half an hour later, after the incident when the committee man deputed to hand me my honorary membership tie congratulated Crawford instead, and merely left my tie draped over my chair while I was in the bath. I hit the roof over that. Anthony Sabelli was sent for. While I was waiting for him Crawford and I had a friendly swallow of the champagne, but I was so mad I couldn't see straight and if somebody had come up to me at that moment and said, 'Here's a fistful of dollars to turn pro,' I would have accepted.

When Sabelli turned up I pointed out that my next commitment was a week's practice at Eastbourne in preparation for Britain's defence of the Davis Cup against the United States. I told Sabelli I would report for duty but that I was not prepared to play in the Davis Cup until I received an apology for what Hillyard had said. It took several days, but in the end I got it.

When I had calmed down I set off for a series of celebrations which lasted all night. I went up to London first to have dinner with Henry Cotton, who had won the Open Golf Championship the week before and pipped me in our personal rivalry about who would win the big prize in golf or tennis first.

If my Wimbledon win hadn't been too well received in some quarters, everybody seemed to be celebrating in London. All the evening paper placards carried just one word – *Fred*. It was very moving. They wouldn't let Cotton or myself pay for our meal at the Savoy, nor were we allowed to pay for our seats at the theatre. When the time came to leave, the doorman took one look at me and asked where I wanted to go. I said, 'Eastbourne.' I don't know what made me say that, because I had completely forgotten that I had to play the final of the mixed doubles with Dorothy Round at Wimbledon the following afternoon. The doorman said, 'You can't drive to Eastbourne, sir; I'll take you down.' So I walked into the Grand Hotel in Eastbourne early in the morning only to be met by a police inspector who told me that I was wanted back at Wimbledon that afternoon; King George and Queen Mary were going to watch the women's singles final and had expressed a wish to meet me.

As time was getting short, we had to leave immediately, so they provided a police escort to speed us on our way. When we reached the outskirts of London we found the roads mysteriously sanded and cleared, and people lining the route, waving. The crowds were waiting for the royal entourage, and there *I* was, doffing my cap because I didn't really know what was going on and thought this was the least I could do in the circumstances. Meanwhile, they had called my father asking him to bring suitable attire for me to Wimbledon for the presentation, and on my arrival I was thrown in the tub, shaved at breakneck speed, before staggering into the Royal Box, there to meet the King and Queen. They had been watching Dorothy Round beat Helen Jacobs in three sets to take the women's title.

For once in my life, I was swaying a bit. Although I didn't usually drink – or perhaps *because* I didn't drink – the champagne of the previous day, starting with the bottle Jack Crawford and I had shared in the dressing room, was still affecting me, and I wondered if the King noticed. He shook hands with me and said, 'I owe you an apology for not being here when you won the championship yesterday. This is the first time an Englishman has won Wimbledon in my reign and I wasn't here to see it, but I do hope you'll appreciate that there are a few other things I have to do.' I recall saying something like, 'Oh, don't bother about it,' which caused the King to observe me more closely and note that perhaps things weren't quite as they should be with Mr Perry's demeanour. 'Don't you think we should *sit down*, Mr Perry,' said the King. 'After all, the public are standing up while I do, and I think it only fair to permit them to be seated.' And thus His Majesty got me off the hook.

Dorothy Round and I did win the mixed doubles that day, though. Dorothy was so excited that she couldn't seem to hit a ball, and she was in bad shape anyway because of the ladies' singles final. 'I don't know what I'm going to do,' she whispered. 'I don't know how I'm going to hit a single solitary ball, Fred. I scarcely know where I am.' I asked her if she felt she could still serve, and she said she could. 'Fine,' I said, 'and the rest of the time, stay in the tramlines as much as possible and I'll do the rest.' Which is exactly what I did. Considering the state we were in, it was a case of 'all's well that ends well', but we managed to hang in there and win the championship.

My Wimbledon win meant that I didn't get much respite from the 'professional' rumours. When I arrived at Wimbledon to meet the King there was a telegram awaiting me from Bill O'Brien, Bill Tilden's manager, making me an offer to turn pro. Pictures taken of me that day with Dorothy Round show the telegram sticking out of my suit pocket. Fred Perry, of Stockport and Ealing, was in big demand in England all of a sudden.

Alec Simpson, whose company – Simpson's of Piccadilly – manufacture Daks trousers, had used me as a sort of clotheshorse to try out Daks tennis trousers. It took a long time to get them right because, while they had to fit snugly, there also had to be room in the seat and at the knee to allow the wearer to move and bend. But I wore the trousers at Wimbledon, and afterwards Simpson invited me to his office to show me a mock-up page of the *Daily Mail* featuring a picture of me executing an overhead smash with the headline, 'Fred Wins Wimbledon in Daks'.

He asked me what I thought of the idea and I promptly told him there was no way he could run the advertisement because it would infringe my amateur status. Simpson said he realized this, which was why he had sent for me, and told me he was prepared to offer me a lifetime contract with Daks, who would pay me a shilling for every pair of Daks sold throughout the world for the rest of my life.

In the end I turned him down because I wasn't ready to become a professional. But when I think of the millions of pairs of Daks trousers in the world, I sometimes wonder if I shouldn't have accepted. Every time I used to spot a pair of Daks in the street I would think, there goes another shilling. Looking back, this was the tip of the iceberg as far as the ensuing professional problems were concerned. Within forty-eight hours of winning Wimbledon I was already embroiled in official offers from American promoters and from clothing manufacturers in England.

9   A Professional Dilemma

Wimbledon was the setting for our Davis Cup Challenge Round tie with the Americans, who had put out Australia in the Inter-Zone final. As a preparation, we played and beat the Japanese at Eastbourne before moving into our team headquarters, the RAC Country Club at Epsom.

The United States team was much changed from the one we had defeated in Paris a year previously. Frank Shields and Sidney Wood filled the singles slots in place of Ellsworth Vines, who had turned pro, and Wilmer Allison, while the tall Californian Lester Stoefen partnered George Lott in the doubles.

For our first defence of the trophy Austin and I played singles, and Pat Hughes and Harold Lee formed the doubles partnership. Austin got us off to a marvellous start, beating Shields for the loss of only nine games, but I had a terrific five-set battle with Wood. He led two sets to one before my superior fitness told in the last two sets, in which I dropped only three games. Wood might have been depressed at that fitness of mine. If he had only known the truth! I had twisted the sinews in my back and after dinner that night it had become so bad that I couldn't get up from the dinner table. Fortunately the next day, Sunday, was a rest day anyway and I was not playing in Monday's doubles match, so I had two clear days to get fit again.

Once more the osteopath Hugh Dempster was called in for consultation. I rested for those two days and was then taken up to his London office in Manchester Square at eleven o'clock, three hours before I was due to go on court against Shields in what had become the crucial rubber since our defeat in Monday's doubles. If I lost to Shields, or was incapacitated because of my injury, the deciding match would be between Austin and Wood, with the American a favourite to win.

Dempster fiddled around with my back and suddenly there were a couple of twangs like banjo strings snapping. Then he strapped me up and told our trainer Tom Whittaker, 'Keep him warm until the match; don't let him cool off whatever happens.' So, despite the fact that it was July, I was muffled up in a couple of sweaters.

They took me straight to Wimbledon, where I had an early lunch before hitting a few balls with Dan Maskell. When I went out on court I was still wearing my two sweaters, which the Associated Press correspondent put down to arrogance on my part: 'Perry was so confident at the start he did not even remove his sweater.'

After winning the opening set, though, I peeled off. My back held up, which was fortunate since Shields and I got into quite a battle that had the crowd of 17,000 in a most un-Wimbledon-like state of frenzy and disorder, with the umpire repeatedly calling for quiet.

The fourth set was a marathon. Four times in succession Shields broke my serve and needed only to hold his own to level the match at two sets all. But on all four occasions, with the crowd going wild, I broke right back again, leaving the set locked at 8–8. Again Shields served for the set at 11–10; again I broke back. Eventually I ended what was the second-longest set in Davis Cup history by holding my serve to love, to lead 14–13, and breaking Shields to win the match 6–4, 4–6, 6–2, 15–13 and keep the Cup in Britain.

Shields, who had battled wonderfully, saved two match points in that twenty-eighth game of the fourth set. At deuce he pushed the ball down my forehand and came in. I just waited for him to make his move; he was watching to see which side I would hit the ball. Eventually he made his guess and went to the right a little, so I squeezed it down his left-hand side. He made a spectacular dive for it, but it was gone. Match point for the third time.

The next point was a similar rally. He came in again, certain this time that I would go across court. So he moved to the right again, and again I squeezed it down the line. It wasn't a hard shot, but once he had moved the wrong way it was a certain winner. Shields made another dive, hit the ball into the net, and fell down in the same place as before. I did my usual leap over the net to shake hands: 17,000 people were screaming and cheering because Britain had retained the Cup.

Shields got up and held out his hand. I expected him to say, 'Well played' or something like that (though I'd admit I rarely did myself), but he just grinned and said, 'You son of a gun. Right in the same goddam place.' The people must have wondered what we were laughing about.

But Frank Shields was that sort of happy-go-lucky fellow. I once watched him leap from the mast of a yacht in Newport harbour for a bet – luckily he landed in the water, not on the deck! There was a 45-foot mast on that yacht. In Paris one year he pulled what I consider to be the all-time caper of my time in tennis. In those days anybody who lost in the first week of the French Championships was invited to a tournament in Berlin the following week, and Shields, having lost on the Saturday, accepted such an offer.

On Monday morning, however, the Germans phoned Roland Garros Stadium to ask where Shields was as he hadn't turned up for the tournament, so the French officials contacted a stockbroker called Portlock, with whom Shields had been staying. Portlock reported that all Shields's clothes and tennis gear were still in his room, but that his dinner suit was missing – as was Frank.

So the Germans started retracing his steps and eventually found that Shields had been to dinner on the Sunday night with a French player, Paul Barralet de Ricou. They had met a couple of American girls and, after a late night, taken them back to their hotel. Shields had wanted to stay, but his girl's parents were there, too, and to make matters worse she was leaving for home the next day.

Shields and De Ricou went to see the girls off on the boat train on the Monday morning and, on an impulse, Shields asked De Ricou to lend him all the money he had. Still in his dinner suit, he climbed aboard the boat train and set off for Le Havre.

By Wednesday the French tennis people wired the steamship to ask if there was a Frank Shields aboard. The answer was no. Then they got hold of the girl's name and asked for the purser to check with her. And there, in her cabin, they found Frank, three days at sea, still in his dinner jacket. He had no passport, no luggage, and could only go out in the evening when the other passengers were wearing their dinner jackets. Quite a romantic, that Frank Shields!

There was little time to celebrate the Davis Cup success before I set off again for the United States, where I fuelled all the speculation about turning pro by winning the US title for the second successive year. This time I beat Wilmer Allison, a man to whom I had never lost, but in the end it was much closer than I would have liked. I blew a two-set lead and eventually squeaked home 8–6 in the fifth set.

Afterwards I planned a little celebration with my New York friends at the Madison Hotel, where I always stayed during the US Championships, and I thought it would be nice if we took the trophy along with us as a decoration. After all, the Davis Cup had been out on the razzle.

We were all sitting in the car, holding the trophy, when a security man came and asked where we were planning to take it. 'Back to the hotel,' I told him, but he explained that it could not be taken out of the stadium. I said that I had won it, so could take it just where I wanted, but he was adamant. 'If you want to take it with you, you've got to win it three times,' he said. 'OK, that's what I'll do,' I promised him, just being bloody-minded at the time, I suppose. But that's exactly what I eventually did.

As champion of Australia, Wimbledon and the United States, I was bombarded by the media, wanting to know if and when I would leave amateur tennis for the paid ranks. I got all this buffeting from the media first hand, together with the questions about when I was going to turn pro (and if not, why not), whereas all the news from England was second or third hand. So for me the pressure was beginning to build up pretty badly. Still no word from the LTA. If I had thought things would ease off when I travelled out to the West Coast for the Pacific Southwest tournament, which I won again, I was sadly mistaken, because by then quite a few of my Hollywood friends were trying to persuade me to go into the movie business.

It was suggested I appear in a film, playing just enough tennis to establish my identity without indulging in any coaching or dialogue, but when I requested permission from the LTA in London it was refused, though for the life of me I couldn't see why at the time.

Then B. P. Schulberg, acting for the Paramount Company, offered me a two-year contract to appear in pictures and on the radio which, I admit, sorely tempted me. And the very next day I was due to sail from San Francisco for Australia with the rest of the LTA team.

Obviously the British faction didn't want me to become a professional, but it wasn't only the LTA who was unwilling to see it happen. As I mentioned earlier, I worked for Slazengers, though officially I represented their Australian operation so that I would still be eligible at tournaments in Britain where Slazenger equipment was being used. I was, in fact, under worldwide contract to Slazengers, and in the event of my turning professional it was fairly obvious that they would want to retain my name. However, although pro-fessionalism was a fact of life in the USA, it was still considered *de trop* elsewhere in the world and a dirty word in the amateur ranks. Had I been able to make a racket deal in the United States, I suspect that it would have been more lucrative than the entire worldwide Slazenger contract. But I had always been with Slazengers and wanted to stay loyal to them. And I wanted to retain my amateur status, so that I could play for Great Britain.

Albert Slazenger, the chairman of the board, was the one who had hired me, with these words: 'We don't care where you go or what you do, but we don't want you sitting in our office unless it's raining outside. Wherever you are, even watching cricket, you are promoting as far as we are concerned. But the day you quit tennis to come into the organization, you had better know what makes it tick.' This was why I spent a great deal of time at the factory.

It was Albert Slazenger who came up with an idea to keep me 'amateur' and playing for my country. He owned a house at Wimbledon, which he proposed to sell to me for £500. He then went to a couple of dozen of the richest businessmen in England, told them he planned to buy the house back from me for £100,000 and asked them for contributions for the 'Save Fred Perry Fund'. A couple were interested. The rest all said I should be proud to be playing for my country for nothing.

I knew of none of this until later, when I was made aware of mysterious 'moves' to help me avoid the terrible pitfall into professionalism. But in any case, before leaving San Francisco I announced that I had decided to remain amateur. I was bewildered by all the contradictory advice I had been offered and at the time I wrote: 'Ought I to accept? Would you? Here was a grave problem to set before a young man thousands of miles from home advice. I cabled home, I telephoned home, to my father and friends, at great expense. But it is impossible to conduct weighty discussions across a continent and an ocean at so many pounds for each three minutes of conversation.'

But if I had thought the matter was closed by my San Francisco announcement, I was rapidly disenchanted. The media radioed me on the ship and tried to contact me on the phone at every landfall on the way across the Pacific. When we stopped at Honolulu and I went for a day's relaxation playing golf I was called off the course to take a long-distance call from a Fleet Street newspaper.

By then I had been in the business only a few years, but long enough at that stage to know how to handle the press properly. Good press relations are one of the most important things of all and if some of today's young professionals could acquire better experience of getting along with the media before they get thrown in at the deep end it would save a lot of problems. In my own case, although I was fed up with being asked the same question time and again, it was distinctly flattering in those days to be called all the way from London if you happened to be in Hawaii or Australia.

It was difficult to get away from the subject. When I went to a cinema in Auckland I found a New Zealand journalist sitting next to me – just by chance, of course. He, too, wanted the inside story on my decision, which, according to him, seemed to be shaking the world.

I managed to get a brief respite when we stopped off at one tiny island too remote for the media to contact. We even managed a tennis game of sorts. The island possessed a concrete court, but the concrete ended with the actual perimeters of the court: you had to stand in the sand to serve, which meant that you would then skid all over the place with sand on the soles of your shoes. The balls we played with were a bit of a joke, too. They had been left there when the French team had passed through some years previously and were the only ones on the island.

In Australia it seemed that nobody wanted to know about my tennis – just whether I was going to turn pro. To be honest, it drove me up the wall to be asked the same question time after time, and soon enough it began to affect my game. Headlines began to appear like, 'English Net Star Soundly Trounced' and 'Perry Exhausted, To Take Long Rest'.

After I had lost to Jack Crawford – breaking a string of six successive wins over him – and then managed to take only two games in three sets from Adrian Quist, the *Sydney Herald* offered the following editorial opinion about me: 'Perry is blessed with glorious powers of recovery and his temperament is ideal, but his brain needs a rest.'

It was certainly true that I was playing under pressure the whole time, because American promoters still hadn't given up hope of persuading me to sign for the professional winter tour of the United States, which did not get under way until January 1935. Every time I lost a match it was a bigger disaster in the eyes of the media than it was even to me, and I was a man who hated being beaten.

In later years the national federations took care of all the pressure from promoters when their players were considering turning professional, but in those days we were pioneers in a field which didn't change until after the Second World War, and that unremitting pressure was on me for three years.

The low point was reached on the night before I met Crawford in the final of the Australian Championships. Yet another rumour was floated about an offer being made to me – a rumour which prompted half a dozen phone calls from London, the final one coming at 4 a.m. This was, as can be imagined, not the best possible preparation for the defence of my Australian title and as a result I was duly beaten in four sets. 'Bang goes £20,000' proclaimed one headline. It seemed I just couldn't win anywhere along the line at that time.

The long-standing arrangement I had had with the LTA which allowed me to travel back home via the United States in the spring of 1935 only gave rise to more stories about me going there to take the money, though if that had really been the case I would not have stopped off in New Zealand to play in a tournament and then had a week's golf in Honolulu after that. Although it was true that I was returning to California to discuss another offer to go into pictures, the media missed the best story of all – I had fallen in love, and with a film actress.

Her name was Helen Vinson and we had been seeing quite a bit of each other when I was in Hollywood. After turning down the latest offer to star in a tennis film because of the continued refusal of the International Lawn Tennis Foundation to permit me to remain an amateur if I did so, I decided to head for home, with Helen, who was going to England to make a picture.

I had had a rough season, playing and travelling. Altogether I had been on the amateur tennis treadmill for three years non-stop and I had looked forward to a short break in Hollywood. However, I quickly found out what a strange place it could be. Previously I had only ever been there when the tennis tournament was on, when the whole town talked and thought about tennis and it was the most marvellous week in my year. But the next week or the next month, never mind six months later, it was not the same place. The fact that a tennis star was having dinner with a film star didn't mean anything. Nobody wanted to know, apart from the people trying to sign away my amateur career. My problem was that all the fellows who were trying to talk me into turning professional were on hand in California and the ones who were trying to talk me out of it were a long way away. It had got to the stage where I was almost a basket case, so I proposed to think it over at leisure while heading back with Helen Vinson for the European season.

My friend Bertram Weal, owner of the Madison Hotel in New York, helped us to give media pursuers the slip by changing my transatlantic sailing from the *Georgic* to the *Berengaria*. But at Cherbourg we were met by the vanguard of the British press – two sports journalists, Bruce Harris and Gerard Walter – and their early stories prompted a massive turnout for our arrival at Southampton.

From 1930 onwards I had been spending less and less time in England, but in 1935 I really had left it late to prepare for the British Hard Courts tournament at Bournemouth, which title I held. There were only a couple of days for preparation, so I called the LTA to ask if they would arrange for me to go straight from the boat to Queens Club to get in some practice with Joe Pearce and Bill Holmes, who were the professionals there. The dear old LTA offered me half an hour in the morning and half an hour in the afternoon and seemed quite surprised when I told them that what I really wanted was about four hours a day of concentrated work.

With Helen being in England I did not find it too easy to concentrate on tennis, but I got to the final of the Hard Courts tournament where, once again, I faced my Davis Cup colleague, Bunny Austin. It was one of those special Bournemouth April days, raw and cold and damp, and the court was very slow and slippery.

Dan Maskell accompanied me on the long walk from the dressing room to the court and he must have thought I was setting off for the North Pole. I was wearing a yellow cashmere top coat buttoned up, a scarf and gloves. I told Dan, 'Don't bother watching this match today; it's going to be the worst you've ever seen. The court is slippery and if I can't get a foothold I'm no good. So I'm just going to sit on the baseline and play Bunny shot for shot.' I felt so gloomy about having to play on such a day that I said to Dan, 'I'll probably lose the first set 0–6.'

Well, I *did* lose the first set to love and I'm sure, on reflection, it must have been quite the worst final in Bournemouth's history. In the fifth set, with me leading 1–0, the conditions finally got to Austin and he went down with cramp. After that it was no problem and I won the final set as easily as he had taken the first one.

Back in London, and suitably thawed out, I went for dinner with my Hollywood friends, Ben Lyon and Bebe Daniels. In our group was a motorcar millionaire, Horace Dodge, one of those Americans who always fancied speaking his mind. Inevitably the subject got around to the vexed question of my turning pro and how much would be involved financially. Somebody mentioned £100,000 – a fortune! Dodge sniffed: 'I spend that kind of money on a boat!' That finished me. I just got up and walked out. After I'd played for love all this time, and been the subject of everybody's Dutch auctions, here was Dodge belittling what I might be worth. But it was another sign of the pressures on me when I could walk out of a dinner with friends like that.

A little to my surprise, I won the French Championships of 1935, beating Crawford in the semis and Baron Gottfried von Cramm in the final. I had never previously seemed able to string good tennis together for long enough on the slow clay of Roland Garros Stadium, but this time it worked and I became the first Englishman to capture the French title.

The win, in four sets, also fulfilled my ambition to be champion of Australia, France, the United States and Wimbledon, although unfortunately my defeat in the Australian final the previous January meant that I had not held all four major championships at the same time. That achievement, the Grand Slam, had to await Donald Budge in 1938.

So, back to England, where my preparations for Wimbledon, as usual, were to play for my club Chiswick Park in the County Championships rather than join all the other big names in the Queens Club tournament.

At Wimbledon I was the top seed and a heavy-betting favourite to retain my singles title and I didn't have too much trouble that year. I beat old adversaries Roderick Menzel in the quarter-finals and Jack Crawford in the semis, before facing Von Cramm again in the final. As one American newspaper headlined that match, 'English Ace Wins in Straight Sets from Teuton Foe'.

I had made a close study of Von Cramm, as I did of all my opponents. He was a very phlegmatic player who never showed any emotion. But if he got nervous or scared, his face would go white and little pink spots would show on his cheeks, and the minute I saw those pink spots I would go after him and keep pushing, pushing all the time, never letting him slow the match to his pace.

The strategy worked perfectly at Wimbledon in 1935 and I routed my 'Teuton Foe', the sporting German baron, 6–2, 6–4, 6–4. I became the first player to play through the tournament and defend his Wimbledon title successfully since the abolition in 1922 of the Challenge Round when, of course, the champion did not get involved until the final.

10   Ribbed and Spliced

The remainder of 1935 was to bring me more glory, an injury – and matrimony.

Britain's defence of the Davis Cup that year was against those perennial challengers, the Americans. Six times since the Four Musketeers had taken the Cup from them in 1927 the United States had battled through to the Challenge Round, and every time they had failed, either against the French or the British. Now here they were again, back for a seventh try, with the veteran Texan, Wilmer Allison, and the young Californian, Don Budge, as their singles specialists, and Allison partnering Johnny Van Ryn in the doubles.

One of their own correspondents, Henry McLemore, gave the Americans no chance in his preview:

The chief problem will be Frederick J. Perry, the number one in the world and leader of the British defence forces. It takes no mathematical genius to grasp the fact that in a series decided on the basis of the best three of five matches, the side which starts two down is at a decided handicap. And that is just what any nation which challenges England for the Davis Cup faces.

Perry is good for his two singles matches before he starts. Unless Joseph Wear, the American team captain, can figure out the ways and means of halting Perry, United States' chances of winning are not only null and void but *nux vomica* as well.

But the English team isn't a one-man affair by any means. In Bunny Austin, Perry has the finest stylist in the world as a partner, and a man who saves his top game for the time when they tell him the royal standard flies above Wimbledon, the King and Queen are in the box, and the honour of the Empire is at stake.

Playing for himself, Austin is only a brilliant player; playing for England, John Bull and the dominions, he's an inspired one.

The only match the Americans can feel fairly sure of is the doubles. England will use the veteran Pat Hughes and the young Army lieutenant, C. R. D. Tuckey. Hughes is past his prime; Tuckey has yet to prove he has one .... Tuckey packs tremendous power, but is just as likely to hit the umpire as the inside of the court. In fact, more likely.

McLemore was almost 100 per cent correct in his predictions. We led 2–0 at the end of the first day's play, but only after Austin had sailed within two points of defeat before downing Allison in five sets, 6–2, 2–6, 4–6, 6–3, 7–5.

Ferdinand Kuhn Junior reported for the *New York Times*: 'Wimbledon has seldom known such a demonstration as followed. Thousands stood on their seats and roared approval as Austin walked off court after having gained one of the finest victories of his career. Sir Samuel Hoare, deputising for the King, was so delighted that he slipped out of the royal box and patted Austin on the back as he entered the clubhouse.'

In such a stimulating atmosphere I had no trouble putting us two up by beating Budge in four sets, 6–0, 6–8, 6–3, 6–4, and when play resumed on Monday after a day's break our doubles pair, Hughes and Tuckey, confounded Henry McLemore and a lot of others by clinching victory for Britain by defeating Allison and Van Ryn 6–2, 1–6, 6–8, 6–3, 6–3. It was the first time a British team had won the Cup three years in a row since the days of the Doherty brothers in 1903–6.

In the 'dead' rubbers I beat Allison, while Austin downed Budge, both in four sets. It was the Americans' most humiliating defeat since the Australians had 'whitewashed' them back in 1911.

Afterwards I went off to America, to be plunged immediately into the familiar speculation about joining the professional ranks. After my Wimbledon and Davis Cup victories even the Americans were convinced there was no way I could fail to collect their national championship for the third successive year, and I must confess I felt that way, too.

By now I was beginning to look seriously at the prospects of a pro life and the cash involved. By the autumn of 1935 Ellsworth Vines and Bill Tilden had toured North America twice in their head-to-head series and the promoters were looking for a fresh face – mine.

Cunning old Bill Tilden shrewdly fuelled the speculation by telling a bunch of reporters, on a rainy day early in the US Championships, that he couldn't make up his mind whether I was 'the worst best player or the best worst player' he had ever seen. Tilden continued his assessment of me as follows:

He hits every shot wrong – every single one. If I tried to make a forehand drive the way he does I'd either hit the middle of the net or somebody sitting up in the top row of the stands. Yet he must be a great tennis player. You don't go on winning all the tournaments unless you are. I think I know the secret of Fred's success. He's got the most amazing right wrist I ever saw. It's strong as iron and abnormally supple.

Of course, he's got a beautiful eye and is as fine a conditioned athlete as there is in the world. The speed with which he starts a fifth set is enough to break an opponent's heart.

As I told the press at the time, 'It appears I have only one stroke in my repertoire, the forehand drive, but that shot alone is worth $100,000 to Mr Tilden and his backers.'

All of which appeared to make me an outstanding favourite for the US National title. But I was literally heading for a fall that year at Forest Hills. I reached the semi-finals comfortably enough and there I had to play Wilmer Allison. If I had beaten Wilmer I don't think there is any way I could have failed to take the championship, since my final opponent would have been either Sidney Wood or Brian 'Bitsy' Grant, neither of whom troubled me too much at that stage of my career.

We all changed in the same dressing room at the West Side Club and before our semi-final Allison had a favour to ask. He had been invited to the Pacific Southwest tournament in Los Angeles immediately after Forest Hills and planned to travel by the new method, aeroplane. He was therefore limited to the amount of luggage he could fly with and asked me if I would mind taking care of a couple of his suitcases on the train journey to the West Coast. 'No problem,' I said.

There had been a lot of rain around and the court was quite slippery for our semi-final. In the seventh game of the first set I skidded going for a wide ball and my full weight came down on my racket handle, driving it into my body. At first I thought I was only winded, but the pain was terrible and it turned out later that I had broken a rib.

It was at around this time that Helen Wills Moody had walked off court at Forest Hills when playing against Helen Jacobs, which created a furore, so as the holder of the title – and an Englishman, of course – I felt I couldn't do the same thing. So I stayed out there, although I couldn't serve properly or hit overheads. Allison had a very pleasant afternoon giving me short stuff and then lobbing me –

tactics which made me as mad as hell. He won easily, 7–5, 6–3, 6–3.

When we got off court and they had strapped me up, I returned to my locker afterwards to find Allison surrounded by the press, explaining that he had won because of a new theory on how to play me. This was too much, so I broke into the interview and told Allison that he could take his own suitcases to California – whether he was flying or not. I never was a good loser.

That broken rib probably prevented me becoming the first foreigner ever to win the US Championships three years in succession, but there was no point moping publicly about it. As Henry McLemore wrote, 'If Perry complained, it was not while the tennis writers were in earshot.'

Helen Vinson, Bertram Weal and my lawyers got me back to the Madison Hotel, where we all had dinner. I felt sore in all senses of the word, awaiting the inevitable headlines and knowing that losing that semi-final had done my professional prospects a bad turn. I'd probably dropped in value from a boat to a dinghy. As far as the Americans were (and still are) concerned, the US title was *the* most important one, which was only natural.

At about ten o'clock that night Irving Squires tried to brighten the gloom by saying to Helen and me, 'Why don't you two go out and get married?' Suddenly it seemed like a brilliant idea. Someone in our group knew the Registrar at Harrisburg, about thirty miles from New York. Telephone arrangements were made, we all climbed into cars, and off we went.

A magistrate was persuaded to leave his bed, and in the police station at Harrisburg, just before midnight that night in September 1935, Frederick J. Perry, broken rib and all, married Helen Vinson. We married in haste and repented the same way. Helen was a very pretty woman, but it was not a successful marriage. I was always travelling and so was she. It was what people in those days called 'a Hollywood marriage', i.e., doomed to failure.

After the ceremony we travelled back to California and although, of course, I wasn't fit enough to play in the Pacific Southwest tournament, I was on our honeymoon, so what the heck? My injury forced me to hang around on the fringe of tennis, which I had never liked, and to get involved in the endless speculation about turning pro. I even spent some time chatting over the prospects with Vines and Tilden, the top professionals at that time.

The offers were still coming in from the movie industry. A friend of mine called Pandro Berman from RKO studios wanted me to sign a contract for two pictures a year at $50,000 a picture. The contract would run for two years and I would not be required to play tennis in any of the sequences. RKO gave me until the spring to decide, so I immediately contacted my father, who put the idea to the LTA. If they had only agreed that I would not be considered a professional provided I didn't actually play tennis in the movies, then I would automatically have remained an amateur in the eyes of the International Tennis Federation as well. There was a precedent: in the United States Frank Shields had been given a contract with MGM, and no obstacles had been placed in his way. So we were hopeful. But instead of making a decision and absorbing any flak from other associations, the LTA put the idea to the vote at the ITF. This immediately killed the deal stone dead. It didn't do anything to improve my opinion of the LTA either.

Still, I did take a screen test for Pandro and his RKO studios. I was immaculate in white tie and tails, playing opposite Virginia Bruce and directed by the great Robert K. Leonard. Unfortunately Leonard made rather a quick movement for a heavy man and pushed his head into the microphone boom, which cut the screen test a little shorter than scheduled. The first picture they had in mind for me was *Top Hat*, with Fred Astaire and Ginger Rogers, which was then in preparation. I did a walk-on, handshake, left and right profile, looked straight into the camera and talked with Virginia as directed by the great man, but there were no hugging scenes, which disappointed me terribly.

Suddenly, however, all hell broke loose and the wires to London were hot. My father was asked to contact me at once and begged me not to turn professional, saying that something would be worked out shortly, and even Sir Samuel Hoare called to tell me the same thing, which was the first direct dealing I'd had with him throughout this whole mess. I called my friends in New York, who told me I was crazy not to turn pro, but that they would stand behind any decision I made. So, as Helen was going to England to make pictures, we decided to drop everything and gamble that the LTA would turn up with something.

Hollywood being Hollywood, there were offers for a piece of Perry. One of the local orchestras had lost its leader and wanted me to take over the job. They told me all I had to do was stand up in front of them and wave a baton, and they would pay me the leader's wages. After all, I had this amazing right wrist. They had it all worked out: they would call the band 'Fred Perry and his Racketeers'; all the music stands would be tennis rackets, and the microphones tennis balls. I must admit it was a hell of an idea, but it never got off the ground.

I was committed to go on from California to Australia, but I was sure I wouldn't be fit enough to play there. Still, I was looking forward to the voyage, which was always useful for the mental, as well as the physical rest it provided.

When I got to Australia I played some kid in the first tournament, but it took me five sets to beat him and I was in pain. Maybe I should have stayed on and seen it through that winter, but I had a wife back in California and I thought, to hell with it. I got on the next boat to America.

At that stage I really didn't care if I never hit another ball. I had had tennis up to my hat brim. Being Wimbledon champion is a very different proposition from being any other champion. It is the yardstick by which everything is gauged in the sport. If I stopped off in Suva or Hawaii or New Zealand and lost a set in a local match it was big news, and there was always somebody wanting to know how that sort of thing would affect my professional plans. The whole shooting match finally got to me.

I returned to England with Helen in February 1936.

Needless to say, the communication from the LTA was nil. We couldn't seem to get to first base. The discussions between my father and Sir Samuel Hoare went on from 1935 to the Challenge Round of the Davis Cup in 1936, but intensified after my return to England. It was all a lot of hogwash. Nothing was ever done, and I'm sure that Sir Samuel never intended that anything should be. As he once said in an off-guarded moment to my father during their discussions on my future, 'After all, we do not consider your son to be "one of us".'

I was now out of condition, a stone underweight, and down in the dumps because my general health had suffered in the aftermath of the rib injury. But those two stalwarts who had looked after my fitness in the past, Hugh Dempster and Tom Whittaker, pulled me back to something approaching my old fighting form by the spring. Daily manipulative treatment from Dempster toned up my muscles, and regular training sessions with Whittaker and my old friends of Arsenal Football Club did wonders.

When the time came for my annual tilt at the British Hard Courts title in April I felt as fit as ever. As usual, Austin was my opponent in the final. He was not only a great friend, but also a great theorist and a firm believer in the purity of strokeplay. Not for him my sort of slam-bang methods. As far as Austin was concerned, strokeplay should be straight out of the instruction manual, line for line, word for word. To see him and Von Cramm play a match, as I did at Wimbledon once, was like reading a book on tennis. Nothing much happened, but it was lovely to watch.

Austin was another player I had had plenty of opportunity to study while playing with and against him. When he got nervous he would walk around in little circles and would get upset by fairly common-place pieces of gamesmanship, such as someone taking a little longer than usual to serve. He had plenty to gall him that day at Bournemouth: I beat him in straight sets to win the Hard Courts Championship for the fifth year running.

I went to Paris in May to defend my French Championship, confident that I was fast regaining my best form. I certainly got a shock in the final there, losing in five sets to Von Cramm. What was worse, Von Cramm won the fifth set – that famous fifth set in which I used to pride myself on always being fitter, faster and fresher – by six games to love, allowing me only nine points! I must admit that for the first time in an important match I failed to make any sort of fight of the fifth set. Von Cramm played fine, attacking stuff on his favourite surface and might have beaten me even if I had been in top form.

Afterwards I was quoted in one English newspaper as saying that I was 'bored', a stupid remark which received appropriate publicity. Technically, I guess I should have said 'mentally flat'. I certainly bored my friends for the next few days as I went over and over the French final, searching for a reason for that pathetic show in the fifth set. Eventually I decided that the seven months' enforced rest I had taken from the game had made me stale rather than refreshing me. I had had an easy time of it in both the Hard Courts tournament and the French Championships – until the Von Cramm match, which proved conclusively that I had not been as match-tight as I had supposed.

Now I had just one month to win back the lost concentration and zest that had wrecked my title hopes in Paris, before I defended my only remaining major title – Wimbledon. I was no longer the French, American or Australian champion, as my father reminded me in a long letter exhorting me to pull myself together.

As Wimbledon approached and there was still no sign of the mysterious assistance being talked about by the LTA, I realized I was getting the treatment: they and the bigwigs at the All England Club thought my era had finished. I had lost my American, Australian and

French crowns, and there were those who were clearly wondering if I was going to lose my Wimbledon title, too.

It seemed that I was dead and about to be buried and that a lot of people at the LTA were happy at the prospect, since it meant they wouldn't even have to pretend any longer that they wanted to do something for me. Naturally this bothered me a great deal. I made up my mind, come hell or high water, that I was going to win Wimbledon a third time, and then turn pro.

Three in a Row

I decided to play as much as possible in the weeks before Wimbledon, with a little help from my friends. Pat Hughes and Dan Maskell spent hours working with me, and an American, David Jones, tested me with the sort of high-speed serving that his compatriots might shortly be unleashing on Centre Court. Despite all this, my timing was still not 100 per cent by the opening day of Wimbledon – I was still too tentative and defensive – but I sailed through the first two rounds without dropping a set.

The turning point was my third-round match with an old adversary, the American Johnny Van Ryn. He and I seemed to specialize in third-round clashes at Wimbledon; this was our third in five years, and I had needed four sets to get past him in 1935. This time I beat him in straight sets, conceding only five games as I flowed into top attacking form. 'You'll do now,' said Maskell, as I came off court.

The New Zealander C. E. Malfroy managed only eight games against me in the fourth round, as did 'Bitsy' Grant in the quarter-finals. Bitsy was a get-'em-back artist and a great believer that since there was no impediment above the net, that was the best place to hit the ball. Some of his shots seemed to go five hundred miles up in the air; I think Bitsy was the originator of that tennis tactic, the 'moonball'. Quite often you found yourself standing there an awfully long time waiting for one of his lobs to come to earth. Then, if he realized he wasn't going to get to your smash, down he would go and everybody in the crowd would laugh because dear old Bitsy had fallen over again while you were still awaiting the arrival of the ball. This particular touch of gamesmanship never worked with me. I would never even look at him; I just ignored him completely, so he stopped trying to pull that one with me.

I had one or two uncertain patches in the semi-final against Don Budge. I dropped the first set (the only one I conceded at Wimbledon that year) after being within two points of it and I nearly let him overhaul me in the second after having led 4–1 and 40-love. But I had regained my ability to battle it out and I won 5–7, 6–4, 6–3, 6–4.

Budge was a great player who was improving rapidly at that time. He used 17-oz rackets and you had to be a dock worker to lift one of those. He would steamroller you, given the chance. He just seemed to drop that heavy racket on the ball, which would really fly.

When playing Budge you had to make sure that he never got his feet planted to hit a backhand: if he did, it was goodnight. You had to keep him moving, and I used to do this by operating my favourite ploy – taking the ball early. Budge could never hurt you with his forehand, though. He looked as if he was beating a carpet when he wound up. It was a bigger and stronger swing than Borg's, but this was perhaps not to be wondered at since Budge came from California, where the ball bounced higher on the concrete courts.

My 1936 Wimbledon final against Gottfried von Cramm was a classic example of the reconnaissance job that Pops Summers used to organize on my behalf before a big match. Thanks to him, I always knew everything my opponents did.

In Von Cramm's case we knew all about his movements between Wednesday evening, when he reached the final, and Friday afternoon, when he walked out on to Centre Court to face me. He was staying at the Savoy and we knew what he ate, how he ate, when he ate, what time he went to bed and how he had slept. It was all done through friendly waiters, friendly chambermaids, friendly assistant managers. Anything was possible.

In the major tournaments which lasted a fortnight I used only to take a massage in the second week, on the principle that it did you more good if you only had it occasionally; if you needed it in the first week you weren't going to win anyway.

When I was on the table at Wimbledon just before going on court I asked the masseur what sort of shape he thought I was in. 'You've never been fitter in your life,' he said. I told him I thought I would need to be, in order to beat Von Cramm. 'What makes you think that?' he asked conversationally. I said that the German had just beaten me in the Paris final and was a pretty fit fellow. 'Well, he's got a cramp right now,' said the masseur. My ears went on full alert. Without opening my eyes I casually asked what he meant. He told me Von Cramm had been out to practise that morning, had overstretched his muscles before he was sufficiently warmed up and had suffered a groin cramp. 'Which side?' I said, pretending to nod off with boredom. 'I'm not allowed to tell you that, I'm afraid,' said the masseur, 'but what I *can* tell you is that he is going to have trouble stretching wide on the right.'

This information was passed along to Pops Summers, who told me to make sure when we were knocking up before the start that anything on Von Cramm's backhand was easy and hittable, but on the forehand side I should make my shots a little wide to see how he moved.

The opening game was a marathon. It went to ten deuces and twenty-four points before I held serve, but the vital factor was that I saw Von Cramm go over for a wide forehand and wince. I immediately looked up into the stands and Summers gave me the 'go' sign. So after that I hit to his backhand to get him over to one side of the court and then followed it up with a wide forehand. The poor fellow was crippled, so there wasn't much of a match.

As you may have gathered by now, I was always a believer in stamping on my opponent if I got him down, at Wimbledon or anywhere else. I never wanted to give him the chance to get up. In foreign countries especially, if you've got the local hero on the ground and can keep him there, you've got no problems. But if he is permitted to recover and the crowd gets behind him, then you've got trouble. Well, the Wimbledon crowds weren't exactly rooting for me, either, but I was determined that day that Von Cramm was going to have no chance of getting up and getting their support. If I could have beaten him six-minus-one instead of six-love I would have done.

Admittedly it was a terrible final, but I simply wanted to get it over with as quickly as I could. I had suffered an injury myself at Forest Hills the previous year in a vital match and it could just as easily have happened to me here. Something like that was always on the cards. It was him or me.

It was all over in forty minutes, the quickest men's final at Wimbledon since 1881 when William Renshaw thrashed the tennis-playing clergyman, John T. Hartley, 6–0, 6–1, 6–1, in thirty-seven minutes. I had won 6–1, 6–1, 6–0, my third straight-sets triumph in a Wimbledon final and sweet revenge for that defeat in the French Championships. After Von Cramm had congratulated me, he relayed a message to the crowd through the umpire. 'Baron von Cramm asks me to state that he has strained a muscle in his leg and is sorry he could not play better this afternoon,' announced the official.

Next day Gayle Talbot reported for the Associated Press that I had received a cable from the New York sports promoter, Bill O'Brien, offering me $50,000 to quit the amateur ranks. 'Perry referred to it as a "yearly query" from O'Brien and added, "It's the usual baloney",' Talbot wrote.

There wasn't too much time to savour what the Wimbledon authorities must have been thinking. This infernal Perry, a chap of quite the wrong calibre, had become the first Briton since Laurie Doherty in 1903 to win the championship three times running. And now I was off and running again, this time down to Eastbourne to prepare for our Davis Cup Challenge Round tie against Australia.

We had arranged a 'warm-up' friendly against the United States and, just having won Wimbledon, I admit I wasn't particularly keen to play in the match. I felt I didn't need any further 'sharpening' at that stage. Roper Barrett, our captain, insisted that I play, however, and after I failed to perform to his satisfaction I got a dressing down at dinner for 'not working hard enough'. That upset me again, on top of everything else that had gone on with British officialdom.

The Australian team consisted of Jack Crawford and Adrian Quist, and after the opening day it looked like another easy thing for us. We led 2–0, Bunny Austin having beaten Crawford, while Quist lost to me, both in four sets. But we went down in the doubles, and then Austin was defeated by Quist in another long four-setter.

So once again the destination of the Davis Cup was dependent on my performance when I had to face my old adversary, Crawford, in the fifth and deciding rubber. There was a good deal of alarm among the officials about whether we would be able to complete the tie that night, since the Austin-Quist match had gone on for hours. It had been agreed between the two captains to draw stumps at a certain time and postpone an uncompleted match until the following day.

It was getting quite late, about a quarter to six, when Crawford and I finally prepared to go on court. All the LTA officials surrounded me to exhort, 'Make sure you get a good start.... Don't take any chances.... Make sure you're not behind if you have to stop for the night.'

I was so fed up with this bombardment of advice that finally I interrupted them: 'What time is it now? 5.45 p.m.? Right, we'll be off court, finished, by 7.15 p.m.' I went out on to Centre Court determined to rush the hell out of Crawford and stop all these LTA people wearing me away.

Crawford served first; my return came off the handle and went halfway over the net. I went charging in as if I were catching a bus. He couldn't believe his eyes.

Players used to talk to each other in those days – though not very much – and when we were changing ends Crawford said, 'That was a hell of a shot to come in on. What are you trying to do?' I told him, 'Jack, I'm coming in on every one, whether it's off the strings or the handle or the frame – whatever.'

Crawford was a good fellow with a keen sense of humour, but I don't think he knew what hit him in that match. I had found when I played him previously that if I really rushed him, taking the ball early and charging the net, he could be flustered. I was determined not to have the tie drag on to the next day, which would mean having to pack up for the night a set up or a set down. Nice man though Crawford was, I was going to knock him over and jump up and down on him. I was going in to that net, and only if he had an elephant gun would he be able to stop me.

I don't think the match lasted much more than an hour. I won 6–2, 6–3, 6–3, and the British team won the Davis Cup again – the fourth year in succession.

As I walked off court Dan Maskell came out to take my rackets, as he always did. As we went behind the barrier leading to the dressing rooms, I said, 'Just a minute, Dan,' and I walked back on to Centre Court and took a final look around at the crowded stands. In that instant Maskell knew that I was going to turn pro, that I was gone from Wimbledon and from the Davis Cup.

I knew I would never play on Centre Court again because I had been back in England since April and nothing had been done to encourage me to stay in the amateur game. I had also heard by then about Albert Slazenger's efforts on my behalf and the reaction of his business pals. I finally knew what not to expect.

Those seven Wimbledons had been wonderful, and in spite of everything that had gone on in the past two years, my great love affair with that place had never faltered. To me it was and will always be the greatest tennis venue in the world, and all my memories of Wimbledon are fond ones. Incidents cross my mind even now to make me smile. I got the greatest kick of all the afternoon I took Loretta Young to watch the tennis there. We had been friends in Hollywood and she just happened to be in London during Wimbledon fortnight. When we walked into the place everything virtually stopped. I don't think a single spectator noticed a ball struck from that moment on. The players hit more bad shots and the linesmen made more mistakes than had been made in years. Loretta took the place by storm.

I set off for America still smarting over my treatment in England,

and as soon as I got to New York I got in touch with my lawyers and told them what I had decided. 'Get me the best terms possible,' I instructed them.

They contacted a couple of men called Frank Hunter and Howard Voshell, who were trying to put together a professional tour for the coming winter. Hunter, a former Davis Cup player, was a very wealthy guy and a part-owner, among other things, of the very famous 21 Club in New York. The offer Hunter made was very much better than anything I had heard before and he also promised to put me in touch with other sources of income and promotion. I was prepared to accept, but first I wanted to see if I could win the US Championships a third time, too, before heading west for one last fling at the Pacific Southwest tournament.

I breezed through the first five rounds at Forest Hills, dropping only one set along the way. Bitsy Grant and his 'moonball' tactics took me to four sets in the semi-final, before I came up against Don Budge in what turned out to be a very strange final indeed.

The weather was unpleasant – humid and hot, with a threat of thunderstorms. The rules in the championships at that time for a five-set match called for a ten-minute break at the end of the third set, *unless* there had been a stoppage for longer than ten minutes during the first three sets, in which case the rest break came at the end of the fourth set.

Budge won the first set 6–2, but in the middle of the second set it began to rain, driving us off court for half an hour. When we resumed I won the second set 6–2 and the third 8–6. By this time Budge's tongue was hanging out; I knew I had him going.

As I prepared to start the fourth set the umpire, Lev Richards, announced there would be a ten-minute break. I went storming up to the chair, demanding to know why, since we had already had one stoppage. Poor Richards, who was a public relations man for Spaldings in the United States and a good friend of mine, was embarrassed. All he knew, he told me, was that the championship committee had decided there would be a rest period at the end of the third set, regardless of what had happened earlier.

To my sceptical way of thinking, that added up to one thing: the committee didn't want to part with their cup, which I would win outright if I beat Budge for my third US title. At Forest Hills they had a tiny dressing room under the stands of the main court for the use of players during the rest periods, because it was quite a long hike back to the main changing rooms in the pavilion.

As I sat down, still seething, several American officials came in and one of them, Walter Pate, their Davis Cup captain, began to explain their decision to me. I didn't want to know. I told him, 'In this match, I am the official representative of the Lawn Tennis Association of Great Britain. You have broken the rules, and my Association is going to hear about it.'

If upsetting me was what they had in mind, they certainly succeeded. I lost the fourth set 1–6. Before the final Frank Hunter had prepared two professional contracts for me. One of them took into account my winning the championship of the United States again, which would indicate to the Americans that there was nobody better than Fred Perry. This contract offered a slightly bigger guarantee and a bigger percentage of my first professional year's earnings. The other contract, to be offered if I lost to Budge, was for less money. So there was a lot riding on that final.

My friend George Leisure and my other legal advisers were sitting in a courtside box. George had the contracts in his hands and they were all having a great time as the final seesawed into a fifth set. If I lost a game George would hold up the smaller contract; if I won a game he would flourish the bigger one. They thought it was a great running gag, but I wasn't at all sure it was the time and place to be pulling stunts like that.

It looked very much as if George Leisure would end the match holding up the smaller contract, because I lost my serve twice in the fifth set and Budge served for the match at 5–3 with new balls, only to drop his service with a double fault.

I broke serve again to edge in front 6–5. Right – now *here's* how we finish off a five-setter, I said to myself. Four times I served and charged in to the net, and four times Budge banged the ball past me. We were back to 6–6.

Finally I edged in front again 9–8 and prepared to serve for the match for a second time, this time with new balls. Before we played the first point I put one ball in my pocket and kept it there until I got to 40–15, match point. By this time the ball was a bit hotter than when it went into my pocket – souped up a little.

I had been serving wide to Budge's forehand most of the time to get him on the move. But at match point out came the hot ball. I let fly right down the centre-line and he went the wrong way. I don't know to this day whether he was ready or not when I hit it. I suspect, to be honest, that my serve might have been a bit 'quick'. But it was an ace and I was over the net before anybody had the chance to say, 'Hey, wait a minute.' Budge said that whenever he played me he was under pressure, always being pushed, never being given time. This was a prime example.

So I took possession of the American trophy (which is now on display in the Wimbledon Museum along with my other 'pots') as the first overseas player to take the title three times. My lawyers told me to go off to California while they finalized the contracts for my new professional life. On my way to the West Coast I stopped off, as I had done on a couple of previous occasions, in Detroit, to play at an indoor club which had only a handful of members and was owned by the automobile tycoon, Edsel Ford. It made a pleasant break from the train journey.

On that particular visit they asked me if I had ever seen a car assembled. I hadn't, and said I would like to, so we went off to the Ford factory. They asked me what I wanted to watch being made. A convertible, I told them. So I was taken along the production line and watched a royal blue convertible with whitewall tyres being put together.

I was due to resume my train journey to Los Angeles the next afternoon and they asked me to come to their offices for lunch before I left. When I got there I saw the convertible that had rolled off the production line. It was licensed in my name. 'Get in and drive it,' they told me. 'It's yours.' I couldn't believe it!

Anyway, after thanking them most profusely, off I went with my brand new convertible with whitewall tyres, aiming to get to California by road. When I switched on the radio, it didn't work. Then it started to rain, so I turned on the windscreen wipers. They didn't work either, so I pulled off the road for an overnight stop and the next morning rang Edsel Ford to tell him he could have his car back because nothing appeared to work on it.

After a while he phoned me back at my hotel and gave me directions to the nearest Ford garage where a mechanic had been instructed to be ready for me. When I got there the man said Edsel himself had been on the phone and that he knew all about my troubles. The car was fixed then and there and off I went, this time with everything on my royal blue convertible in working order, to California and my last tournament as an amateur.

It wasn't a triumphant farewell, I'm afraid. I got to the final, the fifth time I had done so in Los Angeles, but Budge beat me in four sets to gain a little revenge for Forest Hills. He was very tough to beat on his home-state surface and, although I wasn't really in the right frame of mind because I knew I was going to turn pro anyway, I still wanted to go out as a winner of this championship once more.

As a local paper noted: 'Budge found a weakness in Perry's backhand.' I am the first to admit my backhand was no great shakes. I didn't hit very many winners with it, but I didn't generally make many errors, either. My backhand suited the rest of my game. I could make it slide and go away, so that sooner or later – and I didn't give a damn whether it went over the net ten times or forty – my opponent would give me a short ball on the forehand and when he did, that was it.

I remember once playing George Lott, an American who was full of theories, both as an amateur and later in the professional ranks. One day he said to me, 'Freddie boy, I'm going to beat you by playing every single goddam ball to your backhand.' I promised to return the compliment. So we went out and played the whole match that way, backhand to backhand. George's theory didn't work. I won.

Even though I lost to Budge that September day in Los Angeles we still managed to have fun at my favourite tournament. On one occasion a dispute blew up over a line call and there, sitting in as the line judge, was a fellow who was the spitting image of Budge. I wasn't one to let something like that go without comment. I walked over to him, looked him up and down, and asked him to stand up and turn around. Then I called Budge over. 'Who's this, your brother?' I asked him. 'Yes,' he admitted with a big grin.

12

The Show on the Road

Whenever I think back about my decision to turn professional I recall the lecture I received on the subject one day from Harpo Marx at the Beverly Hills Tennis Club. Although he was supposed to be the silent one of the famous brothers, Harpo did plenty of talking that day. According to Milton Holmes, who wrote about the incident in *Liberty* magazine, the conversation went like this:

Harpo to Perry: 'You can't buy groceries with glory. Why don't you turn professional now and cash in? There's your opponent [pointing out of the window at Ellsworth Vines, who was giving a lesson]. You and Vines could clean up. It's your greatest chance. Why not grab it?'

Perry: 'I can't let England down.'

Well, that was back in 1934. Now it was 1936 and my stance had shifted. Pops Summers put it in perspective after I beat Von Cramm in the 1936 Wimbledon final. 'What now?' he asked me. 'You've won three in a row and you could perhaps win four. But can you win six? It's got to be three or six.'

Despite those three Wimbledons and the four Davis Cup years, I deeply resented not having been accepted by the officialdom at home. I was from the North Country rather than old-school-tie country, and I didn't get on with Sir Samuel Hoare, the president of the Lawn Tennis Association. Most of my confrontations were with him and certain other members of the LTA hierarchy, or with a couple of committee members at the All England LTC. It was a question of a lack of understanding with 'the Establishment' and I always had the feeling that I was tolerated but not really wanted – I had forced my way in. Maybe I was wrong, but I never bothered with people who didn't want to bother with me. I was simply never part of the Establishment end of British tennis.

I knew exactly what I wanted to do in the sport and how I wanted to do it. Maybe the way I went about it wasn't very flexible, to say the least. I was uncompromising because I was all for getting straight to the point, rather than beating about the bush. It wasn't my style to deal in platitudes and get around two weeks later to something I could have accomplished in five minutes.

Basically, I suppose, I never took the time to understand the people at the LTA and the All England Club, and they never took the time to understand me. So there was always a bit of a confrontation, a rough edge, when we were in contact.

What they failed to understand most of all was the intense pressure that had been on me throughout the previous two years, and in the end I got the feeling that they actually wanted to thwart me rather than help me, although this probably wasn't so.

It was perhaps just their defensive reaction to the threat of losing their top player and three-time Wimbledon champion. It was also, I must admit, a new problem to lose an Englishman to the professional game. The American authorities had been through it, of course, and so had the French with Cochet, but Henri was almost at the end of his career by the time he turned pro, whereas I wasn't.

I think a lot of the antagonism towards me stemmed from the feeling, 'How could an Englishman even be contemplating such a step?' As far as I was concerned, how could an Englishman not contemplate it? In any case, I was married to an American by then and wanted to make my home in California, and perhaps make films. As I've said before, I liked the American way of life. It was freer and easier and the tempo was a bit faster. But what I particularly liked (and still like) about America is that people accept you for what you are, as a friend or as an acquaintance, until you do something to prove you're not worthy of that acceptance – then God help you. But you click right off the bat, and that's it. In England, by contrast, I was never exactly made welcome, or made to feel that I belonged, and that didn't sit very well with me.

While I waited around in California for the deal to be worked out by my lawyer, I listened to other offers. Racket companies wanted me to do deals which would have been very advantageous, but I was already committed to Slazengers. There were also approaches from motorcar and cigarette people, but it wasn't on anything like the scale you get today. There were no endorsements around in those days, nor agents. The movie stars had them, of course, but not sportsmen. You stood to make a good income from touring and teaching, but nothing more, and with the whole of the amateur tennis world against us we were very much lone pioneers.

Later on, others got away with what I had been prevented from doing. Their associations turned a blind eye to subtle financial arrangements in order to keep them from turning pro. I always hated being told by the authorities that something wasn't possible 'because it wasn't done', although in fact it *was* possible, provided they didn't know about it officially. I'm quite sure, since I was the first Englishman involved, that I got clobbered because I was openly embarking on something that 'wasn't done'.

Of course, none of this deterred me at the time I was going to do it because I thought it would mean I could take care of everybody in my family. I couldn't have foreseen the rocks that lay ahead: my marital difficulties or the divorce which would follow.

I turned pro. Britain lost the Davis Cup the next year, and we have never won it since. Nor has an Englishman won Wimbledon.

The day when, in the words of the *Philadelphia Inquirer*, 'Fred Perry swapped glory for gold,' was 6 November 1936. The signing ceremony was in New York, at the Wall Street offices of my law firm, Donovan, Leisure, Newton & Lombard. The plan that had been drawn up was for me to embark on a four-month tour of North America, starting the following January, in a head-to-head series against Ellsworth Vines, with Bill Tilden joining the troupe at some of the bigger venues. I was guaranteed $100,000 for five and a half months' tennis, but I ended up earning more than that. I never actually realized what '$100,000 or more' meant until we went to lunch with the lawyers that day. I hesitated before crossing the street and George Leisure asked me what I was waiting for. 'For the lights to turn green,' I said. 'Oh, to hell with that,' replied George. 'You're amply insured with Lloyds of London anyway, so everybody's taken care of. What do you care? Go ahead!'

Some of the syndicate putting up the money for the tour weren't sure if it was a good business move. I treasure the story about one of them who told another of the partners, 'If we make any money out of this I'll give you a horse's ass in diamonds.' Well, they *did* make money, a hell of a lot – we all did – and the man who had lost the bet presented his partner with a gold cigarette case with a horse's rear end in diamonds and a ruby set right in the middle of it!

The format for the pro tour was that the incoming professional (usually the Wimbledon champion) played the reigning professional champion, with the newcomer getting the major percentage in the first year.

Naturally, this arrangement was fine by me, but first we needed Vines's agreement. It turned out that he was in Tokyo with Tilden, but nobody knew exactly where. Within an hour, however, after contacting the shipping line which had taken them to Japan, we had Vines on the end of the phone, which I considered pretty nifty going at that time, even for Americans.

'What the hell's going on?' Vines demanded, when I spoke to him. 'Do you know it's six o'clock in the morning here?' So I told him, 'Listen, Ellie, would you like to make some money?' 'That's different,' he said. He was immediately wide awake and didn't take very long to agree to the offer.

For Vines and myself that was the start of a great partnership. We were in business together for the next twenty years, touring various parts of the world. We bought the Beverly Hills Tennis Club, operated it together and sold it together. Yet in all that time the extraordinary thing was that we never had a contract.

By the second year of our pro tour we were sharing the operating end of it, too, and we had complete trust in each other. On the mainland USA, Vines was in charge of finances. Anywhere else, it was my job. I would say, 'Well, Ellie, we took so much money, our expenses were so much, you've already had so much, and you've got so much to come,' and he'd just say, 'Fine.'

We were friends then and we're still friends. We respected each other's ability, yet we didn't pull any punches. I must have played Vines in something like 350 matches, yet there was never any fixing, as most people thought.

There were always people willing to believe that our pro matches weren't strictly on the level, that they were just 'exhibitions'. But as far as we were concerned, we always gave everything we had. If you've got any pride, every match you are involved in counts. You have to go on court with this attitude, otherwise you have no pride in your performance nor any respect for the game you play.

One of the first messages I received after signing my contract was from Sir Samuel Hoare. I wasn't exactly expecting him to tell me, 'Congratulations, I hope you earn a million,' but I was still a bit offended to be asked, 'Why did you do it?' I was a little hurt, too – but not surprised – to be told that I would be relieved forthwith of my honorary membership of Wimbledon and the tie that went with it. And after all the trouble they'd gone to presenting it to me.

As a member of British teams that had toured the world I had also been automatically made an honorary member of whatever club I played at. I was thrown out of every one of those, too. I wasn't reinstated at Wimbledon until 1949, twelve years later.

111

But for the time being, the loss of my Wimbledon tie was not all that important. Having decided to turn my back on the amateur game, I didn't go near a tournament for a long time afterwards. The same thing happened when I decided to quit table tennis. If you're moving on to something new you need a new set of values and a new set of contacts – business contacts in my case.

I admit it was frustrating to read about other players getting world acclaim when I knew in my own mind I could beat the hell out of them, but there was nothing I could do about it. That was only a small aggravation in my new circumstances, with a lot of money coming in.

I shared the view of my journalist friend, Henry McLemore, when he wrote for the United Press:

Perry made the smartest move of his life when he turned pro ... he had everything to gain and nothing to lose. Glory was already his, and in heaping measure. There were no more titles to win. He had 'em all.

Perry's desertion from the amateur ranks must have caused the tennis fathers a headache of major proportions. I sincerely hope it did, for the tennis fathers have been giving the public and the players headaches ever since the first pair of white flannels was cut. It's their turn to yell for the aspirin.

My professional career with Vines, the Davis Cup player George Lott, and Bruce Barnes from Texas, opened at Madison Square Garden, New York, on the night of 7 January 1937, with all the fanfare that one traditionally associates with American promotions. The players stood in a darkened arena with spotlights trained on the furled US and British flags lying on the floor. Suddenly, over the loudspeaker came the announcement: 'The challenger, Frederick J. Perry, from London, England!' and I walked out in another spotlight, to the strains of 'God Save the King' as the Union Jack was gradually unfurled and raised to the roof. It was simple yet quite moving. The ceremony was repeated with Vines and the Stars and Stripes, and I can still remember hearing the snuffles and coughs of the spectators as the emotion hit them. In fact, I think the patriotic preambles unsettled Vines to the extent that he became rather nervous, and I beat him more easily than I expected.

We had a crowd of over 18,000 that night, which was a record for an indoor match and remained so until the famous 'male chauvinist pig' confrontation between Billie Jean King and Bobby Riggs at the Houston Astrodome in 1973, thirty-six years later. The gate receipts were $52,000.

Before going on court I got a telegram from a friend of mine back in Ealing, Stanley Over, saying, 'Pick the kiss out of him.' So I did. Perry beat Vines in four sets. The next stop was Cleveland, where I beat him again, and then we moved on to Chicago, where I did the same thing.

The next morning I woke up to read that poor old Vines had been admitted to hospital suffering from nervous exhaustion. Bill Tilden deputized for him until he was better, and when Vines got back my momentum was broken. At the end of our North American tour Vines was ahead of me, thirty-two matches to my twenty-nine.

But it was a fascinating battle and a very popular one with the paying public, since it was England playing America. All the Americans came to see their hero beat the hell out of the Englishman, and when we went to England it was the other way round. In Canada they just filled the place all the time, cheering for both of us.

I quickly discovered the professional life was far different from the one I had been used to, where I had travelled at leisure to tournaments which lasted a week or a fortnight. Now I was pitched into a fast and furious way of living. In the winter we travelled everywhere by train and when the weather got better we went by car for greater convenience. There were usually four or five hundred miles between stops, which made the travelling hectic and complicated.

Vines and I would start our singles at about 7.30 p.m., a two-out-of-three-sets match in the smaller centres and a best-of-five in the major cities like New York, Chicago, Detroit, Los Angeles, Boston and San Francisco. Then we would follow it up with a best-of-three doubles, the latter often played against the clock because of the train schedules.

After the matches we had to sprint for the railway station still dressed in our sweaty tennis gear, and parched and starving. On the train you couldn't relax properly because your mind was still active, and if your sleeping compartment was over the wheels, so much the worse.

We would arrive at our next destination early the following morning, looking like death warmed up, and head straight for our hotel, where we usually had breakfast with the local press, since it was the only chance they had to talk to us and we needed the publicity to sell tickets. Day after day they would ask the same questions, but we couldn't blame them for that. To them, it was something new.

Then we would head for bed, wake up at about four in the afternoon, and then get something to eat. There was no television

113

then, of course, but Vines and I usually did radio interviews in the early evening. He would go to one station at six o'clock and I'd head for the rival network. Half an hour later we'd change stations, and after all that we would go out and play our match. No wonder I looked a bit gaunt by the end of that first tour.

Since I was the new boy, I was the one in biggest demand. Once I played on ten nights in a row, with Tilden and Vines alternating as my opponent. Vines owned a huge Buick car and generally did the driving between cities, for I couldn't handle that as well. One night Vines and I were appearing in Milwaukee and the next night I was due to face Tilden in a former tramcar garage in Pittsburgh, six hundred miles away. Despite the distance, of course, we still needed to be in Pittsburgh by breakfast for our meeting with the press.

That time in Milwaukee was the only occasion I can remember us planning to fix a match – simply because of the time element. Vines suggested that we played the first set straight, and whoever won it would be allowed to take the match in straight sets.

We battled out the first set and I won it. Then we got to about 3–3 in the second set, which was time for Vines to let it go. The public would have had no idea of what was going on. For us it was as easy to hit the ball two inches out as two inches in, or to hit the net tape instead of just clearing it.

Suddenly Vines hauled off and hit a mighty shot which went in. After that, he couldn't miss. The only way he could have lost a point would have been to hit the ball into the stand. He won the second set and I was fit to be tied, since I had to play the next night and he didn't.

Vines apologized and suggested that the first one to break serve in the third set should be allowed to win the match. 'Nothing doing,' I told him. 'You'll have to win it all the way now.' The third set went to something like 12–10 to me and we got off court at about midnight. It could have been so much easier all round.

We left immediately for Pittsburgh. Vines used to drive like the wind, usually at around 80–85 m.p.h., and because we were so late he took a few chances. On this occasion he took one too many: when he went through a stop sign at a crossroads we suddenly found a police car on our tail. This junction was at the state line between Illinois and Wisconsin and was famous as part of the black-market Liquor Run between Chicago and Milwaukee.

Vines was all for making a run for it across the state line, but it was a cold night, with a big moon, and I could see black ice on the road, so

I told him to pull up. The police put a spotlight on us and while one of them stayed in the car, the other got out, holding a gun. He was quite pleasant, but warned us that in case we got any ideas his buddy back in the car had a gun on us, too.

He looked inside the car and saw a jumble of rackets, tennis balls, wet clothes and suitcases. He asked who we were, so we told him. He wanted a $20 donation to the policemen's benevolent fund to let us go, but Vines was determined not to pay. So he ordered us into the police car and told Vines he would be in trouble for going through a stop sign. I pleaded with him, saying I had to play Tilden the next night in Pittsburgh, at which I was told, 'You'll be lucky.'

Finally I persuaded Vines to swallow his pride and pay the money before I came down with nervous exhaustion, so we got to our destination and our breakfast with the press only half an hour late. But when I went out to play that night I wasn't much opposition for Tilden. I could hardly see where the ball was going.

There were other, obvious dangers involved in driving when tired. Once Vines and I were heading for Omaha and I was driving while he slept. The only problem was that eventually I fell asleep, too, and Vines woke up just in time to grab the wheel before we ran into a hay cart.

On another occasion our group was travelling by car from New Mexico to Arizona along desert roads which were very straight. I was doing about 80 m.p.h. when Bill Tilden passed me in his car as if I were standing still. Tilden's trouble was that he always wanted to get there before anybody else to organize the evening's match. This time he didn't make it. About ten miles along the road I saw a few people gathered at the roadside and Tilden's car upside down in a field, with the engine running. He was still inside, amid a jumble of tennis equipment and programmes.

When we had helped him out I asked what happened. 'I must have missed the curve,' he said. If there was any curve in those roads it was no more than ten inches or so in three miles. When we transferred all the gear to my car he offered to drive, but I told him, 'No way.' He insisted that there had been a curve in the road and said, 'I pulled on the wheel and nothing happened, so I pulled on it some more and it came away in my hands.' The incident didn't appear to have bothered him in the least, however, and when I asked what we ought to do about his car he said, 'Leave it there and let the finance company come and pick it up.'

On the whole, though, driving on tour was fun, especially with Ellie

Vines, because we got on so well together. We played each other almost every night and we were on the road on that first trip for five and a half months, yet we never got into any arguments or fights. Once a match was over, that was it, forgotten. Of course, if we hadn't possessed a certain compatibility as travelling players we would have been in trouble, because we really were at pretty close quarters. There was quite a bit of leg-pulling, too, but we always had to be careful about playing pranks on Tilden because we didn't quite know how he would take it.

George Lott used to travel with us at times and he was a great practical joker. He loved to needle Tilden by calling him 'Tillie'. One night in Kansas City I was playing Tilden in a singles and Lott was hidden up in the back row of the stands yelling things like, 'Good shot, Tillie' and 'Go get him, Tillie'. Poor Tilden was getting more and more exasperated because the one thing he couldn't abide was being called 'Tillie'. Eventually he stopped the match, apologized to me and said, 'That goddam Lott is driving me crazy. I'm going to have to do something about it. But don't take personally anything I may do or say.'

Later on we had to play a doubles and I was paired with Lott, while Tilden played with Vines. Before we started Tilden walked to the net and said, 'Mr Lott, come here.' Lott went sheepishly to the net. Tilden was well over six feet tall and when standing at the net he made a very imposing figure. He told Lott, 'I would like to point out to you that we are attempting to entertain 5000 people who came here to see a gentlemen's game played by gentlemen. You are certainly not behaving like a gentleman. You are behaving like a bum. Furthermore, Mr Lott, unless you reform immediately I will take this racket and break it over your head.' I think he would have done it, too.

13   Canvas Courts,
Millionaires' Mansions

As an alien in America in that year of 1937 I had endless complications with the tax authorities. Every time you left the country you were supposed to pay up your taxes in case you planned to take the money and run. Even in my amateur days I had to fill in a form declaring that I hadn't made any money while in the United States, and as a pro this caused a tremendous amount of trouble.

It wasn't just once a year. After playing in Boston we were due in Montreal, Canada, but before I left Boston, the taxman was in the dressing room like a shot with forms for me to sign, just in case it had slipped my memory. On such occasions the tax authorities always knew the amount of the gate receipts before the end of the singles, so by the time you had played the doubles they had figured out how much you had made that night. You could fiddle with your racket, but you couldn't fiddle anything else.

When I got back to the dressing room the taxman would fill in the amount and I would have to give him a cheque to cover it. As we were always in and out of the country, there were a lot of cheques. We would spend two days in Canada, then come back into the United States, head towards the mid-West, perhaps cross into Canada again and go up to Winnipeg. Then after Seattle we would enter Canada once more to play Vancouver. Trips out of the United States to Mexico City, Cuba and the Bahamas prompted other occasions when I would find our friendly US taxman in the dressing room with his hand out before our departure.

After the North American tour Vines and I headed for Europe, but our visit there turned out to be rather abbreviated because we weren't allowed to play on the courts of clubs affiliated to any of the European amateur associations. Wherever we appeared we drew big crowds, but there was an unavoidable feeling that although we were playing the game we loved, we couldn't appear in the places we would have loved to play.

In European tennis 'pro' was still a dirty word. A pro's job was to sit in his little office until he was sent for, then hit balls with people and perhaps make ten shillings or a pound. But on our European trip we were sure of a welcome in one place at least: an old friend of mine, Sir Arthur Elvin, who ran Wembley Sports Stadium, had sent a representative all the way out to Denver to sign Vines and myself to play at the Empire Pool. We had a three-night series there, with a five-set singles every night. We even played for a trophy, the King George VI Cup. We drew 9000 people each night and I won the cup two matches to one.

Although Wembley was a wonderful occasion, we had problems elsewhere. In Liverpool we couldn't get permission to play at the local club so we turned out at Anfield, Liverpool FC's ground, setting up court at the Kop end and pulling in a crowd of 10,000. Playing on the rough grass of a football pitch was out of the question, of course, and this was where my old school chum Bernard Sunley came to our rescue. By now Sunley was quite a name in the construction business and when he heard of the difficulties Vines and I were running into in Britain because of the attitude of the amateur authorities, he had a special wooden court built for us, with platform sections which dovetailed together.

It was quite a work of art, with 21 feet behind each baseline and about 15 feet to spare at the sides so that we didn't fall off the platform when running for our shots. He also provided us with a van and a couple of men to take the platform from place to place and assemble it for us. The platform was sometimes a bit rickety because we were playing on ground that wasn't level, but I was already learning that when you were a tennis pro you had to put up with a lot of strange things.

On that tour we also played on football pitches at Bristol and Lincoln, and in Edinburgh our court was laid out on a parquet floor in the town hall, with the ball seeming to travel at 1000 m.p.h. It didn't take long in the professional game to discover that you were often a long way, in all senses, from the Centre Court at Wimbledon. Indeed, my most vivid memories are of the variety of surfaces on which we were forced to play because of the lack of proper facilities, even in American cities. I have played in ice rinks with the canvas laid right on top of the ice, where every step off the canvas sent you skidding off into the distance, and even in the venues where boards were laid over the ice the cold used to numb your lower legs and weight the tennis balls like lumps of lead.

When we played in local gymnasiums they were sometimes not big enough to accommodate a tennis court. So, in order to be able to swing a racket, the baseline had to be moved forward a few inches. When receiving service I would stand with my back up against the wall, giving myself a push off to move to the ball. If a serve whistled past your head and hit the wall, it might give you a nasty clout behind the ear on the rebound. Since that sort of hall was used for a variety of sports, there would also be a confusing series of different lines on the highly polished floor.

Sometimes there was no room to lay the canvas court, especially when we were playing in smaller indoor arenas such as college basketball courts. On these occasions we would simply mark out the lines with white paint. Although we frequently moved the baseline forward by as much as six inches, Vines, who had the big serve, would never allow the service line to be shortened. In my own case, I needed as full a length of court as possible for my ground strokes, so after a while I got fed up with what I considered an unfair situation and planned a little revenge on Vines.

It happened in El Paso, the Texas town which lies on the Mexican border. We always supervised the marking of the lines together, to prevent any funny business. On this particular occasion I went back to the hall alone, gave the man who marked the lines a couple of dollars and told him we had made a mistake. 'The service lines will have to be shortened by three inches,' I said. Now, if you *know* the lines have been shortened, there is no problem; you serve and play accordingly. But if you don't know, you can get in a hell of a mess.

That night Vines served fault after fault and I beat him easily. He was so mad with himself afterwards that I was afraid to tell him what I had done. I finally got around to admitting it many years later, at a dinner in London during the Wimbledon centenary tournament in 1977, and I must admit I was still ready to duck in case he exploded.

In all my years in tennis I recall only one similar incident, this time of an accidental nature. It happened at a professional tournament in Scarborough after the war. It wasn't until the final was being played that it was discovered that the line dividing the service courts was off-centre and one of the service courts was six inches wider – which helped to explain why the players were getting nothing but double faults in one court and aces in the other.

Once, in Asbury Park, New Jersey, we played in an auditorium with a terrazzo floor. We couldn't have a court laid over it because there was nowhere to anchor the pulleys, so we just had the lines marked out on the terrazzo, which was wickedly fast. When Vines hit one of his special serves I swung and missed it by about five minutes, and the ball flew past the protective netting and struck a woman spectator in the eye, injuring her quite badly.

Playing conditions outdoors weren't much of an improvement sometimes. One night in Omaha we played under lights in heat of about 90 degrees, with hard-backed beetles buzzing around everywhere. Each time you went up for a smash you would squash a couple very noisily as you landed.

On another occasion we performed in New York's Yankee Stadium, on a court marked out between first and second base on the baseball field. The special difficulty on this occasion was that we had to play the match almost entirely on the volley; we couldn't afford to let the ball bounce because of the sand on the baseball paths.

Because of our abbreviated European tour, Vines and I needed money-earning opportunities in the autumn of 1937. A friend of Vines's, who was a director of the Grace Line shipping company, came up with just what we wanted. He paid us a fee to give lectures to the passengers on a West Indies cruise, while we arranged to play exhibitions at every port of call. Although we played in a mixture of strange and lovely places, it was quite a lucrative three-week deal.

Despite the fact that I had won their championship on my previous visit in 1932, the Jamaican authorities wouldn't permit us the use of their courts when we called there, so we had a special grass court cut opposite the main stand of the Sabina Park cricket ground and drew a crowd of nearly 9000.

It was while we were in Jamaica on another occasion that we received a cable asking us to go to Havana and appear at the opening of a new sports palace. The idea of an overnight trip to Cuba appealed to us so, although no money had been mentioned, we took one of the old flying boats out of Kingston harbour.

At that time Cuba was under the dictatorship of Fulgencio Batista, the man who was eventually overthrown by the rebellion led by Fidel Castro. Batista was present at the opening, where Vines and I played an exhibition match. Still there was no mention of a fee. One of Batista's pet projects after he became president was to upgrade the sports facilities in Cuba, and this particular sports palace had been an old *jai alai fronton*, which he now wanted us to open with our tennis match. As we were there at the invitation of the president, we thought

120

perhaps mention of fees should be avoided.

Next morning, when we were being driven to our aircraft, a government aide said that though President Batista regretted he could not be there in person to see us off, he had sent us each a personal memento of the occasion. Hello, another autographed photo, I thought. We opened the packages and found $2000 inside each of them. We were also invited back any time. So whenever the pro tour took us to Florida, the nearest point on the US mainland, we were happy to oblige.

Although I considered myself a pretty fair tennis player, I wasn't much of a businessman, and when I had the money available I missed out on several opportunities to buy property in American locations that I regarded, at that time, as being too far out of town. My lawyer, George Leisure, and I got a look at the plans for the building of Disneyland in California, but I turned down the chance to buy a piece of land right next to it!

The same thing happened in Australia when I was there in 1935. David Blacklock, the Australian managing director of Slazenger's, took me out of Sydney and into what appeared to be the bush, where it was planned to put up a factory. He offered me some land in the area, but my reaction was to ask him to lend me a pair of binoculars so that I could see where Sydney was. Today that site is part of the city.

But Vines and I did do a stroke of smart business when we bought into the Beverly Hills Tennis Club with our earnings from the professional tours of 1937. It was a small place, with six courts and a compact clubhouse. There were only about 125 members, but then this was understandable since it protected the privacy of its members and had a very homelike atmosphere. Since its inception, only movie people had ever been admitted: actors, directors, writers, studio heads and the like – all pretty high up in the business. To preserve this exclusiveness only movie people making $1500 a week were allowed to join, and that was pretty big money even in pre-war Hollywood. What Vines and I did was to revamp the layout of the club and modernize it with new facilities such as a swimming pool. Yet there was nothing pretentious about the place; it was a comfortable 'home from home' for movie people who wanted to get away from the Hollywood hurly-burly and relax in a place where they were among equals, free from the day-to-day harassment of being stars. At the tennis club they could let their hair down, so a lot of crazy things went on.

People like Errol Flynn, David Niven, Charlie Chaplin, the Marx Brothers, Norma Shearer and Benny Goodman were members. Through John McCormack, the tenor, I got to know Chaplin well and became very friendly not only with Charlie but with the rest of the British contingent – and, believe me, there was a rather large British colony in Tinsel Town at that time. Stalwarts included C. Aubrey Smith, who commanded the Hollywood cricket team, Ronald Coleman and his wife Benita Hume, the newly arrived Merle Oberon, and David Niven, who came along at about that time, too. As we were all British we tended to club together; the Warner Brothers stars had a little clique as well. But perhaps the most publicized name in the business was that of Errol Flynn, the swashbuckling, hell-raising hero who could defeat an army single-handed, and he had a group all of his own. To say that he was a fun-loving fellow is the understatement of the year. He was married at the time to the French actress Lily Damita, had a beautiful home, and threw parties which were the talk of Hollywood. Even Flynn's tennis court was always in demand.

Considering the amount of money that was around, business at the club wasn't as brisk at it might have been, so Vines and I set about changing that. From the clubhouse only two of the courts were visible, and because everybody wanted to show off their muscles or suntans on those courts, we set about rebuilding the whole set-up. We dug up one of the courts and turned it into a swimming pool, because I had a theory that the movie boys liked to show off to the women. We built three courts around the pool so that the men could play and watch gorgeous girls at the same time. The only problem was that, although we had wives and female members, there were no bathing belles *as such*.

Still, in those days there was no shortage of beautiful women in Hollywood. Any girl in America who won a beauty contest went to try her luck there, but unless that luck was in, she usually ended up working in something like a drugstore, coffee shop or a drive-in restaurant. The place was very attractively staffed as Vines and I booked a dozen of these lovelies and made them 'swimming members' of the club. Suddenly business boomed.

I sometimes wonder how much our programme for the grand opening would cost us at today's prices, had we had to go out and book the stars: a fortune probably. The doubles exhibition match was between Groucho Marx and Ellie Vines, and Charlie Chaplin and myself – the British versus the Americans. Charlie walked on court with about a hundred tennis rackets, with Vines and myself following, carrying a huge suitcase and practically killing ourselves with laughter. When we opened up the case, out stepped Groucho Marx. It was his own idea, and he was only a little fellow, so he wasn't very heavy. One of the film companies put the whole thing on record and even today the clip is sometimes used in quiz shows, with contestants being asked to identify the competitors. Our inaugural dinner that night was quite an occasion as well: we had Benny Goodman and his Quintet, as Benny, of course, was also a member of the club.

Vines and I kept that club until the 1950s. When we first bought it there were only about ten city blocks between it and the end of Beverly Hills; now it's in the dead centre of the community and although apartment blocks have sprung up around it, I'm pleased to say it's still a tennis club and that one of our original members, the actor Gilbert Roland, still plays there.

I also managed to indulge in my biggest unrealized ambition during that year of 1937 by appearing in a film. Inevitably tennis was involved. MGM were producing a series of pictures called 'Pete Smith Shorts' and they decided to do one at the Beverly Hills Tennis Club with me demonstrating shots and grips.

To help beef up the public interest in the film, they also set up various stunts on court. I had to hit the ball through hoops and rings, which proved very popular. Then they came up with the idea of putting an old-fashioned bulb-shaped car horn in the service area of the court to see if I could hit it with a serve and produce a honk from this thing while I was being filmed in slow-motion. The trick was to strike the ball with a flat, low trajectory in order to get it to make the desired honking noise. I hit the horn with my fourth ball, knocking it flying. I thought that more or less took care of things for them. No, sir. Next day the film people were back: 'Fred, we've got some bad news for you. We looked at the rushes of yesterday's takes last night and that shot of you hitting the car horn had a scratch on the film. Can you do it again?'

Well, I tried. Perhaps I tried too hard, because it took me three days of concentrated effort to hit the damned thing a second time. I dare say they could have faked the sequence and saved a lot of money. Still, it looked effective in the picture and a lot of people came up and asked me how on earth I had done it. I didn't spoil it for them by saying it had taken me several hundred takes.

An outstanding memory of that era was my visit to San Simeon, the unbelievably extravagant home built near Santa Barbara by the rich publisher William Randolph Hearst, where he lived with his mistress,

Marion Davies. Hearst's place was the talk of the West Coast and to get an invitation to spend the weekend there was the Californian equivalent of being offered a week's stay at Buckingham Palace. Orson Welles's memorable film *Citizen Kane*, one of the finest movies ever made, was based on the Hearst-Davies affair and San Simeon. Marion Davies had a nephew, Charlie Lederer, a movie writer of about my own age and a member of the Beverly Hills Tennis Club. He told me he had a plan whereby we could not only wangle an invitation to San Simeon but make some money out of it, too.

The formal invitation was arranged through Charlie's Aunt Marion, and formal was the word for it, I must say. Dinner was in a baronial hall. The table was so long, with Hearst seated at one end and Marion Davies at the other, that they could hardly see each other, let alone rub knees. Everybody had to be properly dressed for dinner and waiting in an anteroom, and then Hearst and Davies would appear and lead in their guests.

We were never there for any length of time as the parties were usually of the weekend variety, but it was like visiting some feudal castle way back when. The whole organization and atmosphere of the place was other-worldly. I wouldn't say San Simeon was the most beautiful or exotic building I've ever seen: in fact, from the outside it was extremely depressing. Inside, there was always an intangible pressure coming down from the top, and footsteps echoed along the stone floors.

Charlie's money-making idea involved a handicap tennis match. He wanted to know if I could still beat him if he were to hit into the doubles court on my side. I told him I could beat him even if he played the ball anywhere in the whole enclosure of the court on my side of the net – the only stipulation being that the ball must bounce before hitting the fence – and proceeded to prove it. For any top-class player facing a much less skilled opponent, the task wasn't as difficult as it sounds. Charlie had to start by getting the ball into the proper service court, so I had an advantage right there, and when I served he obviously had problems getting the ball back.

After beating Charlie, I explained to him that the way to win such a contest was by hitting the ball as far and as high as he could, so that it bounced just before reaching the boundary netting. Naturally everybody else wanted to have a go at whipping Fred Perry, and Charlie and I ended up with a pocketful of their dollars from ill-advised wagers.

Another place which was a 'must' – and marginally easier to get

124

into than William Randolph Hearst's home – was Romanov's Restaurant, run by a certain 'Prince' Mike Romanov. Mike was from the Brooklyn dynasty of Russian royalty, but he carried it off with panache, sauntering around his restaurant with a regal air and a majestic line in menswear. In case anyone missed the point about his ancestry, each table was thoughtfully decorated with an imitation crown. The place was not to be missed, even though it cost a king's ransom to eat there.

One day I took an English friend to Romanov's for lunch and since he was an Old Etonian himself, he remarked on the fact that Romanov happened to be sporting an Old Etonian's tie. I tried to reassure him by saying that in America it was possible to go into a shop and buy any sort of tie you fancied, but this seemed to vex him further.

Over he went to the proprietor and inquired what years he had been at Eton. Romanov came up with a date and my guest said, 'That's strange – I was there at that time and I don't remember you. I'll give you five minutes to take off that tie or I'll take it off for you.' I don't remember ever being welcome at Romanov's after that incident.

When the time came to arrange the 1938 pro tour of North America two things had changed: one was that Vines and I now owned the tour and the other was that we were in charge of the arrangements. These factors helped Vines to combine his living – tennis – with his new passion, golf. The tour was even planned so that we could start on the West Coast and follow the golf circuit around the southern part of the United States because Vines wanted to try to qualify for the events.

Vines always carried a putter around with him, even practising when we were on the trains. I remember once standing in the snow on a railway platform in Seattle with my feet splayed like Charlie Chaplin so that he could putt into the V. Strangely, this new interest never affected his tennis, although he eventually became a golf professional. In 1938 Vines was still giving me plenty of trouble with his big serve and his hard-hitting forehand. On indoor courts he was rough to handle.

Inevitably I became interested in golf because on so many occasions I spent a lot of time in the company of golf professionals, but it was not until after the war (as I'll explain later) that I really took it up seriously and got my handicap down to three. I first picked up a golf club aboard ship – on my way to Australia, in fact – when I spent hours watching in fascination as a group of American golf

125

professionals hit about two thousand balls over the side every day. They gave me a few basic lessons and when the ship made a stop at Pago Pago we arranged a morning of tennis and an afternoon of golf.

In the morning two of the top golfers, Paul Runyon and Craig Wood, tried their hand at tennis, with dismal results. Sporting professionals who play a moving ball – as in tennis, football, cricket and baseball – find it comparatively easy to take up golf and perform reasonably well, but no well-known golfer, to my knowledge, has ever gone the other way – from hitting a stationary ball to coping well with a moving one.

After lunch, with more than a hint of malicious anticipation, they took me out on to a nine-hole course built around the back gardens of a Navy base on the island. Off the first tee I struck the ball into somebody's kitchen. When I attempted to play another off the tee they insisted I go into the kitchen, open the window and play the ball out. So I did. They seemed surprised that I didn't break anything. So were the owners of the kitchen.

In the summer of 1938, as Europe moved closer to war, I toured the first of what became known as the 'Borsch Circuits' – in other words, a tour of the mainly Jewish resort hotels in the Catskill, Adirondack and Pocono mountains of the north-eastern states of America. In the company of the old American Davis Cup player Vincent Richards, the Czech Karel Kozeluh, and Bill Tilden we would play at one resort in the morning, have lunch, and then move on to another hotel venue in the afternoon.

It was a lot of fun, though we did run into occasional problems because of the fact that Tilden was a known homosexual and sometimes allowed his partiality for one of the ballboys to reveal itself on court. He always made it clear during a match which ballboy was his favourite, and the boy's parents, understandably, would get upset and try to persuade the law to do something about it. Needless to say, many irate fathers wanted to have words with Tilden and asked the police to stop him leaving town.

We always had our own cars on the Borsch Circuit, sometimes as many as three to give us independence in travelling around. On these occasions, Vincent Richards would come to me and tactfully suggest that we drive Tilden's car; 'He can take yours.' You can imagine how we hightailed it out of town as fast as possible in such a legally interesting vehicle.

But I had a great admiration for Bill Tilden's tennis and his knowledge of the game. He was also very intelligent and wonderful to travel with – the occasional brush with the law excepted. When I first turned professional he had criticized my style, saying, among other things, 'All Perry has is a forehand drive. What's more, it is produced very badly – wristy and unorthodox.'

Many years later, having played each other about 300 times, we happened to be in Independence, Kansas. We weren't due to perform until that night, which was just as well because the heat was fierce. Tilden called my hotel room and asked what my plans for the day were. I told him I was going to sit under a tree, relax, and smoke my pipe. 'I want to go out and hit a few balls with you,' he said. I told him, 'For crying out loud, Bill, we've been playing daily for two months and we've got a match this evening. You want to go out in this heat and hit? You must be crazy.' He insisted, however, saying, 'I want to show you something.'

When we got on court he asked me to hit a few to his forehand, low and wide. I did this and he returned them using a perfect continental grip, just as if he were mimicking my own forehand. When I inquired what he was up to Tilden said, 'After playing so many matches against you and studying your style, I realized that the continental grip, and not my own Eastern grip, is the only one for that sort of shot. I felt I wouldn't be the complete tennis player unless I had mastered it to the stage where I could use it in a match if I wanted to.'

I personally never changed anything after learning to hit the ball early, except through sheer necessity. After I broke my elbow in Madison Square Garden – a disaster I shall be coming to shortly – I could not pronate the joint like I used to, so when I started playing again I had to turn the racket *over* after hitting the ball instead of under.

When Tilden perfected that continental grip, after the war, he was fifty-three years old: what a different attitude from that of today's generation, not to mention a lot of players in the past, who have never troubled to learn anything new in tennis. That's why, in my opinion, Tilden was the greatest of the pre-war players I saw. Don Budge and I used to have discussions about changing our style, and Budge's attitude was, if you can beat people all the time playing one way, why change? He was probably right, yet I find the pattern of play nowadays so boringly predictable in most matches. The players are still doing exactly what they did when they first started on the professional circuit.

Tilden was never the same player two days in a row. Even his demeanour would change: one day he would talk to you, the next day

127

he wouldn't speak. Sometimes he would play slow, sometimes fast. He would mix top-spin with slice. He couldn't volley, but on occasion you would find him up at the net; and he would even attempt to confuse you by sending down his first serve slower than the second. He was always trying something different. When Tilden walked on court he was the king; he dominated the scene. I wasn't the only one who sometimes found it necessary to indulge in a little gamesmanship in an attempt to rob him of his charisma.

I remember watching Tilden play Borotra, the prince of gamesmen, in the Wimbledon semi-finals of 1930. In those days players were given enormously long towels, like giants' pillowcases. Between games Borotra would walk past the umpire's chair and drop his towel, leaving it for a ballboy to pick up. After this had happened several times, the ballboy began to follow him at each change of ends, so Borotra started walking further and further clutching the towel. In the end he took it all the way to the baseline, with the ballboy trailing after him dutifully and a lot of giggling going on in the crowd. Meanwhile, Tilden was getting more and more annoyed, and finally he informed Borotra, in his most chilling fashion, precisely what he thought of him.

When I played I had one or two simple ruses to get the spectators looking at me instead of my opponent. When we got halfway on to the court I would throw the racket ahead of me and call, 'Rough or smooth?' Then, after we had warmed up for a couple of minutes, I would say loudly, 'Any time you're ready.' As far as the public was concerned, one player – me – had made two decisions already, so I was the one the people were watching. Tilden noticed this, as he noticed everything else, and in our professional matches he eventually asked me if I would allow him to make the first moves instead of jumping the gun.

Another ruse of mine, when I went to the net, was to hit the ball and then move my body behind it, making it a little more difficult for my opponent to pick up the white ball against the white background of my shirt, and maybe upsetting his timing slightly. The only player who ever noticed this manoeuvre was Bill Tilden. He told me in Omaha during one of our summer tours that he had been bothered with his eyesight lately, particularly playing indoors, as the ball 'sometimes seemed a bit hazy'. He had just visited the optician, but had mysteriously been found to have perfect vision. And then, looking me straight in the eyeball, he said, 'You know something, Fred? When you come into the net you move in behind the ball so I don't get a

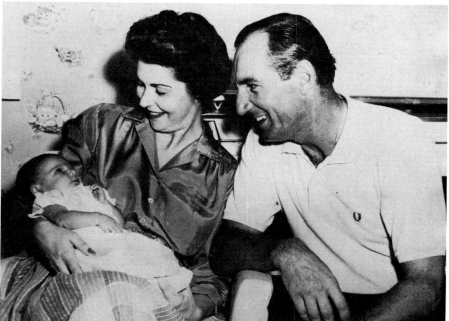

Top: A signing session with Pat Hughes (*left*) and Bunny Austin (*right*) in polka-dot tie

Above: With Bobby and little Penny

Left: Talking with **HRH** The Prince of Wales and Chris Dumfee at Boca Raton Club, Florida

Below: My doubles partner King Gustav of Sweden, with Mrs Satterthwaitte on the Riviera

At the Diplomat Hotel with George Raft, Bobby and Cary Middlecoff in 1961

Right: In Moscow, helping the Russians revamp their tennis

Below: With Christiaan Barnard, Elles Park, Johannesburg

With Bobby, 'Red Hot Momma' Sophie Tucker, and Mr and Mrs David Schine at Boca Raton

Wimbledon Centenary 1977: the Duke and D

t with the champions

Top: HRH The Queen Mother pays a visit to our stand at the Holland Park Show

Above: Being presented with a 1977 Wimbledon commemorative medal by the Duke and
Duchess of Kent

Top: With actor, raconteur, writer and director Peter Ustinov

Above: Putting the members' tie on the young Jimmy Connors

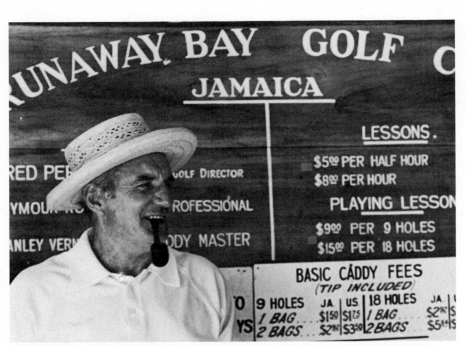

Top: Lord of the Fairways: Runaway Bay, Jamaica, in my golf director's hat

Above: With Bobby and Dan Maskell

clear picture of what I'm aiming at.' Tilden never missed a trick.

Down on his luck at the end, Tilden was playing almost every day until he died in 1953 of a coronary thrombosis while packing at his apartment in Los Angeles to travel to play in the US Pro Championships at Cleveland. As the coroner said, it was 'just a case of a chap sixty years old who outlived his heart'.

A few tennis people, including Ellsworth Vines, were at his memorial service, but no one from the USTA or any other association or authority. I have no way of knowing why there were no officials at Bill's funeral. But it does seem a great pity, with the huge army tennis officialdom boasts throughout the entire country, and with Los Angeles being one of the main tennis centres of the United States, that there weren't a few representatives there with a couple of minutes to spare, to pay tribute to a man who had done so much to popularize the game in America.

14

Divorce and Disaster

I didn't come back to England in 1938 to make a pro tour – not because of Adolf Hitler's ambitions in Europe, but because it was out of the question financially. Helen Vinson, my American wife, had travelled to England to make pictures in both 1936 and 1937, and no taxes had been paid on either trip. Technically she now owed a tidy sum as a big-earning movie star. By 1938 she was conveniently back in California, but, as her husband, I couldn't afford to take the risk of incurring her debts to the Inland Revenue by playing tennis in England.

I don't know where all the money was that she had earned from those English pictures, but it wasn't around, and our marriage, I'm sorry to say, had quickly become a mess, which hurt me and hurt my game. When we became involved in a rather unpleasant 'movie-town divorce', emotional conflicts soon hardened into financial ones.

I think our biggest problem was that we were *both* famous. I had made my name in my sport and she had her stage name, which she insisted on keeping. If a letter for her came to the house addressed to Mrs Frederick J. Perry, egos were bruised and all hell broke loose. If we went to the première of a film in Hollywood, the master of ceremonies would announce as we arrived, 'Here comes Fred Perry accompanied by his charming wife, Helen Vinson.' When we got home, however, the pots would fly again because Helen considered Hollywood to be her bailiwick; by getting my name mentioned first I had usurped her domain, taken the gilt away from the occasion for her. My long absences on tour didn't help matters either, since my wife was also doing a fair amount of travelling on her own account. The marriage just hadn't worked, so we decided on divorce.

I wasn't in California when the divorce broke out, which was a big mistake. Helen had taken aboard one of those high-priced Hollywood lawyers and they really clobbered me. When I got back home I discovered that my bank accounts had been tied up until the final settlement was agreed. All the locks were changed on the house, leaving me with just the clothes I had been on tour in. I had been doing quite well financially, but it took me three or four years to recover from that blow.

My own lawyers moved me to New York temporarily to escape the California problems, and it was during this spell that they advised me it would make better sense if I became an American citizen. As they pointed out, 'You're obviously not going back to England. In any case, you're unhappy about the way you were treated there. Your future is here in America.' I agreed with all the points they put forward and in November 1938 I took out United States citizenship.

Ellsworth Vines's fascination with golf helped to get me started on a new phase of my life after the bitterness of the divorce. He worked for the Wilson Sporting Goods company, and they decided to send him to Mexico City to compete in the Mexican Open golf championship. Wilson's wanted somebody to go with Vines to play some tennis exhibitions down there and I was the natural choice. It suited me, too, since I had to keep out of California for a while.

We stayed at the Churubusco Country Club, just outside Mexico City, and while we were there the owner, Harry Wright, asked me to stay on and revamp his tennis set-up at the club. In the end, I spent the next three winters down at Churubusco, and got my own cottage there, called Casita Numero Uno, right alongside the tenth hole of the golf course.

One highlight of my spell at Churubusco was the arrival of the deposed King Carol of Romania. He arrived accompanied by his lady friend Madame Lupescu, all the royal retinue and five freight wagons filled with his belongings. They stayed nearby at San Angel and quickly took an interest in the Country Club. One day Al Espinosa, the golf pro who had formerly been at the Firestone Club in Akron, Ohio, said, 'I need your help today; King Carol has sent for me. He wants to learn to play golf.'

The King was accompanied by his equerry and the red-haired Madame Lupescu, dangling a cigarette from a long holder. Espinosa started his lesson by showing King Carol how to hold a club, but was swiftly interrupted by the equerry, who told him, 'You are not permitted to speak to His Majesty direct. You must pass on your advice through me and he will answer through me.' 'The hell I will,' said Espinosa, and that was the end of the King's golf lesson.

131

Madame Lupescu said she wanted to take tennis lessons, so I told her the first thing she would have to do would be to cut her long finger-nails. She refused, so I refused to teach her tennis. Neither Espinosa nor I was ever invited to their home again.

In 1939 I did a short North American tour with Don Budge, but once the big cities had seen the same professionals for three years their attitude tended to be, 'What, those guys again? Who needs 'em?' We were old hat in the big centres, so we decided to concentrate on the smaller places, the resort areas and the Middle West, where they hadn't seen too much top-level sport.

When Britain went to war in September 1939 I was terribly torn about what to do. My instincts were to go back, but if I had gone into the British forces as a naturalized American I could have lost my citizenship. It was a feeling strange to me, this being undecided. But what helped me make up my mind was the fact that I had burned all my bridges behind me in England in 1938 when I took out United States citizenship, and now I was facing having to burn them all over again by leaving America.

In the end, I decided to stay put and to go into the American services if and when they got into the war. In the meantime, I played a lot of matches in Canada for British war relief.

But at that time my heart wasn't in tennis. I felt a bit fed up with the whole thing and spent a lot of time down in Mexico. I was still bitter about the divorce and didn't want to be pestered. In that respect, Mexico was perfect, because nobody could get to me.

While I was based in Mexico City, incidentally, I received a request from an old friend, Huge Strange of Neenah, who had promoted our appearances on the pro tour in that region. The president of his Alma Mater, Washington Lee University in Lexington, Virginia, was keen to upgrade tennis at the college and had asked for my advice. I told the president, Dr Gaines, that he could have the best college team in the United States: no problem. Just offer scholarships to the best youngsters in the country. This was not practicable, so we decided to do the next best thing. A great deal of business was being done during golf and tennis weekend parties, so, as the chief responsibility of an American university was to prepare its students for the real world, we would give ours the best-looking basic shots in golf and tennis. If they looked good, this was half the battle. So the tennis team, instead of playing other colleges, played matches at country clubs to further the image of the university. Luckily it worked, and I spent five happy springs and autumns there, giving such worldly wise advice.

It was in Mexico in 1941 that I was married for a second time, to a beautiful American model, Sandra Breaux, although that marriage collapsed, too, during the war. I was married for a third time, in Florida after the war, to Lorraine Walsh, but that didn't last very long either. Marriage seemed like a very slippery diving board and I didn't find true happiness until I met Bobby, the woman who is my present wife and has been for the past thirty-two years.

Barbara (Bobby) Riese was born in London. Her father was a stockbroker from the Sunningdale set, and her sister is the former film actress Patricia Roc. We first met at Wimbledon after the war, when she was divorced with a young son, David, whom I adopted. We were married in 1952 and our daughter Penny was born in Fort Lauderdale, Florida, in 1958.

Bobby and I were married in three different places: first in Scarborough, then in Florida, and finally in Arizona, because Bobby's California divorce had just become final and Californian law didn't recognize our Scarborough or Florida nuptials.

It was probably because of my earlier marital failures that I wound up as wonderfully as I did. It has been a great marriage; we have the same interests, the same national background, and we both knew more or less what we wanted. Bobby has always been excellent at the entertaining end of my post-war teaching career at the major resort hotels where I worked in the United States. She also likes to travel, which suits me perfectly because I know nothing else. I have practically lived out of a suitcase since 1930. If I stay in an office for a couple of days I'm impossible to talk to. I fall asleep at meetings, get headaches – and give them to other people.

To round off my marital history, we now have four grandchildren (all of them David's) living in Beverly Hills and our daughter Penny is married and living in Frimley, Surrey.

In the early years of the Second World War the United States watched anxiously from the sidelines as Hitler swept across Europe and North Africa, while Japan made increasingly militaristic noises in the Far East.

Yet the tennis scene was by no means dormant in America. In 1941 I won the US Professional Championships for the second time (1938 had been the first). Later that year Don Budge decided to put together a winter professional tour and he interested a rich young sports promoter, Alexis Thompson, in backing it. I was canvassed in Mexico

City and agreed to join the tour, while fresh blood was available in two newcomers to the pro ranks, Bobby Riggs and Frank Kovacs. Riggs had won the last Wimbledon championship before the war, but Kovacs was perhaps less well known in Britain. He was a great player and a natural athlete, but a bit lazy. He couldn't imagine success well enough to motivate his efforts.

Although the United States were by then involved in the war after the attack on Pearl Harbor on 7 December 1941, the pro tour went ahead as scheduled, opening at Madison Square Garden on 26 December 1941. It was here that I ran into a disaster of my own. Normally for indoor matches we used a heavy canvas court, with pulleys and ropes at each end and on either side to stretch it tight. The overlays were in strips, facing away from the centre of the court and double-stitched.

For some reason known only to himself, Alexis Thompson opened in Madison Square Garden with a lightweight canvas, which didn't possess enough body to allow it to be pulled tight and the lines to be kept straight. And, fatally for me, there was only single-stitch overlay – facing the wrong way, into the court instead of away from it.

None of us noticed this until we went on court that evening. The first match was between Budge and Kovacs, and during it Kovacs had opened up an eight-inch split along one of the stitched seams which didn't really show. I was playing Riggs in the second singles and midway through the first set I moved over for a short, angled ball on the forehand. I was leaning into my shot when my foot went into the hole in the stitching. I cartwheeled up into the air, landing on my right elbow and smashing it to bits.

I woke up later in hospital with my lawyer, George Leisure, screaming down the phone for a doctor to get some X-rays taken. I went straight from hospital back to Mexico, trying to regain the strength and mobility in my arm by driving heavy nails into teak wood, but I realized that, for the immediate future, with a major joint thirty-five degrees off line, tennis was not for me. Accordingly I wrote to the US Professional Lawn Tennis Association in 1942 and resigned, telling them in my letter, 'I shall not be able to play any more competitive tennis.'

Notwithstanding, I was called into the US Air Force that year and passed my physical examination, even though I couldn't raise my right arm high enough to salute. They gave me a red band to put on my sleeve, excusing me from saluting the officers. All that seemed to matter to them was that I was a big-name athlete. That was why I had to go in, for propaganda purposes: because all the folk in the Mid West and outlying places wanted to know why their sons were going into the war and not the athletes. And as I had a dodgy arm and could no longer play, they couldn't use me to entertain the troops, as happened with some sportsmen.

At first I was in the physical training side, working with future pilots. At one point, General 'Wild Bill' Donovan, Commanding General of the OSS (Office of Strategic Services) in the US Air Force (and incidentally also my lawyer) visited the base and suggested that he could get me away from a situation in which I wasn't making much of a contribution. He wanted me to join his personal staff on a tour of the South Pacific for about sixty-five days, after which I would return as a captain with a battlefield commission. We would have gone to the Pentagon and I would apparently have been elevated to major. But at this juncture, casualties were beginning to pour back in to the base, and I decided to stay where I was doing rehabilitation work – a most worthwhile and rewarding job for me.

Suddenly, I was summoned to Washington. They had a problem in Australia. American non-combat troops arriving there with a lot of medals and money had been stepping out with the local girls, which did not sit well with the Aussie lads on leave from fighting in New Guinea, where the only time an Australian got a medal was when he was dead. The US government wanted men with both Australian and American backgrounds to go out there as troubleshooters and smooth things over, and I fitted the bill because I had been to Australia before – four times. The idea was that I should be commissioned and posted, but in the event I failed my medical on account of my arm. I was recommended for discharge.

But the Air Force wouldn't let me out: I was an athlete; I was a public relations exercise. Next they wanted me to go to Officer Candidate School in Miami for six weeks, but I couldn't see the point of this. If there was supposed to be an emergency, why send me to school? Why not pin the bars on anyway, instead of wasting six weeks? But I suppose it was the old story of me not getting on too well with authority.

At the interview board there was a typical Perry versus Authority scene. I was asked if I held an American high school diploma. I told them I had spent all my school years, from six to sixteen, in England. So they wanted to know if this was equivalent to an American high school education. I said if they didn't know, how the hell would I? The assumption was clearly that as a non-American, I must be dumb.

135

Next they asked me what made me think I was fit to be an officer? Well, this was amazing, since I'd been sent to the school for reasons of Air Force protocol anyway. So I started asking my interrogator a few questions. Did he speak German? No, he said. 'Well, I do.' I told the board. Did he speak French? No again. 'Well, I do.' Had he been to Australia, New Zealand, India, South Africa, South America and all over Europe? No, he hadn't, but I had. I won the interview, but lost the commission. Not unnaturally, I suppose, after this little confrontation, they didn't think I was American officer material. I was eventually discharged in the autumn of 1945, as a staff sergeant, and I ended up fighting my war in Santa Anna and Bakersfield, California, on training and rehabilitation work.

I became very interested in this particular kind of rehab work and many years later, when we did some question and answer broadcasts for the BBC overseas stations with Henry Cooper, Cliff Morgan, etc., it stood me in good stead. Several times we went to the Stoke Mandeville hospital to do a show for the patients, who were some of the most pleasant, devil-may-care people I've ever met. They would rush around the hospital corridors in their wheelchairs and stop on a sixpence right in front of you, which was enough to scare the hell out of anybody. But the work was fun and very absorbing: we used to stay long after the show was over, just wandering round the wards. In fact, for many years the British team members in the Paraplegic Olympic Games were dressed by our sportswear company.

The Beverly Hills Tennis Club, which Vines and I still part-owned at that time, had survived through the war – for a very special reason. When we had embarked on our first professional tour, back in 1937, the organizers, Howard Voshell and Frank Hunter, were also agents for Ballantine's whisky. Three days before we hit any town, the local sales reps would take a suite in the best hotel and stock it with twenty-year-old Scotch for the press in order to ensure good publicity. When Vines and I arrived we would take over the suite for the duration of our stay, and when we moved out so did the surplus whisky.

The longer that 1937 tour lasted, the more baggage went into the support truck in order to make room in the car for the booze. Every time we got back to California we would have a carload of liquor, which went straight into the club. So we were the only tennis club in California during the war with a supply of twenty-year-old Scotch. I think, you know, that helped to keep the club from going under.

In 1945, just as I had packed my car ready to return to Mexico for Christmas and was attending to some business in the Beverly Hills club, Bill Tilden walked in. 'Just the man I'm looking for,' he said. I told him that whatever he had in mind didn't interest me, but once Tilden got hold of an idea you just couldn't get away.

The proposition was this: an army friend of Tilden's, General 'Howling Mad' Smith of Pacific War fame, had called him to ask a favour. A lot of his soldiers, back from the Pacific, were stuck aboard ship in San Diego harbour and wouldn't get home for Christmas. Would Tilden mind coming down to play an exhibition match or two to help entertain them? And could he bring a friend?

I was reluctant to do it, even for such a good cause. Not having played for so long, I had lost a lot of interest and confidence, and I felt there was simply no question of taking tennis seriously any more after breaking my elbow. But I finally agreed to accompany Tilden, on condition that he took it easy against me. I could hit the ball as long as I could keep it in front of my body, but I couldn't strike it hard any longer. Nor could I pull against the weight of the ball; I could only push it down the line, so half the court was closed to me. Hitting a ball still hurt me and as I played my arm started to shake (in fact, there is still a piece of bone floating around in there somewhere). But the soldiers seemed happy enough with the tennis we offered them, and the following year Vincent Richards, Tilden and I hit on the idea of a series of professional *tournaments* around the United States, rather than city-to-city appearances by a troupe of four.

Between the three of us we knew every pro in the country, so we devised a thirty-week tour, spending a week in each place – a luxury after those years of one-night stands. We played for no guarantee and 75 per cent of the gate, which was the only way we could interest any promoters. To get enough professionals to make up the numbers for a thirty-two-man draw we had to recruit teaching pros from the Los Angeles area for the Western part of our tour. Then, when we got as far east as Texas, we recruited another bunch of Eastern pros to fill out the draw sheet and keep the tour going until its grand finale in Forest Hills, New York.

At the end of each tournament Tilden, who ran everything, would ask the promoter or the committee involved how it had gone. If they had not taken much at the gate he would give them a few hundred dollars off the top, just to keep them sweet in case we ever passed that way again.

I took part in the tour, but not seriously. I would play if it was a nice warm day and the arm felt good, but I still had to be careful. It no longer mattered, however, whether I won or lost, which as far as I was concerned was something new altogether. It was a cruel way to play the game because a lot of my opponents wanted to show how much better they were than a three-time Wimbledon champion. With half the court closed to me, it wasn't too difficult for them. Still, that 1946 tour was real pioneering stuff. It marked the start of the men's professional circuit as we know it today. We didn't make a fortune, but we had the satisfaction of getting things started again after the war.

That year, to make a little money, I also took part in what I can only call a light-hearted tour of the Caribbean and South America. We used to get up to all sorts of pre-Nastase antics to amuse the people: we would run for a wide shot and end up sitting in the crowd; Frank Kovacs would throw up four balls at the same time when he served and start to argue if you got one of them back. In the places we went to, spectators hadn't seen much tennis, so we had to meet them halfway and make it as bright as we could. Even then, it wasn't as silly as World Team Tennis.

In Bogotá Kovacs and I played in a bullring as a prelude to the main event, which was the bullfight itself. We had to end the match at a prearranged time to let the bullfight get under way, which didn't upset us at all since the ball took all sorts of crazy bounces off the sand.

But the most touching moment for me personally came in Trinidad. I was playing in Port of Spain when a lorry drove up to the side of the court and a group of local musicians burst into a calypso specially written in honour of my visit. It was called 'A Tribute to Fred Perry – the Empire's Greatest Tennis Player of All Time', and here's how it went:

> We welcome with deep sincerity
> The presence in this colony
> Of the world-renowned Fred Perry
> A genius in his own right definitely.
> A British Empire ambassador,
> Going we know from shore to shore,
> Demonstrating his wonderful ability
> That has his name enshrined in history.
> He has thrilled millions already
> And we are indeed lucky
> That such a great personality

Should give an exhibition at Tranquillity.
We understand even the great Perry
Had a hard time in days early
In developing his genius to the degree
That has him beloved universally.
What an infectious and charming personality
Is the genial Fred Perry,
The most human of men we ever did see,
Courteous, cultured to an unusual degree.
Mr Perry will leave us very soon,
But he has to us bestowed a boon
By not only displaying his artistry,
But making himself beloved generally.
Fred Perry, when you return to your country
Please remember this – that we
Will always cherish a pleasant memory
Of your short stay in this colony.

What could I say after such fulsome praise, except thanks, and could I have a copy of their words for my memoirs?

15

Post-War Posts

As the plane came in over the suburbs to land at London Airport I caught my first glimpse of the red buses on the roads. The sight gave me one of my biggest thrills because at last I knew I was back in England after an absence of eleven years.

It was 1947 and I had come over at the invitation of Slazengers to help revitalize the game of tennis in Britain after the war. I was happy to accept the invitation, since it offered me a chance to see my father and sister after all those years. I stayed at the old house in Ealing for the London part of my visit, though my father had remarried a couple of years after my mother's death in 1930 and things weren't therefore quite the same.

I was impressed by how little Britain had changed, though, from what I remembered, despite six years of war. Of course, you couldn't help noticing the bomb damage which still scarred so much of London: nor could you go very far without seeing people queueing – for food, buses, everything. It brought home to me the spirit of the nation. No other country in the world would have accepted it the way the British did, and for all the bomb damage and queues, I noticed an optimism in the air. By 1947 the people knew they were round the corner from the bad years and could see the light of a better life ahead.

There had been rationing in America during the war, but on nothing like the scale as in Britain. I can't say I noticed any great shortages on that first post-war visit, though. I am a very plain eater anyway, even in posh restaurants, and, of course, rarely touch alcohol.

At the instigation of Slazengers I toured Britain with Dan Maskell, playing a series of light-hearted exhibitions at local tennis clubs and donating the proceeds to the clubs for repairs and improvements.

Whether because of the war, or the lack of television, or the fact that I wasn't there to copy, my successes hadn't inspired a stream of Perry 'clones' in British tennis, as Bjorn Borg's achievements have done in

Sweden more recently. Any child in Britain of ten years or under was lucky to see tennis played at all, and because of the war our most promising pre-war players had lost a chunk out of their prime years. People like Tony Mottram and Geoff Paish were excellent talents, but by the time the war ended they were in their mid or late twenties, with the experience – and the game – of eighteen-year-olds. Like everybody else in Europe, they had a great deal to catch up on.

Dan Maskell told me that in attempting to coach youngsters in the style I used to play, he suffered, in particular, the handicap that none of them had ever seen me play. They had nothing to hang their ambitions on except a name.

That year of 1947 marked the renewal of my love affair with Wimbledon. I was still barred from competing, of course, being a professional, so I went on to Centre Court for the first time since that Davis Cup win in 1936 – armed not with a tennis racket but with a press pass. I was to comment on Wimbledon for one of the London evening papers, the *Evening Standard*.

Wimbledon 1947 was the first amateur tournament I had attended for twelve years. After that, I never missed another Wimbledon, covering it for newspapers, radio and TV, until last year, when I was taken ill after the opening day.

Slazengers, with whom I had maintained my connections through the professional years and the war years, started a professional tournament at Scarborough in 1946, and one of the reasons for my invitation to Britain was to persuade me to play in the 1947 event. I told them I couldn't compete at that sort of level any more, but they were very persuasive and eventually I capitulated. At least I had come to terms with my elbow disability and had learned how to 'fiddle' my shots. But the arm still hurt me and playing wasn't any fun. I still had difficulty hitting backhand cross-court shots and I was only effective against people who didn't hit the ball back to me too hard and too often.

In those early years the Scarborough field was made up of little-known professionals from Europe, and Slazengers wanted my name to help boost the event. In fact, I did rather better than that – in 1948 I won it, beating Yvon Petra, the tall Frenchman who had won the first post-war Wimbledon, rather surprisingly, in 1946 and subsequently turned pro. When people asked me how on earth I beat somebody like Petra with a bad arm, I used to tell them it was because I knew a little more about the game than he did.

At any rate, the Slazenger tournament at Scarborough became part of the reason for my annual return to Britain, and I won the championship there twice more before the event began attracting younger and fitter people like Gonzales and Trabert.

The British had become a nation of spectators, rather than participators, and in an attempt to change this Maskell and I started something called 'Focus on Tennis' in 1948. It was organized by the Central Council of Physical Recreation, and Slazengers supplied all the equipment we needed. One of our most valued helpers was R. E. 'Buzzer' Hadingham of Slazengers who became chairman of the All England Club in 1984.

For the next three years Dan and I took tennis to the kids of Britain in the three summer months following Wimbledon. We played in indoor markets, on football pitches, on the sides of hills – anywhere we could gather an audience. We even kept the sessions going in pouring rain, with me standing out there in waterproofs and Maskell standing under shelter and throwing balls for me to hit – just to bring the game to the children. Once we played in Peterborough the night after the circus had been in town and Dan found himself standing in a hole left by an elephant!

Through the local tennis associations, the best boys and girls in each area were invited to hit some balls with us, and if they showed any extra potential they were sent for coaching with Maskell at Wimbledon, bypassing the normal channels. Out of that scheme came such Davis Cup stalwarts as Billy Knight, Tony Pickard, Mike Sangster and Mike Davies, so our efforts were not wasted. The girls proved successful, too. One was Angela Buxton, who went on to win the Wimbledon women's doubles titles with Althea Gibson.

Our show, for that's what it was, lasted about an hour and fifteen minutes, and was compèred by Emlyn Jones, later Chairman of the Sports Council. Through the participation of local schools, the youngsters arrived in buses for the 'matinée', and there was an evening performance for the older children and any parents who wanted to come along.

After the austerity of Britain, my life went to the other extreme on my return to the United States in the autumn of 1947. The Boca Raton Hotel is in the swish resort of Palm Beach, up the Atlantic coastline of Florida from Miami, and if there was a more luxurious place around at that time I certainly hadn't come across it. One look at the place really brought the contrast home to me: the difference in the standard of living in England – which I had seen after my long absence – and America was staggering. No shortages here. Money

142

flowed like water. The best sports equipment in the hands of the hotel guests, no bargaining or querying the price of things, and the food served in portions that would have fed an army. Even to someone like myself, travelling over the world and often surprised at the abundance and luxury I saw, this place, Boca Raton, was in a class of its own.

When I accepted an offer to become teaching pro at the Boca Raton Club (a Spanish phrase which translates as 'Mouth of the Rat' it proved to be another watershed in my life. I moved my base of operations from California right across America to Florida, and I have been there ever since.

The Boca Hotel had cost $18 million when it was built in 1928. All the furniture was hand-carved Italian and all the swimming pools and fountains were lined with hand-painted Italian tiles. The moulds were deliberately broken after construction, which created a problem when it came to replacing some of the tiles after the war. The hotel had been used as a government rehabilitation centre during the war years and afterwards it was bought for a song by a man called J. Myer Schine, who will perhaps best be remembered these days as the father of G. David Schine. In the black days of Senator Joseph McCarthy's 'Reds-under-the-beds' crusade in America, the senator's legal sidekicks were Roy Cohn and G. David Schine.

Being resident in one place for the Florida tourist season between October and May was obviously something new for me, and I considered J. Myer Schine's offer carefully before accepting it. I had very firm ideas about being a teaching professional. I didn't want to get tied up, for instance, giving lessons to people who were already top-level players. I was more interested in those who simply liked to play the game; I wanted to make tennis a little easier for them.

I agreed to run the tennis at Boca, but told Schine that it would have to be done my way. No problem, he said. In fact, there *was* a problem immediately I looked at the books and saw the figure of something like $700 a week under the heading 'Income from Tennis'. When I queried the amount Schine explained this referred to money collected for rental of the courts to hotel guests. I told Schine not to be ridiculous; he couldn't charge people to play tennis when they were already paying something like $125 a day for a room at the hotel. In any case, I went on, neither I nor my assistants proposed to act as cashiers. 'No problem,' he said again. 'Run it your way.'

So I did, and the guests got their tennis courts for free. But after a few days the general manager of the hotel, Gaston Lauryssen, told me Schine was complaining there was no income from tennis any more;

his instructions were to restore charges at once. I told him to call Schine and congratulate him on becoming the new tennis pro at Boca Raton. Having done that, I went off to play golf. It wasn't long before Schine arrived. He used to walk everywhere with his hands behind his back, rather like HRH the Duke of Edinburgh. 'How's the tennis?' he asked me.

'Well, you ought to know the answer to that one,' I said. 'You're the pro here now.'

'What do you mean?' Schine said.

'You interfered with me, so I've quit and turned the job over to you,' I told him.

'Don't be silly,' said Schine. 'Do whatever you like whenever you like.' And after that I never had any problems.

I spent thirteen years, most of them wonderfully happy ones, at the Boca Raton Hotel. Eventually my wife Bobby and I got a house on the inland waterway which runs just behind the seafront along that part of the Florida coastline and I would make the half-mile journey to work in my own little boat, mooring it right alongside the tennis courts. That sort of commuting was difficult to beat!

The hotel also boasted a golf pro (that unforgettable character, Tommy Armour), a swimming coach (the Olympic diver Bill O'Brien) and a resident orchestra (Freddy Martin and his band). Though the place opened in October there were very few guests and little for us to do except prepare for the high season, which got under way at Christmas. So I was able to spend a lot of time with Armour. Not only did it improve my fund of anecdotes a hundredfold, but it also got my handicap down from twelve to three.

Because of my bent arm I was a hacker until Armour went to work on me. Of course it involved a lot of practice and if I fluffed a shot or missed a green I used to get really mad. Then one day I thought, what the hell are you doing this for? You don't need it. I had spent years of constant practice to make myself a world champion at table tennis and done the same thing all over again at lawn tennis. I simply wasn't interested, I decided, in involvement at that level of intensity again, so I settled for relaxing rounds with friends instead, and to hell with my handicap.

Armour's reputation as coach, raconteur and character attracted other top golfers from all over the world. Whenever people like Dai Rees, Max Faulkner, Bobby Locke, Harry Weetman, Jimmy Demaret or Jack Nicklaus were in the area they always dropped in to join Tommy at his nineteenth hole bull sessions.

Tommy Armour, or the Silver Scot as he was affectionately known, was the epitome of what the golf pro at such a fabulous hotel club should be. He made all his clients feel they were the most important people in the world, yet at the same time he insulted them in the most outrageous fashion when it came to their golfing prowess – or lack of it. He was possibly the greatest con artist around, but he was the best teacher, too. During our thirteen years together there, I can't count the number of name professional golfers who stopped by for advice and help, and they were not just Americans either. Bobby Locke, though, came as a friend of mine rather than one of Tommy's. These two would clash consistently over golfing matters, and everyone else would run for cover.

There was an extraordinary amount of gambling on the golf matches, and every day one would look at the flag placings on the green and understand immediately how much money was riding where. The higher the stake, the closer the pins were to the right-hand corner of the green, because Armour was a master of left-to-right shots. His opponents with more money than sense would eventually get on the green to find themselves with a 500-mile putt. If Armour had a particularly delicate 'fiddle' to work with people who really knew what they were doing, he would send for me to partner him, trusting to his pupil's three-handicap game and a little psychological by-play to clinch the outcome.

The preamble would be for him to argue with me about grip, saying I mustn't 'strangle it'. Every time I hit a ball on the first few holes, Armour would launch into a lecture about holding the club lightly, and I would accuse him of being stupid because in tennis if you don't hold the racket with authority, the damn thing will fly out of your hand when you hit the ball, and the same must apply to a golf club as well. The 'pigeons', meanwhile, would fall about laughing at these little rows, but after five or six holes, sure enough, you would notice them fiddling with their grips. Once their mistakes began to flow, Armour would never open his mouth again.

A peerless instructor, Armour's methods were nevertheless unorthodox. His teaching hours were from 9 till 12, one hour per session, with selected clients mostly from a list compiled by Dunn and Bradstreet. Armour would sit in a canvas chair under an umbrella with cigarettes to hand. He taught with new balls and only ever used a couple of dozen at most, as he had one caddy to place the ball for the guest, and one to pick it up at the other end. This way there would be a lull every two dozen balls while the far caddy retrieved them all, for he never hurried. The interval would be filled by Armour with a stream of stories, none of them anything to do with golf, during which the client would fall under his spell. Armour had a charisma about him which everybody loved, and they couldn't wait to get on his books, weathering the insults with a good grace. Most play-for-fun golfers with high handicaps are inclined to slice the ball. Armour would look scandalized at this outrageous flaw, and then instead of just telling them to move the right hand under, to counteract it, he would go off into lengthy complex explanations, saying he couldn't understand how they could own private planes, three or four cars, have two or three factories and employ 10,000 people, and not have the brains to hit a golf ball straight.

His sporting interests didn't stop with golf; he followed other sports keenly and knew big names in them all. He was also a very generous man, and in the spring when assistant pros and caddies were heading north after a working winter in Florida, Armour would always come up with a few dollars to smooth their passage, provided they had a PGA card. If they didn't, they left poor, and quickly. There will never be another Tommy Armour.

The Duke of Windsor was also a regular visitor and used to reminisce about the pre-war (and pre-abdication) days when we had met. One day, when he was on the practice putting green, I felt a bit bolder than usual so I asked him if he ever regretted not remaining King of England. I got what I considered a very diplomatic answer. 'Well, Mr Perry, I think my brother's done a pretty good job,' said the Duke.

Another frequent guest at Boca Raton was the actor Danny Kaye, who spent a great deal of time down there with his agent Bert Allenberg, playing golf with Armour. One day Danny happened to be flying to England to play the London Palladium, and he said he would call my father on his arrival to say that I'd be there in a few days. He impersonated me on the phone, and his mimicry was so marvellous that for the first five or ten minutes of the conversation my father really thought it was me. It was only when Danny invited him to his show that Perry senior realized he'd been taken in.

On the whole our clientele at Boca Raton was drawn from the wealthy Jewish community and in the peak season it built up to a capacity of about eight hundred people. For the four months beginning with December my time was booked up teaching tennis to the sons and daughters of millionaires. I had one particular regular, an older man called Mr Rentzler. He was the head of Pratt &

Whitney engines and spent the winters at Boca Raton in a magnificent house across the road from the hotel. He arrived in December, but would never come near my courts when the Christmas crowd was in. He would send one of his servants over to get a couple of rackets restrung and to make his reservations for after the Christmas holidays when the kids had gone back to school.

Mr Rentzler always booked from 2 p.m. until 4 p.m., the most difficult time to fill as people were at the beach club for lunch, so the arrangement suited me perfectly. What's more, he refused to play with anybody except me, and only against my two assistants, which effectively prevented anybody else from getting lessons in that period. But he bought new balls every other day and his daily bill was $75, from the moment he first came to the hotel each year until the time he left it at the beginning of May. If he wasn't able to come he would always call by noon to cancel, on the understanding that if we couldn't arrange other lessons to fill in the time he would pay anyway. Somehow we never managed to arrange other work for that period!

Eventually, under new ownership, the hotel adopted a different policy and decided to go after the moneyed 'WASPS' (White Anglo-Saxon Protestants) – the top names. But you can't make wholesale changes in your clientele like that without courting disaster, and the business fell apart. The first Christmas they had twenty-two people in the hotel instead of eight hundred. The hotel had been bought at the end of the previous season by the Arvida Corporation of America, headed by multi-millionaire Arthur Vining Davis, who had purchased almost everything in sight in Florida. His general manager had been one of Schine's assistant managers, and had been in confrontations many times with Tommy Armour. When it came to a showdown, Armour had always stayed, but under the new regime he was the first man to go.

They decided to revert to their more reliable clientele in the end, but the goodwill had been damaged and it needed a lot of hard work to rebuild the business. By that time, too, my own life had branched out in another direction – the clothing business.

16

The Sportswear Magnate

Being a realistic man, I have never worried about admitting that my name is better known worldwide, not for winning Wimbledon three times, but because of Fred Perry shirts and sportswear. My on-court achievements are history now, but the sportswear company is still going strong.

Like most of these things, it began in downbeat fashion. I was in England at the end of the 1940s, doing the 'Focus on Tennis' tour with Dan Maskell, when a former Austrian footballer called Tibby Wegner came up to me with an idea for a sweatband that he wanted to market, using my name. He said nobody would listen to him, and when I saw his product I knew why. It looked like a bath towel and weighed a ton. Though Wegner claimed it was an innovation I told him I had played the 1934 Wimbledon with a piece of gauze wrapped around my wrist, not for wiping my brow, but to stop the perspiration running down my arm on to the racket handle, causing the grip to become slippery.

I told him to go away and redesign it into something light, soft and pliable, and promptly forgot Tibby Wegner and his idea. But when Maskell and I were in Leicester for a 'Focus on Tennis' session a little later, Wegner came back and showed me the prototype for what is now universally known as the sweatband. 'That's it,' I said. 'Where did you get these things made?' 'Right around the corner, here in Leicester,' he said. From that moment Wegner and I were in business.

He wondered how we could best market the sweatbands. By persuading top players to wear them, I said, urging him to give them away at the best tournaments in Britain. He did, and that's how Fred Perry Sportswear got started.

Wegner asked what I knew about shirtmaking as a business. I told him I was generally regarded as the best-dressed player of my time, but that did not necessarily mean I knew how to make the shirts I used to wear. Between us we had no idea whether our proposed Fred Perry sports shirts should be cut on the bias or the warp or the weft or what the hell. We put up £300 between us and agreed that was to be the total of our investment. It was, as can be imagined, very much a hit-or-miss affair at first. What we needed now was a logo or emblem.

As a pipe-smoker I thought it might be a good idea to use a pipe, but Wegner didn't think the girls would go for that. We thought of roses and a thousand other things and discarded them all. Suddenly Wegner had a brainwave: 'What about that laurel wreath you wear on your touring blazer and Davis Cup sweater? What's the story behind that?' Since 1934 when I first won Wimbledon, I had always sported the famous wreath. In the old days, you see, the Wimbledon champion got his name on two trophies he never saw. He was given a replica of the Renshaw Cup, a beautiful thing; a gold medal; a £25 voucher to spend at Mappin and Webb, and, lastly, this gold laurel wreath embroidered on a 4 inch by 1½ inch purple silk ribbon – the 'blue ribband' of the championships. I had always worn my wreath with pride: it was, after all, a historic symbol, honouring excellence from classical times.

'Well,' said Wegner, 'why don't we use that?' I asked Colonel Duncan MacCauley, then Secretary of the All England Club, if Wimbledon would object. He said there would be no problem, since the Club didn't own the emblem and in any case had not really used it since the war, and he gave me a release in writing, which meant that the wreath was ours. So we had the design made up. The symbol we sent to the embroiderers happened to be the green wreath of the mixed doubles, which is why all the original Fred Perry shirts had green wreaths. Then, over the years that followed, we had the somewhat difficult task of getting the emblem registered throughout the world.

Fortunately Wegner had a shirt design in mind and he was a real go-getter. He persuaded a company in Leicester to make up seventy-five dozen white tennis shirts for us. His job was to get the stuff manufactured and mine was to organize the marketing.

The first samples of the white sports shirts were ready by the first Saturday of Wimbledon, and on the following Monday I took them to the championships. At this time I was commentating for ITV and Dan Maskell was doing the same for the BBC, so we gave each cameraman and each director a shirt. The girls who punched the buttons got a shirt too, with the instructions to try to get our laurel wreath emblem on TV.

The next job was to get the players to wear them. Being allowed in the men's dressing room at Wimbledon was a great boost to my promotional work. This was the era of Hoad, Rosewall and the young Australians, and at the start of the Last Eights – the second week of the men's and women's championships – the only courts of interest to the TV cameras were Centre and Number One. We didn't have any ladies' shirts at the time, so we concentrated on the men, and most of them were pleased to get their hands on a garment like ours, after they had been reduced to laundering boring old sagging shirts picked up from the bazaars of their travels. The result was a slick piece of television promotion, with everyone on Centre and Number One court parading before the camera in our shirts, and with anyone *less* elegantly accoutred cropped at the neck to avoid offending the viewers' dress sense. The image was always there. Of course, we did have our problems. We offered one to the giant Argentinian, Enrique Morea, who was doing well at Wimbledon that year, and he volunteered to wear it. Players like poor Morea were just clotheshorses really, as we experimented with the cut, durability and shrink-proof quality of our new product. What we didn't realize about Morea was that he had this quirk in his metabolism whereby anything new that he wore invariably shrank. Extra large was only just the right size for him, in any case, and by the time he got through his match his eyes were bulging because the shirt had started to shrink on him.

My next marketing ploy was to tap all the old friends from my playing days who now either owned sports goods stores or worked in them, together with the people of my pre-war acquaintance who had been salesmen and were now managers or buyers for the big department stores. One of these was Sam Cox, the head buyer at Lillywhite's, the big West End shop. When I went to see him and pushed the shirt on to the table he said, 'So it's yours, is it? We've been trying to trace those shirts with the laurel wreath on them ever since Wimbledon. We've had a lot of inquiries.' He asked what colours we had and I told him, 'White, in four sizes.' Cox promptly ordered ten dozen from me, but while I was delighted, I pointed out that left me with some sixty dozen still to sell. So he picked up the phone and called the head buyer at Harrods, who also took some. Next he called somebody in Leeds, and then Manchester. In half an hour they were all taken. 'Now go away and make 200 dozen,' Sam advised me. We did, and sold them. Next time we made 400 dozen, and that's how Fred Perry Sportswear hit the jackpot.

We were lucky, of course, that the man whose name had been given to the company (i.e. me) was still very much around, which was the case with hardly any other sportswear company with the exception of Lacoste. This made a big difference. Wherever I was seen, at tennis or other sporting events, in a restaurant or simply walking down the street, publicity for, and interest in, Fred Perry Sportswear was generated, and we deliberately set out to personalize it. I like to describe my style of marketing as a combination of friendship and bullshit.

It was a good product, however, and the public liked it. When Queen Elizabeth the Queen Mother asked me at the opening of a clothing exhibition, 'Mr Perry, what makes your shirt better than anyone else's?', I told her with a warm smile, 'Ma'am, it's the shirt that fits.' We had learned a lot since the days of Enrique Morea!

The following year a lot of players started wearing Perry shirts at Wimbledon. We quickly spread into the continent and eventually worldwide. First it was shirts, then we started making tennis shorts – more on which subject in a minute – then women's shirts and skirts. Next came socks and other accessories, sweaters and zipper jackets. It took a long time and needed a tremendous amount of work, but eventually the income was very good, and my part of the business (sales through personal contact) fitted in well with my coaching and broadcasting careers in Britain.

In my day, of course, you weren't allowed to wear tennis shorts. The man who first broke with convention at Wimbledon was Bunny Austin. Shorts suited him. He wasn't a flamboyant fellow – far from it – in fact, he was quite circumspect. But he reasoned that he would play better in shorts, and having considered the matter carefully, out he went on to Centre Court, knees bare. It caused a tidal wave.

British rules and regulations on dress were taken very seriously, and as I wore Daks trousers anyway, I was more or less stuck with my elegant image. But even had I been permitted to wear shorts, it would never have entered my head. When I turned pro I continued to wear long trousers because I'm a great believer in trying to look the part – it's a fetish with me. When I was teaching, all my assistants wore long trousers, too: I wanted them to stand out as professionals among the bare-kneed guests. The only time I ever wore shorts was during the US pro tours many years later. It was summer, and the twilight of my career, and we were playing one Sunday in Connecticut. I suppose the trousers I was wearing must have been getting a little threadbare with the years, because when I bent for a low forehand I split the knee. I couldn't even get up, because my knee was sticking through the rent like some kind of deformity. A lady sitting near the umpire's chair came up with a pair of curved manicure scissors, and I stood there in full view of the crowd while one leg of my trousers was cut to a scalloped edge. And as I found I couldn't play with one leg scalloped and the other long, the other leg was cut off as well.

I don't think wearing long tennis trousers ever encumbered me as a player. There were lighter materials than flannel even then, and my trousers were baggy, with plenty of knee and rear-end room for bending and stretching. Shirts weighed about the same as now, and my footwear was actually lighter.

In those days, perhaps the women were the more incommoded by dress regulations as they had to wear long skirts and stockings. When South African Billie Tapstock went on Centre Court with no stockings she caused a furore. And the covered stands almost collapsed when Dorothy Round and Helen Jacobs stretched for a wide one wearing their revolutionary divided skirts. The shockers had been designed by Jack Izod, who also dressed myself and Henry Cotton, when we were poor as church mice, and the Maharaja of Patiala, who spent £25,000 a year on polo shirts alone.

When our Fred Perry women's shirts were designed originally, we gave a shirt to about twenty girls of different nationalities and asked them to cut the garment up in any way they wanted, to conform with their idea of what a women's tennis shirt should look like. So the players, men and women, made use of our outfit to be well dressed, and we made use of their help to design and promote it.

Wegner and I didn't always make the right decisions in the sportswear business. We brought over from Hungary the low-cut football boot and hired Tommy Lawton to promote it; but nobody wanted to know. We were told it wasn't possible to play football in things like that. But a couple of years later, in 1953, Hungary's footballers came to Wembley and slaughtered England 6–3 – a historic first-ever home defeat – wearing the low-cut boots, which were suddenly all the rage. Yet when we had had them we couldn't give them away with a pound of cheese.

We were also a little ahead of our time when we tried to market an open-knit shirt for hot weather. We manufactured 100 dozen, but, like the boots, couldn't shift them at all. We eventually got rid of them because the floor beneath our offices in Golden Square in London was occupied by Ghana Airways and their pilots bought armloads of the shirts to take home. We thought we had done well to unload them at cost price. That was in November. The following May Wegner and I were in Paris, window shopping to see what other manufacturers had come up with, and every window we looked in was full of open-knit wear!

We generated all our publicity by getting players to wear our gear. The only advertisement we ever commissioned was a tiny one which pictured a spiv in a dark alleyway, saying, 'Psst, wanna buy a Perry shirt?' We got into the routine of giving the players shirts at the French Open and pre-Wimbledon events in Britain, so that by the time the championships came along all the pictures in the papers and the film footage showed them wearing the Perry laurel wreath.

Later we decided to personalize each gift by putting the players' initials on the chest. Everybody got two initials, except me – I was FJP. There was a reason behind the monograms. We discovered the players were getting the jump on us. We would meet them in Paris for the French Championships with enough gear to last them until they reached London for Wimbledon: most of them would take in a couple of minor British tournaments on the way. Another quota of clothing would be waiting for them on their arrival in London, so we expected and hoped they would appear in the right stuff when their pictures were taken in the pre-Wimbledon build-up. But oh, no, here they were, wandering around in lovingly well-laundered old togs, saying their Fred Perry gear had been stolen. We would even give them a shirt ready to go on to a show court and see them stepping out in their tatty old one, so we strongly suspected our shirts were being hocked. The initials not only put a stop to this freelance merchandising, but gave the players a feeling of recognition and individuality which they didn't have in the ordinary shirts.

The idea of the initials really caught on. Tibby Wegner would never throw anything away and he even converted the mill ends of our cloth into baby shirts for the players' children, suitably initialled. We also sent shirts to politicians and film stars, and even the Crown Prince of Japan used to wear a Perry shirt.

One of our keenest customers was Jack Kennedy. We sent shirts (bearing the initials JK) to him through a friend in Providence, Rhode Island, his home area. After his election as President in November 1959 and before his inauguration in January 1960, Kennedy was taking a holiday in Palm Beach, Florida, and we found ourselves sharing the same golf course, him going one way and me the other. While we were on adjoining fairways his ball finished up quite near mine, so I walked over to say hello to him, much to the consternation of his Secret Service bodyguards. Kennedy was wearing a Perry shirt, so I told him I wanted to congratulate him, not on becoming

President of the USA, but on his excellent choice of shirt. I said, 'I guess we'll have to change the address and send them to the White House now.'

'No, no, don't do that; send them through the usual channels,' he said, then added, 'By the way, can I ask you a favour?'

'Well, since you're going to become President in January I should think we might possibly arrange something,' I said, pulling his leg. 'What is it?'

'Can I have three initials, JFK, on my shirts instead of two?'

'I'll do better than that,' I promised. 'From now on, you're the only man with three initials on your shirt.' And in order to accommodate the incoming President, I reverted to two initials on my own shirts. The only other exception we made was for a woman, Billie Jean King, or Billie Jean Moffitt as she was in those days.

When Wegner and I started the business we simply regarded it as something extra, something to do on the side. Yet it mushroomed until we were runaway leaders of the sportswear field, and it stayed that way, more or less, until the advent of Open tennis in 1968 and the explosion in leisurewear.

I think every single Wimbledon champion in the fifties and sixties was at one time or another a 'Perry player'. That was why we didn't need to spend on advertising. We also tried to help players in the days before official prize money. If they were going somewhere overseas where we didn't possess agents, we would sell them our goods at a very special price and they would make a handsome profit reselling. So their assistance was reciprocated. But we never got involved in actually paying players to wear our clothing. How things have changed since Open tennis came in!

When agents and companies began putting players under contract for sportswear we decided to get out of that end of the business. If players wanted to wear our clothes, as in the past, that was fine, but if they wanted to take up other offers that was up to them.

Towards the end of the 1950s we began looking around for a tie-in with a winter operation in order to make our company year-round rather than just seasonal. Tibby Wegner was friendly with the Gannex raincoat man, Joe Kagan, but eventually we decided against making that connection and went instead for another raincoat company, Charles Mackintosh.

By this stage the outside selling operation was far outstripping our in-house ability to handle it. One example was the success of our sales drive in America. Although we started in a very small way, we were soon receiving orders worth half a million dollars, and by the time we had filled those orders there was another half a million's worth coming in, so we never caught up. Because everything was made in the United Kingdom, thereby increasing its status value to the Americans as an imported item of clothing, we were always trying to keep abreast of demand.

Eventually, in 1961, Wegner and I sold out our financial interest in the company to Mackintosh. Although we could handle the manufacturing and selling end with comparative ease, the internal workings of the business became too much – though I signed a working agreement to continue promoting the clothing wherever I happened to be in the world. It was around this time that I began to spend some of the winter months in Jamaica and the new owners of the clothing company wondered why I needed to spend so long promoting the clothing in such a location. What was I up to?

Soon after this whingeing from London, there was a particularly brutal murder along the coast from where I lived, at a resort called Port Antonio, which was once the home of Errol Flynn. Some fellow had murdered a couple of people with a machete and taken off into the mountains. Despite a big hunt, he wasn't found for several days, until finally he was spotted lying flat on his back and very dead at the bottom of a gully – wearing a Fred Perry shirt. The shirt and its emblem appeared in all the papers under the headline, KILLER FOUND. So I sent the clippings to the company in London, to worry them still further as to my activities in Jamaica.

At the end of the 1960s Fred Perry Sportswear changed hands again, sold this time to an American company, the Figgie Corporation in Cleveland. By then I had already formed another company, owned by my son David and daughter Penny, and run by David from the United States. We marketed rackets, shoes, balls – everything except clothing. It wasn't a very large business, but it had good success in half a dozen countries. When the Figgie International Corporation of Cleveland, Ohio, took over the clothing company they wanted me to go back into business with them, so a deal was struck whereby they bought out the Fred Perry name worldwide and I joined them as a sort of glad-hander, the chairman of their friendship department.

It's a role I still enjoy. My activities for the corporation are confined to the occasional TV appearance, opening shops, giving tennis clinics, speaking or lecturing. It helps me to do what I most like, to travel, and keeps me connected with the sport I love. It also keeps me involved with Fred Perry Sportswear, which was commercially the most successful thing I ever did.

My sportswear activities were also responsible for a fascinating visit to Russia in 1958. It all started just before the 1957 Wimbledon when a thirty-two-man Russian delegation turned up at our offices in Golden Square. They said they had come because mine was the only name they knew in British tennis. Since their country was not a member of the International Tennis Federation they had no credentials and they were looking for a bit of friendly assistance. I did all I could to help them. I arranged for the All England Club to provide ground passes so that they could get into Wimbledon, and through my connections I got them on to TV and radio. I also made them a gift of a piece of the Centre Court – the lump dug up for the netpost – and this was carried back home as a prized possession.

The heads of the Russian delegation to Wimbledon naturally spent a lot of time at our Golden Square offices, never leaving the premises without some little memento we had given them, and in passing they expressed the view that I would be the one to help them with their preparations and teaching methods in their own country. I thought no more of it, but the following year I was surprised to receive an invitation to take some European players to Russia for their championships and to stay on afterwards and look at the tennis set-up in the country. I was intrigued at the prospect of a first-ever visit to the Soviet Union, but a bit worried, too, as an American citizen, because of the fears stirred up by Senator McCarthy and his investigations of alleged Communist sympathizers.

So I asked the advice of Irving Geist, a guest at the Boca Raton Hotel who was well connected in government circles, about whether it would be wise to accept the invitation and also whether I could be sure of getting back into the United States afterwards. Geist promised to explain the situation on my behalf, and the upshot was that I received a letter signed personally by President Eisenhower authorizing me to travel to Russia and stressing that this should not be held against me or any member of my family.

Armed with this assurance, I set off for what turned out to be a fascinating trip. My guide and companion on the tour of Russia's tennis facilities, taking in all the big cities, was 6 feet 4 inch Eugene Korbut – no relation to Olga. He had been an aide to the Russian hero Marshal Voroshilov during the war, so he was a very interesting character and we got on well, speaking in German because his English wasn't so good. Our ability to share a language did away with the tiresome need for an interpreter.

Every evening after our day's tour of inspecting, Eugene had to call the Ministry of Sport and pass on to them my recommendations. Then, and not before, they would tell us what our next day's programme was to be. We were never permitted to deviate from this Moscow-planned itinerary.

The Russian tennis scene was a depressing one. All their courts were grey and so were all the surrounds, so that after two or three games you couldn't see the ball because of the uniform colour of everything. The nets were flimsy and the tape was poor. Some genius had designed their championship courts with a slope downwards from the baseline to the net in order to help drainage, and there was also a drain channel under the net. That meant you were hitting downhill from the baseline to an easier target, a fact which never seemed to have occurred to them. At any rate, all my recommendations were swiftly acted upon: the court surrounds were repainted, courts levelled and improved in other ways, so that they were nearer to the standard of those in other parts of the world.

I was never given any form of currency, but they provided whatever I asked for. If I wanted postcards they would buy them for me and then post them after I had written them. (The postcards, incidentally, got back home long after I did.) I knew they only wanted me in the USSR to pick my brains, but I didn't mind because it gave me a chance to see how their country worked. I was impressed, if not by the equipment, at least by the scale of the Russians' coaching effort for youngsters, with everything provided by the state.

When I returned to England I told the press to expect the Russians to do well in the next few years since they had some promising players. My forecast was proved right because they got Alex Metreveli to the Wimbledon men's final in 1973 and Olga Morozova into the women's final a year later, while Metreveli and Morozova twice gained the final of the mixed doubles. After the successes of these two, though, it seemed the Russians got big ideas that they knew what they were doing, and they promptly tried to change everybody's style to conform to a set mould. The result was that, instead of innumerable individual Russian players, there was now really only one, and any opponent who could master this one style found himself well-equipped to deal with other Russians in the future, because they would all play in exactly the same way. Their Tennis Federation got even bigger ideas and began trying to force issues through the International Federation which were completely unacceptable to the governing body. To put it bluntly, politics got into the act, which for my money does sport no good at all.

Exactly ten years later, in 1968, I was invited back to Russia because they wanted to know where they should go next after their 'ten-year plan'. There is no copyright agreement in the Soviet Union, as authors and other artists have discovered, so I wasn't too surprised – although a bit miffed – to see that their tennis clothing was copied from the Fred Perry wear they had been given in London. Their tennis equipment was also copied from Western models and the coaching manuals were pirated translations of French, English and American books, under the names of Russian coaches.

I took my wife Bobby along with me on this occasion. The Russian Tennis Federation wasn't permitted to invite her officially, so she went along through Intourist, the government travel organization, and was allocated a tourist number. This led to all sorts of complications in such a rigorously controlled society. When we went down to dinner at our Moscow hotel we found a pleasant dining room with an orchestra playing. After sitting down we were told we weren't allowed to eat there, but would have to move to another dining room without music. So we huffed and puffed a bit, throwing around the phrase 'tennis delegation', and they relented; but it wasn't long before they came up with another problem.

The waiter told us he couldn't serve Bobby dinner because, according to his records, she didn't exist as a member of the tennis delegation. Eugene Korbut, my travelling companion of ten years previously, actually had to ring up the Ministry of Sport and obtain official permission for her to eat dinner with us.

I was tremendously impressed by the fantastic progress the Russians had made in the game since my last visit. I was also impressed by how pro-Wimbledon they were. Though it might have been considered the centre of capitalist decadence, they thought of Wimbledon as a blueprint for what they wanted to achieve, which I thought was quite sensible. It was only in 1983 that Russian competitors reappeared at Wimbledon after a long absence caused by their political wrangling with the International Tennis Federation.

My most vivid memory of that 1968 visit was the day the Russians invaded Czechoslovakia. We were in a car tour with the Minister of Sport at the time, and suddenly this martial music came over the radio, followed by a terse announcement. The driver almost hit a tree and everybody in the car looked worried. I asked what had happened and was told their army had just moved into Czechoslovakia by invitation. 'Who invited them?' I asked. It was just about the end of our visit so I wasn't worried about giving our hosts a bad time over this. They wanted to know what the people in the West would think about the move. 'They'll think you're behaving like Hitler,' I told them.

While we're on the subject of international incidents, I should say that I was involved, at least indirectly, with one of the biggest of all time. I had been playing in the Czechoslovakian Championships in the 1930s (which I happened to win), and the cup was presented to me in Prague by the Czech President, Dr Benes. At that time one of his Cabinet was Jan Masarek, who was their ambassador in London and who later became a good friend of mine. I was invited to dinner in Prague with Masarek and the British ambassador, Sir Joseph Addison, and another guest that night was the redoubtable Hadau, one of the secretaries at the British Embassy in Vienna, who had just arrived from there after a 'sudden rush car trip'. The previous night he had been summoned to the Austrian Chancellery by Englebert Dollfuss and entrusted with certain signed documents for the British Government. As he had left the building and walked towards the British Embassy, trucks carrying German troops had come down the street and surrounded the Chancellery. Hadau had made all haste to his car and driven straight to Prague, his nearest port of political sanctuary. That night, Dollfuss was shot.

By the end of that trip to Russia in 1968, however, I was still on good enough terms for the Tennis Federation officials to ask what I would like for a memento of the visit. I didn't want any signed pictures, so I suggested a sable coat for my wife might be a nice idea. But they simply smiled and said such an item wasn't exactly what they had in mind. When we arrived at the airport, though, we found an extra suitcase, brand new, amongst our luggage. It contained 40 pounds of caviar, our parting gift. This pleased my wife Bobby, who adores caviar, immensely.

17

Changes in the Game

When I watch the game now there are several big differences from my own playing days which strike me forcibly. I never thought, for example, that I would see the introduction of seats for the players. In the pre-war years you went out to play a match and stayed on your feet until the end of it. If you didn't, it was because you had collapsed.

Matches now last much longer, too. One of the big reasons for my success was that I was fitter than any of the other players, and if I got my opponent on the run he didn't have time to recover by taking a rest. For instance, in the 1936 Wimbledon final against Gottfried von Cramm I won three sets in just forty minutes. Nowadays players are lucky to complete *one* set in that time.

The practice of allowing players to sit down for a ninety-second break every other game turns a match into a drawn-out business. Not only that, the players are also permitted thirty seconds between every point – and quite a lot of them take it, too, with their time-wasting tactics.

The 1980 US Open final between Bjorn Borg and John McEnroe is regarded as one of the marathons. It was a great match all right, but hardly a 'marathon'. They played five sets and fifty-four games, in a match that lasted four and a half hours. Yet they didn't actually *play* for that length of time. How so, you may ask. Well, with a ninety-second break at every changeover and twenty-seven end changes, that's roughly forty minutes. In addition to this, in fifty-four games the players contest a minimum of 220 points, which is four per game – and no match goes like that because there are deuces and extra points in between. So you get closer to 250 points, which, with thirty seconds between, adds up to 125 minutes. Plus the sitting-down time, forty minutes, which gives a total of two and three-quarter hours. Take this all into consideration and the actual playing time is greatly reduced. True, the players are out there, just as we were, but they're not on their feet the whole time – as we were.

It was even worse in the 1982 US Open, because the changeover break was extended beyond two minutes so that the television commercials could be fitted in. The fellow who stood by the umpire's chair with a stopwatch wasn't timing the players, he was clocking the commercials!

I was sitting with some of the other old-time champions, like Don Budge and Jack Kramer, when we decided to put our own stopwatch on the changeovers. We found they were taking two minutes and twenty-five seconds on average, which means they were breaking the rules in order to accommodate TV, an indication of how that medium runs sport in America.

Quite honestly, I don't know whether to laugh or cry when I watch the start of a tennis match these days. There they are, two young sportsmen, trained to the limit. And what do they do? They play one game – just *one game* – then they sit down for a rest. It just doesn't make sense to me. They'll be providing armchairs and lilos next.

Another big change I notice at Wimbledon is among the crowds. In the old days spectators never dreamed of going there without a collar and tie, or a suitable dress, because this was the Holy of Holies. And if a voice was raised, it was to say 'Well played' or 'Good shot'. Now they scream, wave banners and bellow 'Attaboy, Jimmy' and stronger stuff. I'm all for freedom of speech and nobody could accuse me of snobbery, but this is stretching the point too far. You get your timing from the sound of the ball leaving the racket at the other end and then coming off the ground. If you don't hear the sound, you don't know when to hit. This is why, incidentally, players performing indoors tend to think they're playing better: unless the courts are carpeted, the acoustics are better.

One of the most dramatic changes in recent years, among players as well as spectators, has been in the matter of discipline and respect. In my time, even if you fervently disagreed with a particular authority (and I often did), you still acknowledged it and obeyed the rules. Present-day players have too much scope for misbehaviour – they are allowed three infringements before they even risk disqualification. Now, that's not much encouragement to self-control. In my opinion, it should be like it is in football – give an offender one warning and then show him the red card. If players knew that sort of punishment was hanging over their heads, there would be fewer arguments. Quite simply, discipline has gone in the game because junior players have not been stamped on at a time when they could have absorbed it and it wouldn't have hurt them. I had my fiery temperament stamped on a few times and I reckon it did me good.

161

Harry Hopman, that great Australian coach, used to handle the succession of youngsters he turned into some of the greatest players the world has ever seen by imposing strict discipline on them. Although they didn't like it, they respected it. When any of his squad were told, 'Do it this way or you go home,' they never took the chance of trying him out.

Once I was with Hopman at Wimbledon, watching his players practise. Frank Sedgman was working on a high backhand volley and it was the young Lew Hoad's job to feed him the sort of ball that would help him. After a while Hoad hit a tremendous whistling forehand across court and past Sedgman. This happened two or three times before Hopman beckoned Hoad to the side of the court and told him, 'Frank is working on his backhand volley and you are supposed to be feeding him. The next time you hit a ball across court like that you can work off your surplus energy with a two-mile run on Wimbledon Common.'

Hopman and I walked away from the court, but Hopman continued to watch the practice from behind a hedge. Hoad was only seventeen or so then, and that sort of dull routine was all too much for his youthful impetuosity. Suddenly he let go another cross-court forehand – whoof! Hopman emerged from behind the hedge and hadn't got within twenty yards of the court before Hoad put down his racket and said, 'OK, Cap, here I go,' and set off on his two-mile punishment run.

That's discipline, and I went through the same sort of thing at the formative stage of my career. It was made quite clear to me the first time I went on tour in 1930, wearing my national team blazer, that if I didn't toe the line I would be on the next ship home. I certainly wasn't Establishment-minded: in fact, I was probably the only British player of my era who ever kicked over the traces at all. But being told in no uncertain terms where I stood served me in very good stead.

When Britain won the Davis Cup four years in succession in the mid-1930s, our non-playing captain, H. Roper Barrett, was a formidable personality. I can't say we loved him dearly, but we didn't answer him back. If he said, 'Breakfast at nine,' he didn't mean wander down when it suits you. This was all part of the disciplining process and we accepted it because we desperately wanted to play for Britain. It meant so much to us, but that patriotic feeling doesn't seem to exist any more; a lot of youngsters don't want to play for their country at any price. Look at Yannick Noah. He was unavailable to represent France in the World Team Cup competition in Düsseldorf in 1983 as he had some commitment to play in another tournament, so his national federation responded by suspending him, even though by then he had won the French Open – the first Frenchman to do so for thirty-seven years.

Discipline in tennis took a few steps backwards when that awful vaudeville invention, World Team Tennis, flourished briefly in America: spectators were encouraged to blow horns and shout things like, 'Serve a double fault, you bum,' and the players attempted to give the matches a little 'atmosphere' by staging arguments. I've nothing against a few light-hearted tennis matches – after all, I love the entertainment business – but WTT turned the players into idiots and the game into a joke.

It is perfectly possible to play tennis without hawking four-letter words all over the place or making obscene gestures. Unfortunately, the juniors tend to copy the players who make waves, rather than those who don't, and nowadays the one they tend to copy most is, of course, John McEnroe – a very intelligent man and a brilliant player who suffers from perfectionism. John McEnroe cannot be wrong in public – or so he seems to think. There is evidently some quirk in his character which comes into operation whenever he's publicly accused of being wrong, and this prevents him from grasping what this might mean.

I have some sympathy with him inasmuch as he gets upset – and, rather as I used to do, he tends to play better when he *is* upset. But I have no sympathy with the resulting tantrums, or his explanations for them. It seems to me that McEnroe gets out on a limb and doesn't know how to get back. He'd rather crash down than climb down.

Take, for instance, the 1983 Wimbledon and the matter of McEnroe's foot-faults. He knows the rule: the only way you can be foot-faulted today is to have any part of your front foot touching the line as you prepare to serve, which gains you perhaps a millimetre of advantage. McEnroe stands so close to the line that, by the very way he serves, he must touch it or go over it once in a while, in which case he gets called, as he was last year. Nobody likes being foot-faulted, but most people accept it. Not McEnroe. He would rather keep repeating the fault and go through a big argument than go back a couple of inches. If it comes to a confrontation, that's OK by him. Yet in his next match he *will* stand a couple of inches further back. If he had done that in the first place it would have saved a lot of headaches, but that would have shown him to be in the wrong, to have made a mistake.

A Code of Conduct for tennis was long overdue and I'm glad it is now being implemented, if only half-heartedly. The really big names still know that they are safe from disqualification, because the tournaments need them. So they get fined, and their reaction is merely, 'Do you want the money in five- or twenty-dollar bills?' There is no point hitting rich people in their wallets.

To reprimand a player publicly takes a lot of guts and the professionals realize that not many officials possess that sort of courage. But it is imperative to remind these players that certain things won't be tolerated, as Jimmy Connors was sharply reminded when he was given a warning for audible obscenity in the Benson & Hedges tournament at Wembley in November 1983. Connors didn't like it one bit, but it was his own fault for swearing out loud, just as it's often his own fault for making suggestive gestures with his racket. To have said afterwards, as Connors did, that he was being victimized, and to have threatened to pull out of the Grand Prix and just play exhibitions if it didn't stop, was patently absurd. The only way to get big money from exhibitions is by winning the top Grand Prix events. Once a player stops playing in those, the public quickly forgets who he is. I have always said that tennis players are like buses – there will be another one along in a minute!

An unwillingness to abide by the rules indicates lack of respect for the game. If players don't like the rules or the conditions, they needn't play Grand Prix tennis. I think the boys (and one or two of the girls) would do well to remember that they owe their sporting eminence to the Grand Prix, not to exhibition tennis.

It has always been the case, of course, that the more rules and regulations introduced into a sport, the more loopholes people find. If you put up a sign, 'Do not walk on the grass,' and then let somebody walk on it, everybody is going to do it, whatever the notice might say. But if the first transgressor, no matter how important, is well and truly clobbered, nobody else will walk on the grass.

18

A No-Win Situation

The trouble with tennis nowadays is that there are too many tournaments and too much money on offer to the stars. I never thought I'd find myself putting forward such a criticism, but it's true. The proliferation of tournaments, especially now that the women have largely gone their own way, means that there are simply not enough top-level competitors to go round. Those that there are wear themselves out with too much tennis, too much travelling and too many other exhausting – if lucrative – commitments. On top of that, there is the constant mental pressure to succeed and retain a high ranking on the computer which decides the level of entry for competitors.

It is no longer a question of beating somebody for the pleasure of winning. Now players do it principally for the money and the computer points. This has led to a growth of 'computer-orientated' players who can retain a high ranking by performing only on surfaces and in conditions that suit them, and it is one of the great pities of tennis that they are able to do this rather than expose themselves to the variety of surfaces on which the sport is played. Some even choose to miss Wimbledon, which would once have been unthinkable.

The ninety-second rest at the change of ends, and the fact that the tie-break rule has virtually eliminated marathon deciding sets like 22–20 or 18–16, mean that the players are guaranteed less exhausting matches. However, the sheer speed of modern travel means that they are playing many more matches than we did. They can finish a tournament in London on Sunday, be in Los Angeles or Rio de Janeiro on Monday, and be playing in another tournament somewhere else on Tuesday.

Too many people continue to play these days when they are injured – because of the money. As long as they win a couple of rounds, collect the cash and the computer points, they are content. When you look at the scores these days it is amazing how many 6–7, 1–6 results you see.

This isn't just coincidence. If, as a second-round loser, the player collects $1000 and in any case would be facing McEnroe in the third round, it's simpler – once he has lost the first set narrowly, despite playing hard – not to sweat his guts out, but take the money and move on to the next tournament.

Jet lag is another reason why there are more surprise results now than there were in my day, and the sheer pressure of competition means that some players never get around to working out improvements in their game. In the old days, if you wanted to learn something, you took time off the circuit to perfect it. Anthony Wilding, the pre-First World War Wimbledon champion, learned a new backhand on the boat trip from his home in New Zealand to England. Don Budge was another example. His forehand was not so much Western as Wild Western. He wanted to copy my style of forehand and ended up with something in between my stroke and his old one. But it suited him, which was the important thing.

Nowadays, if a player is making a quarter of a million dollars a year and if a ranking level is at stake, it is admittedly very difficult to make the decision to quit the circuit completely in order to perfect a new stroke. There is always the chance that it wouldn't work anyway, and he might be throwing $60,000 prize money down the drain. The only example I can recall in recent times of a player who took this risk is the Australian Paul McNamee, who spent six months with Harry Hopman to learn a new, double-fisted backhand with a bigger racket. In McNamee's case it worked; he beat John McEnroe soon after in the French Open.

Despite all the tournaments and the cash on offer, the great majority of the professionals earn no more than a comfortable living in very agreeable surroundings in exchange for all their travel and stress. The women are luckier than the men, since there are only two top ones now, Martina Navratilova and Chris Evert Lloyd. Take them away and a women's tournament is struggling to find a crowd-puller, though British fans are all keeping their fingers crossed that Jo Durie will continue her remarkable progress towards the top. Let's hope that she can become as popular as Virginia Wade.

Because of the enormous number of people who play tennis around the world, the sport has generated a massive back-up business in clothing and equipment. This is natural enough and, of course, I've benefited from this as much as anyone. But now manufacturers are keen to clothe and equip promising youngsters, sometimes at an incredibly early age, with the full encouragement of the agents,

managers, lawyers, coaches and trainers they all seem to be surrounded by. The endorsement business is getting ludicrously out of
hand and is placing extra pressure to succeed on players who are
really still children.

This is much more prevalent in women's tennis. Girls of fourteen
and fifteen – even thirteen – are offered enormous amounts of money
to endorse a certain racket or to wear certain clothes, shoes, even
perfume or jewellery. Many players go into action now wearing more
trade names than a Formula One racing car. I know that pro-tennis
and commerce have always enjoyed a close relationship, but until
today I didn't think they were married.

The catch is that, in order to live up to all this commercial backing,
players must win some matches, and it's a tough grind for the teenage
girls, especially when so many of the American ones are Chris Lloyd
clones with two-handed backhands. They even look the same
physically. By the time they're seventeen many of them are carrying
stress injuries because of the demands on little bodies and bones
which are still developing. At about the same age a lot of them
discover there are other things in life besides tennis.

When I was living in America after the Second World War I
thought they had the greatest bunch of under-fifteen boy players I had
ever seen. That was the Jack Kramer era, so they all had their hair
crew-cut like Kramer and tried to walk and play like him. (Now they
want to walk and talk and serve – and argue – like McEnroe.) When I
was tennis coach at the Boca Raton Hotel in Florida I got to know a
fifteen-year-old called Lester Ruthven, the son of the hotel's sign
painter. Lester was a wonderful prospect, so I offered to give him free
coaching twice a week and also, since the family didn't have any
money, arranged for rackets, shoes and clothes to be supplied free.

But Lester was a contrary so-and-so. One day, for example, I would
tell him to hit half-speed forehands across court, but after doing this
four or five times he would wallop one down the line. When I asked if
he understood my English he said he preferred playing the other shot.
He was hard work to coach. On another occasion he would forget his
rackets; sometimes he would turn up for a lesson having forgotten his
shoes. But he got into all the finals, every family wanted him to meet
their daughters, and he was on everybody's free list for ice-cream.

Then suddenly, when he moved into the under-eighteen bracket, he
was up against bigger and better kids, and he wasn't getting into the
finals any more. Nor was he getting the invitations or the parties. And
instead of being on the show courts, he suddenly found himself stuck

out on the far courts early in the week – and losing.

He told me he was going to give up tennis for a year and put on some weight so that he could hit the ball harder. I didn't say anything, but I knew Lester Ruthven would never be back. There were too many counter-attractions – cars, girls, movies, milk-shakes.

The ones who make it to the top, like little Jimmy Arias of the United States, knuckle down and realize that it's a tough business, in which it sometimes helps to be big-headed. You are, after all, in a one-to-one confrontation every time you step on court, and if you don't think you're any good it's certain nobody else will.

Before the Second World War tournament tennis was true-blue amateur, and woe betide you if you tried to make it anything else. After the war, when there was more money around, what quickly became known as 'shamateurism' crept into tennis, and competitors would only enter events if they were guaranteed the prizes that went with a semi-final appearance. To sweep the game clean, tennis went Open in 1968, with Wimbledon, to its great credit, leading the way. From that moment tennis became big business – with agents and entrepreneurs and, of course, TV.

There is always the possibility that television's huge influence and its potential effect on tennis can be a worrying thing, particularly in the United States where television has far too much to do with the actual scheduling of matches. In the US Open it's just not possible, as it is at Wimbledon, to have one of the major players performing on an outside court and a potentially good contest between lesser-known people on the main court – because this wouldn't suit the TV people.

It has reached the stage where TV is practically running the US Open. The huge prize money comes from the fees paid by the television companies, so the scheduling of matches depends on TV requirements, which depend on advertising, which depends on the right names, as far as tennis watchers are concerned, being on the screen. It's all a question of wheels within wheels. Television even fixes the time of the final at the US Open – a ludicrous 4 p.m. start to a five-set final, guaranteeing that it will have to finish under floodlights and in very different conditions from when it began, because the TV people are busy pumping out football earlier in the afternoon and tennis must await its turn in the programme slot.

The power of TV in the United States is obviously responsible for many players getting away with misbehaviour and rule-bending.

Nobody with two hours' prime-time television and all the attendant commercial revenue can afford to have a player disqualified.

A supreme example of this came in the 1983 US Open final when Jimmy Connors suddenly sprinted off court, allegedly to obey a 'call of nature', at a tight stage of his match with Ivan Lendl, who was given no reason for the stoppage. To begin with, it would have been mere courtesy to explain the reason why Lendl was left to kick his heels for several minutes in heat exceeding 100 degrees while Connors took a break. Lendl eventually protested and, in my opinion, would have been perfectly within his rights to demand Connors' disqualification. The tournament referee was called on to court, yet Connors got away with it. Why? Because TV wouldn't have tolerated the final being terminated unexpectedly by default or disqualification. It would have left them with 'dead air' in prime time. So Connors came back and went on to win the match.

They wouldn't have got away with pulling such a stroke on me, even if it had meant a confrontation to end all confrontations. It would also have been interesting if Lendl, having been refused a victory by default, had then said, 'OK, I retire in protest.'

It is possible, with enough money, to run a tournament specially for TV, like the now-defunct Pepsi Grand Slam at Boca Raton, Florida, by assembling four big names, packaging it and selling it to the screen, too often without any consideration about what such 'special events' are doing to the Grand Prix circuit.

Of all the ills which exist in the game today (and in some cases have existed almost as long as tennis), the worst is the proliferation of special events and exhibition matches at the expense of the regular circuit. Tournament directors, promoters and sponsors must often wonder whether it's worth it when their events get a poor entry, as the Australian Open did for years until 1983 and as the South African Open continues to do. Luckily for the players, however, for every tournament that collapses as a result, another fills its place.

Promoters may put up $300,000 for a tournament, knowing that the Association of Tennis Professionals will guarantee them thirty-two competitors – but they don't know which ones. Most of the leading men aren't interested in playing much of the Grand Prix circuit beyond the major tournaments which keep their names in front of the public – and those who pay out the money for equipment and clothing contracts. They would rather take part in an exhibition, often earning as much, or more, than they would by appearing for a whole week in a circuit event and with the possibility of a drop in prestige by losing.

That sort of attitude has to be bad for tennis. Modern exhibitions aren't like the tough head-to-head matches we used to play when I was a pro. No matter how promoters disguise it under the title of 'shoot-out', 'classic' or whatever, an exhibition is exactly what the name implies – a practice match beefed up by public relations experts. And for this, the star players may pick up $50,000 a night, or even more, for practising in public. An indication of how meaningless it all is, despite the hype poured forth by agents and PROs, was given by Gladys Heldman in the American magazine *World Tennis* (November 1983) when she said, 'McEnroe will never misbehave in one of these so-called "tournaments" because nothing is riding on it.'

True, when I turned professional after winning Wimbledon for the third successive year in 1936 I moved into a world of exhibitions, too. But they were different. The professional championship of the world was at stake in the tours (often lasting four or five months and stretching into dozens of matches) that I undertook against people like Ellsworth Vines and Bill Tilden, so there was never any easing up. Those matches were far removed from being just public practices. A whole stream of talent, from Jack Kramer to Rod Laver, maintained that high professional standard until the sport went Open in 1968.

Despite the escalation in prize money since Open tennis arrived, it is the phenomenal growth in appearance money that has caused such great concern to people like myself, who believe in winning and genuine competition and have the game's interest at heart.

Appearance money has existed since the 'shamateurism' days, when it lurked under a different name. All the pious claims that there is no such thing as appearance money are a lot of hooey. It *does* exist, but it has been difficult to prove on the Grand Prix tournament circuit, since the top players blankly deny it and the promoters are afraid to admit it for fear of losing the big-name competitors next time round. The money being demanded is astronomical, and whether it goes directly into the players' pockets or reaches them by some other roundabout method, such as personal appearances or coaching clinics, is immaterial. Like exhibitions and 'special events', appearance money is hurting the sport.

You may say, 'Oh, Fred made his money at tennis and now he wants to spoil it for those kids.' I don't. It's one thing for a player to trade on his competitive abilities – as we did in my day – and quite another to cream off huge sums from the game without even competing.

Players and promoters are a bit more open about admitting to the existence of appearance money outside Grand Prix competition. I was interested to read about a four-man tournament (Jimmy Connors, José Luis Clerc, Gene Mayer and Ilie Nastase) in Atlantic City in the autumn of 1983. The winner, Connors, took home $50,000 and the others proportionately less, but what caught my eye in the newspaper report was the sentence saying, 'Each player *also* received an unspecified amount of appearance money.' So why worry about winning?

19

Living Legends

One of the questions I am regularly asked is, 'Do you think you could have beaten Borg?' Or McEnroe? Or Connors, or Lendl? People find this sort of speculation fascinating in all sports and I can understand their wanting to know, but I like to turn the question around by asking them, 'Could Jack Dempsey have beaten Muhammad Ali?' The answer, of course, is that we will never know – though this doesn't stop the speculation!

In my own case I had to pack up playing seriously in 1942 when I broke my arm in that match at Madison Square Garden, New York, and in one way I found it a good thing because of the well-known cruelty of the sporting public towards their former heroes. They see someone who's a bit past it trying to stay at the top level and they come out with such cutting comments as, 'You're a bit slow,' or 'Put on a bit of weight, haven't you?'

With me that never happened. Because I went out at the top, I was never a has-been. People think I was perhaps a little better than I really was, a bit faster than I really was, that my forehand was more devastating than it really was, and that I was a much nicer person than I really was – even if they didn't like me at the time! And I think it's much better to keep it that way.

One thing about me was *not* exaggerated: I gave no quarter. I never believed in taking prisoners on a tennis court. I was a great believer in getting my nose in front and making sure the other fellow's nose didn't catch up.

I don't think I was the world's most gifted player by a long stretch. For one thing, I didn't possess the variety of shot required for that. But I never went on court to come second, and if I did lose to somebody I was determined that he would never put it across me again.

I hear a lot about Englishmen being good losers. Hogwash! There's nothing good about losing, and if somebody makes a habit of it, there's a simple explanation: he's no good. It should be the end of the world if you lose a tennis match at top level. How you get round it is entirely up to the individual. I was a loner, though I travelled most of the time as part of a team and had a lot of friends, and I always made it my business to know more about my opponents than they knew about me. I was pretty crafty. If I ever said, 'Good shot' – which I very seldom did – they were never sure if I meant it or not.

Nor did I ever believe in the gesture of throwing a point away in order to acquire the reputation of being 'a good sport'. I didn't aspire to being a good sport: 'champion' was good enough for me. Say, for instance, you are match point down and you hit the ball out, but the linesman calls your shot good and saves you. Are you then going to throw away the next point and go match point down again? You quickly learn not to do these things.

Believe me, throwing away points and attempting unnecessarily fancy shots are two of the greatest reasons for players losing matches. The fancy shot that I remember best of all was in the 1972 Wimbledon final between Stan Smith and Ilie Nastase. In the fifth set Nastase was ahead and 30-love up on Smith's serve. On the next point he pulled Smith wide, but instead of just popping the ball over the net he went for a fancy winner – and missed. Nastase lost the match and never won Wimbledon.

Another factor to consider in the 'Could-you-have-beaten-so-and-so' debate is the question of which rules you would play under. In my time we had to stand with both feet behind the baseline to serve and keep one foot on the ground until after making contact. Now you can skid forward like Lew Hoad used to do; go into a rocking motion like John Newcombe and let fly when you have worked up to about 20 m.p.h.; jump in the air – that's a popular one; or do an Arthur Ashe – stand well behind the baseline, throw up the ball ahead of you, and then leap after it. All this is now permitted. Players can get a foot and a half closer to the net than we could, legally. This is why, on grass and other fast surfaces, it's now a different ball game. The server bangs the ball into play and grunts; the other man hits it back and grunts. End of point.

But whatever the rules and whatever the era, a champion earns his fame because he possesses that extra something the other fellow doesn't. And I believe champions always have that quality, in any sport. You can't put a name to it, but I can tell you this: anybody who played me would have known about being in one hell of a tennis match.

People are especially fond of making comparisons between myself and Borg because it was he who exceeded my total of consecutive Wimbledon wins, although with all due respect, Borg *didn't* beat my record since it wasn't strictly the same as mine. Technically, I was the first player to win three successive Wimbledons (1934, 1935 and 1936) having played through the whole championships, for although William Renshaw won the Wimbledon title six times in succession between 1881 and 1886, in those days the holder didn't have to defend his title until the following year's final. A tournament was held first, and then the winner played the title holder. This exemption was in force until 1922, so Renshaw is the record holder up to that time. After 1922 I am the record holder until 1968, when Wimbledon went Open. My three titles were amateur ones, and my run came to an end when I turned pro – not because I was beaten, but because I was banned. So Borg didn't beat *my* record. Borg won Wimbledon five times altogether: he was always eligible to play. If he had been playing in my era as an amateur, though, how many of those years would he have waited before turning professional?

Since the players of my era weren't allowed to play any amateur events after turning pro, who is to say that Don Budge wouldn't have won three in a row if he hadn't joined the professionals? I for one am certain Budge would have added the 1939 Wimbledon to his 1937 and 1938 wins. Who is to say that Lew Hoad wouldn't have won it three times, too, or Rod Laver, but for professionalism? In fact, Laver won Wimbledon twice, turned professional and won it twice more as soon as Wimbledon went Open, so he might have established a modern record beyond *anybody's* reach.

When Borg won his Wimbledons there was no need for him to turn pro: he already was one. I was happy for him and was among the first to shake his hand when he won his fourth successive title. After all, these records and so-called sporting milestones exist to be broken.

I was also thrilled to see my judgement vindicated where Borg's talent was concerned. When he won the French Open at the age of seventeen I was doing a BBC broadcast and was asked, 'Will this fellow ever be good on a fast surface, such as grass?' My answer was a very positive yes, since Borg had learned all his tennis in Sweden, where the bounce of the ball is low outdoors and even lower and faster on their indoor courts, on which the Swedes spend most of their time.

Borg learned very early how to run on grass – which is something Ivan Lendl has never learned to do. It's not just a matter of breaking into a run; you have to glide into your shot and then start moving back into position right away. You can't hit the ball, watch it, and then move, as Lendl does. Even when he reached the 1983 Wimbledon semi-final against John McEnroe, his best performance, Lendl was still moving too late, which is fatal against someone like McEnroe, who has such awesome racket control and who can make you pay the full price for not being in position.

Borg was the best player I have seen when it came to battling his way out of a tight corner; when he was love-40, 15–40 or 30–40 down he was marvellous. Look how he came back so many times from seemingly impossible positions against players like Mark Edmondson, Vijay Amritraj and Victor Amaya during his great Wimbledon years.

It was a shame that Borg had to retire with one ambition – winning the US Open – unfulfilled. But once the Americans moved their championship to the concrete courts of Flushing Meadow, I knew that for technical reasons this was one title Borg would never take. Those courts were specifically built for Americans to win on – as they have proved since Flushing became the Open venue. They give a waist-high bounce, whereas Borg liked a low ball which he could come up-and-over on, to give it the exaggerated top-spin which was one of his greatest weapons.

When he played in the US Open Borg had to retreat well behind the baseline in order to take the ball on a lower bounce. So for two weeks out of his playing year he was hitting the ball from two feet further back than usual. This also gave his opponent that much more time to see the ball coming and meant that whenever Borg went forward he had further to run. Two feet might not seem much, but when you are adding it to your every movement over a period of hours, it begins to take a toll.

Borg was, inevitably, a lesser player on those hards courts at Flushing Meadow. The reason he succeeded as well as he did (he was runner-up three times) was a mark of his pride and the fact that he was fitter and concentrated better than anybody else.

If it were possible to have these time-free championship match-ups, I'd love to get at him! In my day I was just as fit as Borg and just as dedicated: I would have stayed out on court for three days in order to beat him. As for my contemporaries, I think Henri Cochet, one of those famous Four Musketeers of France, would have beaten Borg with his subtlety and because he took less out of himself than Borg did during a match. But for my money, the man who would have given Borg the most trouble was Lew Hoad. He hit the ball so hard and was so quick that he would have knocked him off his rhythm.

175

Movement is all-important at the top level. Vitas Gerulaitis and Billie Jean King have earned much praise as good movers, but for my taste they are a little too mechanical, not naturally smooth. The best movers I have seen were Henri Cochet, Pancho Gonzales, Evonne Goolagong and Ilie Nastase – all of them smooth and silky, like oil.

After movement, the next most important possession for a tennis professional is racket control, and in this respect the best two players I've seen since the war are Nastase and McEnroe. Both of them make the racket look like an extension of the arm; it's as if they were born holding the implement. They have a shot for every kind of ball that comes over the net at them, whereas so many players need to receive the right kind of ball before they are able to make a shot. In other words, they lack improvisation, which can never be said of McEnroe.

He can start to make his stroke and then hold back if he has to; and he can bring the racket through a bit quicker, too, if needs be. He can drag the shot, or fiddle it at the last second. He is the *one* player, man or woman, in the game today, who knows exactly where his racket is at all times, and exactly what his options are.

Yet despite McEnroe's undoubted genius and Borg's unparalleled achievements, the best player I've watched since the war is Rod Laver. Rod wasn't called 'The Rockhampton Rocket' for nothing. He hit the ball awfully hard and was a beautiful volleyer, a good mover and a competitor full of fire. He pressured his opponents the whole time. He also had one of the best left-handed serves ever; he could slide flat serves into the corners and had a wicked kick-serve. That type of delivery from a left-hander is the most difficult for a right-handed player to return.

I think Rod Laver learned that particular serve from Neale Fraser, who beat him in the 1960 Wimbledon final and who is now non-playing captain of Australia's Davis Cup team. That's one of the reasons why the Australians were so good in the post-war era. They travelled everywhere as a team and were willing to help and teach each other.

I am a great believer that, to reach the very top, you must have one winning shot, the outright winner that comes from nowhere like a knockout punch. In my case this was my forehand, and with Laver it was his volley. Jimmy Connors possesses the ability to hit the outright winner, the killer shot, especially on return of serve. Borg could hit winners, too, though he had to work the opening first, and they weren't of the same order as the ones you get from McEnroe. Whoosh! A forehand or backhand in the past tense.

Ivan Lendl has a lethal forehand, but for my money he's one of the game's Frankenstinian monsters – a manufactured and totally programmed performer. I have watched Lendl since his early teens, when he went on to win the Wimbledon junior championship. His Czechoslovakian mentors have indoctrinated him with years of studious and constant practice. He has a great forehand and his backhand has improved enormously in the past couple of years, but his strokes are somehow regimented. I always get the feeling when I'm watching one of his matches that he should be wearing an army greatcoat and walking up and down outside the Politburo offices in Prague with a gun on his shoulder: forty-two paces to the left, about turn, forty-two paces to the right.

Lendl is fast, no doubt about that, but that's not to say he's a good mover. What's more important, his blinkered outlook makes it difficult for him to change his tactics or his style. He possesses ability in abundance, but lacks flexibility. In the past four or five years I don't recall seeing him attempt more than three or four drop shots. When you watch Lendl you know in advance that he will leather the ball for all it's worth.

I once thought he was strictly a European slow-court player, and certainly Europe is where he got most of his early results. But he has put up some excellent performances on all surfaces, establishing a domination of McEnroe with a string of wins, including one in the Davis Cup at Flushing Meadow which was a classic. He has also won the Masters title indoors in New York. Yet Lendl has difficulty in winning any Grand Slam championship, which is extraordinary. He has been in four finals – the US Open twice, the French and the Australian – and failed every time. By now it's clear that he gets nervous on such occasions, and when a wily campaigner like Jimmy Connors (who beat him in both US Open finals) scents nervousness he pounces. There is obviously a mental barrier for Lendl to overcome now.

There hasn't been a British Wimbledon men's champion since me in 1936, and a lot of people keep wondering when we will produce another one. Well, it's not a matter of *producing* anybody, to begin with. It's a case of there being somebody, somewhere, who wants to succeed badly enough and is determined and bloody-minded enough to make sure he does. You can take anybody and give him the best rackets, the best facilities, the best coaches, Rolls Royces, Porsches or Cadillacs; but you can't make him into a top-class tennis player unless he really wants it himself. If somebody is there to help him, that's wonderful. But if nobody helps, his attitude should be, 'Too bad, but I'm still going to get there.'

I cannot go along with the old excuses that in Britain it's the fault of the climate or the shortage of facilities. To me, that's hogwash. Look at Jo Durie. Two years ago she was flat on her back after a spine operation and it looked as if she might never play, or even walk properly, again. But she was determined enough to say, 'I'm going to do it.' She has done such a wonderful job in such difficult circumstances that she forced her way into the world's top ten in 1983. British tennis badly needs more of that attitude.

The situation is better in the women's game. There have been three post-war winners – Angela Mortimer, Ann Jones and Virginia Wade – and, especially in the case of Virginia, Britain has had somebody with charisma for the youngsters to want to emulate. But those three women were either in their late twenties or early thirties before they won Wimbledon, an indication of later tennis maturity in England. I don't think a British player reaches his or her peak until the mid-twenties. The prodigies of seventeen or eighteen don't exist in Britain as they do elsewhere, and I think that needs to be acknowledged.

The French have done a great job in bringing on players of the calibre of Yannick Noah and Henri Leconte from their youth training scheme, and the Lawn Tennis Association – not before time – has started to see encouraging signs from similar schemes and regional centres it has set up around the country. On the other hand, don't forget that Connors wasn't 'produced' by any tennis association. Nor was McEnroe. Neither was I.

20

The World, My Oyster

People often express surprise that my involvement with the British Davis Cup efforts has been almost non-existent. After all, I helped Britain win the Cup four years in a row in the mid-thirties. Why wasn't my expertise called upon in the post-war years?

This was, in the main, my own decision. Although I thoroughly enjoyed such work as 'Focus on Tennis' with the children, I deliberately resisted involvement in official coaching. You rarely get any kudos or credit for it and I certainly got no kick out of it either.

To be frank, I regarded coaching really good players as too much like hard work. They already have their own personalized way of hitting the ball, and they resist change. In any case, when a player reaches that level and starts attempting to make changes, there is always the thought in the back of his mind that this is going to be a long hard process and may not work anyhow. Whenever I had good players coming to me for technical advice, it was like pulling teeth to explain the whys and wherefores of the changes. That was why I never had any protégés. For me, coaching was strictly a business, trying to make it easier for people to play and enjoy the game with the ability they already possessed. I think they should get enjoyment out of hitting a tennis ball; if they don't, it's going to become a chore and they won't play anyway.

I did do some work with the British team on two occasions, however. In 1955 I was approached by Basil Reay, then Secretary of the LTA, asking me if I would help with the British Davis Cup team and try to pull things together. The team, under the captaincy of John Barrett and the coaching of the Australian George Worthington, seemed to have become a little bogged down. It sounded like a good idea, though I didn't know exactly what I was expected to do. I couldn't see why we should need a squad of four players and three officials to go with them. According to my brief, all the team announcements were to be made by the captain, Barrett, as was only right, and all tactics and training were Worthington's responsibility. So goodness knows where I came in. Problems began early. When we got off the plane in Vienna the local press made a bee-line for Fred Perry. There was a bit of a stink about that. And when I was asked to make the draw for the tie, that caused another upset in our camp, so the venture couldn't be called a success.

The other time I helped a British team was when it was captained by the late Herman David, who asked me to work with Bobby Wilson and tune him up. So I told Wilson we were going to hit forehands for an hour, one bounce, at top speed – the idea being that you make the stroke so many times it becomes automatic. If you fiddle around in practice and let the ball bounce more than once, as so many club players do, you won't learn anything; your whole rhythm and timing should be geared to hitting every ball that comes your way either on the volley or first bounce.

Wilson and I practised for half an hour flat out, had a short break, and then put in another half hour because his forehand was a bit dicey and I wanted to build up his confidence. Next morning Herman David said he had had a call from Wilson's mother telling him Bobby would not be at practice. When he had got home the previous evening, she claimed, he had been so tired that he had had to go straight to bed and have his dinner there. She felt this wasn't right, since it was only practice. Herman then gave Wilson an ultimatum to turn up or be thrown off the squad. He turned up and, to his credit, worked hard – which, of course, you should always do when representing your country.

I assisted the Indian, Belgian and Swedish Davis Cup teams at various times. I was also invited to Egypt to help sort out their professional system, but, like in so many other places I went to, I was soon in trouble, though not of my own making. The popular revolution against the regime of King Farouk broke out while I was in Egypt and I was on the wrong side on two counts. First, I had been invited there by Farouk himself, and second, I was a Westerner at a time when they weren't exactly popular with the locals.

I was allocated an army captain as a bodyguard and never went anywhere without him. If the crowds saw a white man inside a car they were liable to overturn it, so if I had to be left alone in a vehicle temporarily, my bodyguard would hide me under a blanket on the floor. The captain even accompanied me to the airport to catch my plane back to London late at night. When we got there we were told the plane was late and would not be leaving until eight the next morning. 'I'm not driving Mr Perry back into Cairo,' said the officer. 'What's that plane over there?'

'That plane' was a four-engined BOAC Hermes which had been flown out from Britain carrying a load of VIPs for the opening of the new Entebbe airport, and it was on its way back to London, empty. It, too, was scheduled to depart the following morning, but the army officer told the BOAC people, 'It will leave in two hours, otherwise it is impounded. Get the crew out here, get the plane refuelled, and take Mr Perry with you.' So inside a couple of hours I was on my way back to London, all alone in a plane with a crew of nine. They took more care of me!

I had a scarab, given to me by King Farouk and although I didn't know it at the time, I suspected that this scarab had a history. Soon afterwards I was in Sweden to help with their Davis Cup preparations and, as usual, I spent a while on court with their new tennis-playing king, Gustav. I used to flip my scarab up and down from time to time because I carried it loose in my pocket – rather as George Raft used to do in the film *Scarface* – and one day the King asked me what it was that I kept flipping in the air. When I showed him my present from King Farouk, Gustav was intrigued. He wondered if I knew anything about the history of these scarabs – I didn't, I had to admit. I wasn't aware either, at the time, that His Majesty was a keen archaeologist, with a special interest in these matters. He explained that my scarab was millions of years old and had been formed by the pressure of the rocks on the remains of a beetle. Apparently this fossil I had was a very good one, and therefore quite valuable. The King said, 'That would make a wonderful ring.' I agreed, and said I might have it done one day. So he suggested that if I had that in mind, there was only one man in the world who could do a proper job on it – his personal jeweller. 'Perhaps so, Your Majesty,' I said, 'but that's not in my league!'

The King took the scarab, saying he would see what could be done, and before I left Sweden he handed me a beautiful ring with my scarab splendidly set. It became one of my most precious possessions – a jewel given to me by the King of Egypt and made into a ring by the King of Sweden.

My wife used to wear it as a talisman whenever she flew anywhere alone, and my son David also coveted it. He finally took possession in a dramatic way. At the age of twenty-four, while driving in Jamaica, his car skidded under a truck, and David wound up gravely injured and unconscious in hospital. I flew out from England to be with him, and when he regained consciousness after two days the first words he uttered were, 'I almost didn't make it, did I?' So I gave him the ring he had always wanted as a good-luck keepsake.

A bit of good luck, allied to a lot of practice and firmness, was what I needed when I agreed to manage a European professional tour for Jack Kramer in the late fifties. The playing troupe consisted of the Australians Frank Sedgman and Rex Hartwig, and the Americans Tony Trabert and Pancho Gonzales. The great Gonzales, a wonderful player but a loner, was the one who tested my patience and firmness to the full on that tour. I quickly found that the way to handle him was to make sure he was happy, and almost as quickly discovered that it was not wise to give in to him. I really do think that deep down Gonzales had a certain respect for me and my accomplishments in the game, and I'm sure this was the only reason I had any influence over him. But he also knew that I meant what I said, and was prepared to back it up.

Gonzales loved to gamble. He said he had decided not to get involved in any gambling on the tour, so he asked me to hold his money for him. One morning, at about four o'clock, there was a banging on my bedroom door. There stood Gonzales, large and menacing. 'I want some more money,' he said. I started to argue, but rather than get punched I caved in, went down to the hotel safe deposit box and let him have his cash.

Perhaps Gonzales regarded this as a sign of weakness, because other incidents quickly followed. Hartwig and Trabert didn't get on very well with Gonzales, as I soon discovered. In Scheveningen, Holland, they were teamed against him in a doubles match. A Gonzales serve to Hartwig was called a fault, which really riled him. Just as he was winding up for his second serve, Hartwig called out, 'The rules apply to you, too, you know. You're supposed to hit the ball inside the lines, champ.' Gonzales' next serve almost hit the baseline, drawing the comment from Hartwig, 'Not very accurate for a world champion.' By now Gonzales was carrying a personal thundercloud over his head.

Next it was Gonzales' turn to serve to Trabert, while Hartwig stood at the net. The first serve almost took Hartwig's head off. 'Not very accurate for a world champion,' repeated Hartwig, so the next ball was aimed at his head, too. There was uproar in the crowd and Gonzales decided he would take a long walk around the confines of the stadium while he cooled down.

I hurried on to court and talked to him in a corner, wanting to know just what the hell was going on. After he had explained what had happened I told him he had two options: either go back and finish the match or pack up and go home to America, which, I said, was perfectly OK with me. 'Who's going to take over?' he wanted to know. 'I'll take over,' I said. 'I used to play quite a bit around here.' I didn't add that it was about twenty years ago! Eventually Gonzales calmed down and said he would play on, but he was rumbling away like a volcano and it was clear another eruption wasn't far away.

After Scheveningen we had four days free until we were due to play in Luxembourg. The boys were upset that they weren't making money and asked me to fill in something. So I got hold of Martin Plaa, a French professional who had once toured with Tilden and who ran a club at La Baule. He agreed to set up a match there, but because of the short notice the attendance was poor, which upset Gonzales again. He moaned that if he was going to be hanging around like this he would rather spend his money in his own country with his friends, so again I reminded him he could leave the tour any time he felt like it.

Our next stopover was in Luxembourg; but as Gonzales and the others were flying and I was driving I said I had had enough. He could tell me before dinner the next evening whether he intended to play the tour my way or not at all. Naturally all the others were agog at the dinner table, awaiting Gonzales' arrival. He strolled up and started to sit down. 'Just a minute, haven't you forgotten something?' I said. 'You promised me a decision before dinner about which way you were going to play this tour.' 'Your way, of course,' he said, and that was the end of our troubles.

After my Russian visit in 1958 I went straight to Florida to help supervise the construction of the tennis facilities and the hiring of sports personnel for a new hotel called the Diplomat at Hallendale. I found the place in chaos because of a simple mathematical error: Instead of excavating six inches to lay the tennis courts, the construction teams had gone down six feet, which is well below the water table in a low-lying place like Florida. The result was that we were looking at the world's biggest swimming pool; I think it cost the owners almost as much to fill in the hole as it had done to dig it.

As the time for opening neared in the autumn of 1959 all sorts of minor problems cropped up to plague us, but the most memorable of these, in which I was involved, was the matter of the horse pee.

It happened this way. The new clubhouse had a very attractive dining room and bar, behind which was a copper partition. However, when the copper was installed it was too bright, too new, for the likes of the hotel's interior decorator, Franklin Hughes. 'We've got to do something about that goddam copper before we open,' said Hughes, and when he was asked for ideas he said, 'Well, the best thing in the world to dull it down is horse pee. That will turn it green overnight.'

So he asked if any of us knew anybody who owned horses nearby. Guess who held up his hand? One of my greatest pals – and godfather to my daughter Penny – is Freddie van Lennup. He and his wife Frances, a daughter of the Dodge automobile family, owned Castleton Farms, a breeding, trotting and show horse complex in Lexington, Kentucky, and their winter headquarters were in Pompano Beach, Florida, a scant half hour's drive away. So I went to see Freddie. 'There's no problem providing what you want, Fred,' he said. 'The problems are collecting it and getting it to you.' He told me to come back the next morning in an old station-wagon and to bring tarpaulins.

Freddie was as good as his word. He had collected the urine in large carboys, and when I asked what I owed him he said, 'All you have to do is pay for a new suit for the guy who collected it.' I drove back – carefully – to the Diplomat, where Hughes instructed the decorators to paint the urine over the bright copperwork. When they objected that it would ruin their brushes he promised to buy them new ones. So they brushed it on and it worked a treat: overnight the copper turned green.

The day before the hotel opened, the owner, Sam Friedland, came for an inspection. When he walked into the dining room he told the man who did the landscape gardening to change the fertilizer on the indoor plants because of the smell. 'That's not the plants, it's Perry's horse pee,' he was told. So they ended up spraying the place for twenty-four hours with air fresheners to get rid of the smell before the opening.

Sam Friedland wanted me to help bring Ben Hogan to the Diplomat, with the grand title of Director of Golf. Hogan wasn't interested, however, so I suggested Dr Cary Middlecoff, who had just won the US Open. I flew to California to talk to Middlecoff, who wasn't sure if he needed such a commitment. He hummed and hawed and beat around the bush before asking me, 'Are you going there?' 'Yes,' I said. 'Well, that's good enough for me, I'll go too,' he said.

Middlecoff stayed there for three years altogether but I left after only two. For myself, teaching tennis was getting to be more and more of a chore, and my arm still hurt whenever I played. Rather like Bjorn Borg in 1983, it got to the stage where I couldn't face the thought of tennis. Having to turn up at 9 a.m. to give somebody a lesson was no fun any more.

Still, I must say, my last tennis coaching assignment ended in some style. The family Gidwitz from Chicago, who owned the Helen Curtis cosmetic company, were staying at the hotel. There were eleven of them and the father was the only one who didn't play tennis. I had to give lessons to the other ten, and by the time I left the Diplomat I was suffering from Gidwitzs before the eyes.

Though disillusionment with tennis teaching was one reason for my leaving the Diplomat Hotel post, another was the prospect of an attractive job on what I consider to be the greatest island in the Caribbean, Jamaica. It had all started a couple of years earlier when, walking down Conduit Street in London, I ran into my old school chum turned building magnate, Bernard Sunley. Pulling his leg, I told him I was angry with him for building a hotel in Nassau and failing to ask me to put in a Fred Perry School of Tennis.

Sunley took my arm and told me to come with him to his office, where he had a project in which I might be much more interested. Sunley and a Jamaican called Roy Lindo, whom I had met when I visited the island in the 1930s with the British tennis team, had bought property at a gorgeous spot on the north shore of Jamaica called Runaway Bay, and they intended to build a hotel and golf course there.

He suggested I help to get the whole thing off the ground, and after making the short hop from Florida by plane to look at the site I knew Runaway Bay was right up my alley. But I told Sunley that, because we had known each other since school, I couldn't possibly work *for* him. I was, however, prepared to work *with* him, and it was agreed I would be in charge of the Runaway Bay golf concession. So F. J. Perry acquired an unusual title to add to his collection – Director of Golf.

Sunley wanted me to spend the winter season at Runaway Bay, so we made a wonderful deal that my family could live in the hotel as guests while I was operating the golf. The place was supposed to open in December 1961, but when I turned up in the middle of November nothing was finished, so I sent Sunley a telegram asking whether I was supposed to live under a palm tree and eat coconuts until the place was ready. Then I went back to Florida for the winter, only returning the following March, when the place was completed.

After that, Jamaica became my main winter base, though I would fly up to the United States from time to time for appearances and TV commentary commitments. Gradually we built up the golf and got the course open, though the importation of equipment was always a problem and has now become extremely complicated and expensive. Mine was the first golf course in Jamaica to have golf carts. They were bright, fire-engine red, and it was a proud day when I went down to Kingston Harbour to watch them being unloaded. I was a good deal less proud, however, when the first cart was swung out of the ship's hold and fell from a considerable height on to the dockside, which didn't do it any good at all. But they managed to offload the other five without smashing them to bits.

The story of how the broken golf cart was eventually mended will give you some idea of the fascinations and frustrations of life in Jamaica. Bobby and I used to take drives after dinner – all very romantic, moonlight and palm trees. One evening we got a flat tyre, so I turned into the car park of a night club to try to fix it. As I was struggling to change the wheel, a huge Jamaican loomed up out of the night, offered to fix the tyre for me, and did so in no time at all. Like just about everybody else in Jamaica he had a nickname by which he was known all the time; in his case it was 'Africa'. Africa said he had worked for Mercedes Benz in Kingston for three years, but was now looking for work.

I told him to join me for a sandwich at Runaway Bay the next day and we would talk about it. When he turned up I showed him the damaged golf cart, which nobody had been able to repair, and asked him if he had ever seen such a machine either at Mercedes Benz or any other place. He hadn't, but said he would spend a minute or two looking at it while I organized the sandwiches. I waited about an hour for him in the clubhouse and was beginning to get really teed off. I wanted my sandwich and wasn't about to go all the way over to the golf course to fetch Africa. Suddenly, hearing the sound of motorized transport, I looked out of the door. It was Africa, proudly tootling up in the red golf cart. 'You're hired,' I said.

He was an absolutely brilliant engineer, but totally without a sense of discipline. Gradually we got the fleet of carts up to fifty and he looked after the lot. He was a priceless man to have around, but eventually, at the hotel's insistence, we had to part company with him. There was a 'halfway house' on the golf course which wasn't doing much business in thirsty golfers. Nobody could figure out why. Until we found out that Africa was taking one of the carts to the nearest supermarket, filling it with soft drinks and beer, and selling them at a comfortable profit on the course.

Once I literally ran into a bunch of less charming rascals in Jamaica. I had a Triumph Herald at the time, and was driving over the mountains on a business trip to Kingston. I wasn't going very fast because of the winding roads, which was just as well because, when I rounded one sharp corner, there right in front of me was a cement lorry parked in the middle of the road.

I slammed on my brakes, slid slowly into the truck and jammed underneath it. Unfortunately the lorry had a puncture, and as the tyre went down the vehicle descended on top of my car, trapping me even more firmly. I couldn't get out and appealed to the men at the scene to help me, but they wouldn't even open the door until I wound down the window and passed each of them a few pounds to come to the rescue. I didn't much like doing that, but it was preferable to spending the night under a cement truck. Apart from that little incident, our time in Jamaica has been wonderful.

One of the highlights of our lives there was the fun we had playing host to the various visiting cricket teams at Runaway Bay. The first to arrive were the Cavaliers, a notable band which included Tom Graveney, Freddie Trueman, Godfrey Evans, Ted Dexter, Colin Cowdrey and Denis Compton. We also had Cowdrey's England XI, and Colin Milburn, 'Knotty' Knott and Ken Barrington. We even had Bobby Simpson's Aussies, who were greeted coming in for dinner by a calypso band playing 'Waltzing Matilda'. Some of the lads were laughing and crying at the same time, especially the young ones who had never been away from home before. Cricketers of no matter what nationality looked forward to their little breaks at Runaway Bay. They could play golf and forget all their troubles, enjoying a touch of Old England in the sunshine.

I must tell you a funny story about my old friend Denis Compton, among the original Cavaliers who came out with Jim Laker and Tom Graveney. It was a fun tour of friendly games, kicking off with three days of whooping and hollering at Runaway Bay. The night before the friendly match between the Cavaliers and Jamaica, Sir Frank Worrell, the Jamaican skipper, insisted on returning to Kingston to spend the night with his team and make sure they at least got to bed at some point, despite the fact that it was only a friendly the next day.

The same constraints were not placed upon the Cavaliers, and at eight o'clock in the morning some of their number practically had to be poured on the bus to wheel them to Sabina Park. They arrived at the venue at about 10.15 ready for an 11.30 start, but Compton, in particular, was still not seeing the ball terribly well.

Sadly, the Cavaliers lost two quick wickets, so Compton had to go in before lunch, an unlooked-for burden. They showed him where the wicket was and Sir Frank Worrell walked at his side in case of any sudden unevenness in the turf which might incommode him on his way to the middle; everyone thought what a wonderful gesture it was for the great Frank Worrell to go out on the battlefield with the great Denis Compton. Actually they were having an argument as to how many runs they were going to allow Compton before they tried to get him out. After considerable disagreement, it was decided that 25 was the decent figure. But Compton took over two hours to get 25, by which time a good lunch and a lot of fresh air had improved his vision no end, and they couldn't get him out at all. As they came off the field, the crowd could see Frank Worrell's lips moving, no doubt expressing his heartfelt congratulations for a fine knock, and they thought what a marvellous gesture that was. Actually Worrell was saying, 'Never again, Denis. Never again.'

I became great friends with Cowdrey's England XI and as I'd never seen a Test match in England, I went along to the Oval some years later to see them playing the Australians. They were trying to winkle out Wally Grout, and it came on to rain. Then in the middle of the morning an announcement came over the loudspeaker: 'Would Mr Fred Perry please go immediately to the Secretary's office.' It turned out that the television people were looking for me because Princess Marina, President of the All England Club, had sadly passed away, and I was needed to do an obituary that night on the Eamonn Andrews programme. This was a surprise to me, because I thought an official might be a more appropriate spokesman for the Club; but it seemed they had expressly asked for me to do the tribute. When I walked into the England dressing room, the match had taken a sorry turn: the ground was flooded, and Cowdrey was busily organizing 200 schoolboys to poke the turf with stumps to let the water off, ready for Derek Underwood to mop up the Aussies. The lads took a dim view of my name being broadcast over the loudspeaker at the Oval, hogging the limelight, and when I left they still hadn't got Wally Grout out. I've yet to see a wicket fall in an England Test.

Through the sportswear business and our offices over in London,

I'd got to know both the Australian and West Indian cricketers, who used the place as their headquarters while they were there. Gary Sobers and Jackie Hendricks happened to be spending a weekend at Runaway Bay while I was in a spot of difficulty getting a couple of steamer trunks over the mountain. My wife Bobby had already left for England, and I was trying to transport our trunks in my little Triumph to Kingston, to get them on the boat. One trunk would get up the mountain, but two would not. Sobers and Hendricks said they would help me out by delivering one to the dock, so I arrived at the quayside, and waited and waited. Everyone was in a muck sweat to load on the missing trunk, and it grew later and later. Still no sign of Sobers and Hendricks: perhaps they'd slid back down the mountain. Finally, a few minutes before the absolute deadline, up rolled Gary Sobers with the trunk. They only let him in because he was Gary Sobers. He calmly announced that they'd met a friend on the way and had passed the time of day with him, talking over old times. 'Soon come,' as everyone says in Jamaica. Even our donkey was called 'Soon Come'.

One of the most interesting guests we ever had at Runaway Bay was Congressman Fulton from Pittsburg, Pennsylvania. He was in Jamaica for a vacation and had brought his secretary, who happened to be a paraplegic and who normally had a permanent male nurse to accompany him. Unfortunately the male nurse had disappeared in Kingston with a friend, so Congressman Fulton and his secretary were about to return to Washington with no nurse. We had had a caddy at Runaway Bay at that time who was a man of many talents and had an American visa to work in the citrus groves in Florida when he wasn't being a caddy or a cook. His name was Egbert Smith, and we set up the jungle drums over the island to summon him from his home in the hills. These days the caddies get pictures of Egbert in a dinner jacket at this or that function in Washington, because he is now the permanent nurse of Congressman Fulton's secretary.

Congressman Fulton happened to be the chairman of the Space Committee, and this was before the days of space travel which we all now rather take for granted. On rainy Jamaican days, of which we had quite a few, he would sit down and explain all about the forthcoming space shots. He would tell me how the various booster stages were worked out, how eventually they would send a rocket up with a man in it (this was to be Shepherd), how they would orbit the earth (Glenn), and how ultimately they would go and look at the moon and decide where to land when the time came. Fulton even sent us a classified picture of the landing site, marked with an 'X'. This was over twenty years ago, so you can imagine how incredible it all sounded when he explained about having a man walking outside the rocket with a line attached (the astronaut White), and having a capsule land on the moon's surface to rejoin with the main craft at a specified time. I suppose, if you happen to be an astronaut, everything else must be an anti-climax once you can look up at a wonderful full moon at night and think, 'I've walked around up there.'

We have lived twenty-three happy winters in Jamaica; but the island, the politics and the hotel set-up have all changed. Since Runaway Bay opened, there have been seven or eight lessees and I have not found the past few years easy. The country's economy has declined and the government doesn't consider golf and tennis equipment to be urgently needed imports. We are now down to nine or ten golf carts, not enough by any stretch of the imagination for the tourists who want to play in the heat. We need import licences for new carts, but these are virtually impossible to obtain and even if they weren't, the rate of exchange with the US dollar pushes the price out of reach.

The government eventually bought the hotel from the Sunley company and in 1982 closed it between May and December for renovation, though the golf course stayed open and I ran it according to the original contract. Nothing was done for the clubhouse because they had spent all the available funds on the hotel. When the place reopened I found myself in the middle of arguments between rival government officials. That, plus the fact that we simply didn't have any merchandise to offer the customers, meant that we left the hotel early in 1983, around Easter time. I don't look to the future at Runaway Bay with much optimism.

Though I have done plenty of work with both radio and television, I prefer the former medium. Perhaps it's because I was growing up when the radio was born, or simply because on television there is really very little need to say anything, whereas I love to talk.

I did my first BBC broadcast in 1948 with Max Robertson, and it quickly became an annual arrangement which I continue to enjoy. I have had some hilarious times and some anxious moments, just as I did in my playing career. In the old days of the French Championships our operating space in the Roland Garros Stadium used to be in the open air. Max tends to get very excited when he does his commentary and once, as he kept jumping up and down, spectators started hitting him over the head with umbrellas and bags because he was obstructing their view.

At the end of the day's play in Paris we used to make our way to the BBC sound van to do the round-up. On one occasion, since it was lovely weather in London, they had trouble believing that there was rain in Paris, so I added what I hoped was an authentic touch to my commentary by dangling the mike over a pool of water and letting the audience listen to the plip-plop of the raindrops. I suppose I could have been blown off the air.

Much similar improvisation was needed in the years when ITV used to cover Wimbledon and employed me as a would-be counter-attraction to my old friend Dan Maskell on BBC television. We were simply not able to compete and I wasn't unhappy when ITV gave it up as a bad job. The BBC had two channels against ITV's one, and were not inhibited by commercial breaks every fifteen minutes and the imposition of a strict time limit on the coverage, as ITV was. Viewers simply switched over when the adverts came on, in case they were missing something. So we were dead ducks on ITV really.

The BBC also had plenty of archive material to slot in when the weather turned bad, whereas ITV relied on people like me to fill the air time with chat whenever the heavens opened over Wimbledon. In ITV's first year of Wimbledon coverage, there was a long break because of the weather and I was ordered to report to our 'studio' – which was a tent – to help Emlyn Jones pass the time with some chit-chat. In the end we had to prattle on for an hour and a half and eventually even I ran out of things to talk about, so I said to Emlyn, 'How many people do you think there are in this studio?' A little startled, he looked around and said, 'About eighteen.' 'Well, in that case, why is it we can't even get a cup of tea in here?' I said. Somebody at the back of the tent got the message and called, 'Coming right up.' Our refreshment arrived and another minute or two was thankfully filled up on the cup-of-tea theme until our air time ran out.

On other occasions, however, we, and the viewers, were a bit luckier. One day, as I was going into Wimbledon, I saw Bing Crosby standing outside the Church Road entrance. He said he was trying to buy a ticket from a tout. I told him not to worry – ITV would get him admitted – and a little later Bing did a 'thank-you' appearance on our show.

All the fabulous trips that my wife Bobby and I have been able to make over the past twenty-five years would not have been possible had not Miss Eve Bishop come into our lives in 1959 and subsequently become part of the family. She is the anchor that holds it together. She knows more about the Perrys than we do ourselves. Without her we would really be up a gumtree.

There have been more than the usual amount of comings and goings, to some of the most exotic and interesting places in the world. One of my trips took me to Lebanon for an exhibition match. President Caecamille Chamoun decided to honour me with the decoration of the Order of the Cedar, but when he realized that our sportswear emblem was a laurel wreath, he upgraded my award, just like that, to the Chevalier of the Order of the Cedar, which happened to have a laurel wreath on it, though I had special instructions not to wear my insignia to any Lebanese nightclubs. A similar sort of thing occurred in New York, when I was presented by the Mayor John Lindsay with the Key to the City. I asked the Mayor what this would do for me, and he replied, 'That and 50 cents will get you on a bus the same as everybody else.'

There were also the wonderful South African trips, eleven in all, while I was covering their championships for radio and television, sponsorship courtesy of the South African Breweries. We'd spend three weeks each year in Johannesburg, Durban and Cape Town, and after years of trying, we finally got to travel on the sumptuously posh Blue Train, which for me comes pretty close to being one of the Seven Wonders of the World.

In Johannesburg I became friendly with the famous heart surgeon Christiaan Barnard, who was fascinated by the way the tapes were spliced and edited in the recording booth at Ellis Park. One night, while I was running up and down the staircase, Bobby chanced to remark that I'd have a heart attack. 'If ever you do,' said the world-famous Christiaan, 'send for me.' Well, immediately following the much-hyped 'chauvinist pig' match between Bobby Riggs and Billie Jean King in Houston, Texas, some promoters got in touch with me and asked if I would be interested in playing King myself. I hadn't played tennis for many years, but thought it worth looking into. Tongue in cheek, I made a couple of conditions. I said I must insist on the match being a straight tennis contest without any carnival atmosphere. Fine, they said, and don't worry about money: that's all taken care of. My other condition was more perplexing for them. I said, 'You must invite Christiaan Barnard over from South Africa to sit on my side of the court and change ends whenever I do.' I didn't hear any more about that match.

Our last visit to South Africa was in 1980, which was memorable chiefly for the way in which we travelled home. We had been invited to return to the USA by way of Buenos Aires, as fifty years previously I had won my first national championship, the Argentinian, at Buenos Aires LTC. I stood at the top of the stands looking down on the court and half a century flashed by: it was a tremendous feeling. The celebrations went on for three days and nights – we never even went to bed – and after that we were supposed to stop off at Rio de Janeiro as well, on the way to Miami. Bobby looked at me and I looked at her, and we looked at our baggage coming off the plane and said this was one stopover we weren't going to make. By that time we were practically unconscious.

Although I celebrated my seventy-fifth birthday in May 1984, I still manage to go on living out of a suitcase – good health permitting!

My year continues to be a busy one and, I'm happy to say, a combination of attractive places and big tennis events. My role as one of the three people nominated by the International Tennis Federation to award the annual title of men's world champion means that I am able to travel to the French, Wimbledon and US Championships to watch the top people perform. Philippe Chatrier, President of the ITF, felt that the Federation should choose a world champion, since so many newspapermen and associations had their own ranking lists, and the Association of Tennis Professionals had their computer rankings. Chatrier invited Lew Hoad to represent the Australian part of the world, Don Budge the American part, and myself for Europe, and this has worked extremely well over the past six years, though the women's panel has been dissolved because of an arrangement between their Association and Virginia Slims.

My year gets under way in January at the Masters Championship in New York, when Budge, Hoad and I meet to choose the world champion for the previous year. After the Masters, I do a series of clinics for children and women's clubs, some privately and some on behalf of Fred Perry Sportswear, in the United States. With the women's clubs we usually work the theme round to Wimbledon – either a Wimbledon tea or a Strawberries and Cream day – or else we have a Fred Perry day. I try to offer advice to each member before we all sit down to tea, followed by a question-and-answer period.

Then I go to Jamaica for the months of February and March,

though sadly, with the problems facing us in the business now, this may not be on our future schedule. Next we embark on a series of children's teaching clinics in the United States which continue until the time comes to set off for Europe and the French and Wimbledon Championships. After Wimbledon it's back to the United States and more coaching clinics, before going to Flushing Meadow for the US Open at the end of August. Then I work my way down to Florida with more teaching sessions and promotional appearances for the sportswear people, before taking a break at our home in Pompano Beach.

Come December, off we go to Runaway Bay for a month until the wheel rolls full circle and we pack up and move off to New York in January for the Masters again. It's a pretty hectic schedule, even for a fit young fellow of seventy-five who practically skips up the hospital steps to see his specialists, but then I've always tried to look at tennis as a game of no excuses. Whenever I'm asked about a player's chances when going into a match with an injured shoulder, or a pulled stomach muscle, my reply is always the same: if he goes out on court and stands behind that baseline, he's fit and ready to go. There are no excuses.

I mentioned earlier about being nominated by the ITF to help choose the world champion of tennis. In 1984, during the Masters, Budge, Hoad and I were supposed to be in New York as usual, but two days before my departure I was thrown into hospital once again, this time with pneumonia of the right lung, so I wasn't able to be present at the matches. However, the telephone lines were kept open on the Sunday morning while the world champion nomination meeting was in progress, so that I could give my personal views and make my vote. It so happened that Budge had decided to go with John McEnroe, while Hoad was holding out for Max Willander; I voted for McEnroe from the hospital bed, though it wasn't easy for me to talk with tubes sticking out of my arm and drips going in and out of every aperture.

This year, 1984, is a special one, not only because of the big celebrations on my account – of which I am more proud than I can say – but because 1984 is also the 100th anniversary of the Women's Championship, and all the living lady champions have been invited along for the festivities. It should be quite a centenary if it is anything like the one we had in 1977, the 100th anniversary of the championships, when Virginia Wade won the singles title so miraculously.

194

HM the Queen, in her Jubilee Year, was present on that day, and the former British holders of the men's and women's titles were invited to tea with the royal family. The girls sat at one table with the Duke of Edinburgh, and I was host to the gathering that sat with Queen Elizabeth. She was particularly interested to find out how the players felt on Centre Court, with fifteen or sixteen thousand people looking on, and she intimated to me that it was quite an experience even for her to step from behind that barrier on to the hallowed court itself to the thunder of cheering from that vast arena.

Her Majesty asked me how I'd felt that day long ago when the trophies were presented to the Wimbledon men's champion, and she was completely taken aback when I told her that the great day was the Silver Jubilee of her grandfather George V, but that before the Second World War there *were* no presentations. And then I explained about the champion getting his name on cups he never saw, about the replica of the Renshaw Cup, the gold medal, the voucher, and the purple ribbon with the laurel wreath on it. I also told Her Majesty that I was taken to the Bank of England under guard to have my picture taken with those two Wimbledon trophies that these days the champions proudly hold aloft. The Queen appeared to be most intrigued by all this, as today the presentation ceremony is one of the highlights of the tournament and the photographs of it go all around the world.

All the major trophies that I won as an amateur were presented to the Lawn Tennis Museum at the All England Club, along with all my medals, and they are there and will always be there for everyone to see, for perpetuity. But when anyone asks me what I got when I won the championship, I always have to smile, because they expect me to say, oh, so many thousand pounds. You know what I got? Tea with the Committee – with two sugars, I must admit.

How times have changed, because my lifelong love affair with Wimbledon has now been crowned with a ceremony beyond my wildest imaginings, when His Royal Highness the Duke of Kent unveiled the Fred Perry Gates at the Somerset Road entrance and dedicated the statue of me 'as I used to be'. The occasion meant more to me than all the prize money in the world, though I rather wonder what my inner feelings will be when I walk into Wimbledon in future to do my various chores for the championships, and not only pass myself going in but going out as well. To be able to do that, as *Time* magazine pointed out all those years ago, 'a bloke needs a little bit of luck'.

I've had that luck and I'm grateful. It's true I've got a lot of mileage on me, but there's still plenty of rubber on the tyres.

Fred Perry's Record

compiled by Alan Little

Davis Cup

1931
European Zone
First round v. Monaco at Plymouth, 23–25 April
beat R. Gallepe 6–3, 6–2, 7–5
Second round v. Belgium at Brussels, 9–11 May
beat L. de Borman 6–2, 6–0, 6–2
beat A. Lacroix 8–6, 6–4, 7–5
with G. P. Hughes beat Borman and Lacroix 6–1, 6–4, 6–2
Third round v. South Africa at Eastbourne, 4–6 June
beat N. G. Farquharson 6–2, 6–3, 6–3
beat V. G. Kirby 3–6, 6–4, 6–1, 6–4
with G. P. Hughes beat Farquharson and P. D. P. Spence 8–6, 6–4, 6–3
Semi-final v. Japan at Eastbourne, 12, 13, 15 June
beat J. Satoh 6–1, 4–6, 7–5, 7–5
beat H. Satoh 6–2, 6–3, 4–6, 6–2
with G. P. Hughes beat J. Satoh and M. Kawachi 6–4, 6–4, 8–6
Final v. Czechoslovakia at Prague, 9–11 July
beat L. Hecht 6–1, 8–6, 6–3
beat R. Menzel 7–5, 6–3, 7–5
with G. P. Hughes beat Menzel and F. Marsalek 6–4, 4–6, 6–4, 6–2
Inter-Zone Final
v. United States at Paris, 17–19 July
lost to F. X. Shields 8–10, 4–6, 2–6
beat S. B. Wood 6–3, 8–10, 6–3, 6–3
with G. P. Hughes lost to G. M. Lott and J. Van Ryn 1–6, 3–6, 6–4, 3–6
Challenge Round
v. France, Paris, 24–26 July
lost to H. Cochet 4–6, 6–1, 7–9, 3–6
beat J. Borotra 4–6, 10–8, 6–0, 4–6, 6–4

1932
European Zone
Second round v. Romania at Torquay, 14–16 May
beat N. Mishu 6–0, 6–1, 6–1
beat G. Poulieff 6–1, 6–2, 6–1
with G. P. Hughes beat Mishu and Poulieff 6–0, 6–1, 6–1

Third round v. Poland at Warsaw, 10–12 June
beat I. Tloczynski 7–5, 8–6, 6–2
beat M. Stolarow 6–3, 7–5, 6–4
with G. P. Hughes beat L. Hebda and P. Warminski 6–0, 6–2, 6–0

Semi-final v. Germany at Berlin, 8–10 July
lost to D. Prenn 2–6, 4–6, 6–3, 6–0, 5–7
beat G. von Cramm 6–1, 6–2, 6–3
with G. P. Hughes beat Prenn and W. Dressart 6–3, 6–4, 6–4

1933
European Zone
First round v. Spain at Barcelona, 21–23 April
beat E. Maier 7–5, 7–5, 6–2
beat F. Sinreu 6–1, 6–3, 6–0
with G. P. Hughes lost to Maier and A. Durall 3–6, 1–6, 6–1, 6–4, 3–6

Second round v. Finland at Queens Club 13, 15, 16 May
beat B. Grotenfelt 6–0, 6–3, 6–1
beat A. Grahn 6–1, 6–2, 6–4
with G. P. Hughes beat Grahn and Grotenfelt 6–1, 6–1, 6–3

Third round v. Italy at Eastbourne, 8–10 June
beat U. L. de Morpurgo 6–4, 7–5, 6–4
lost to G. de Stefani 7–5, 4–6, 4–6, 4–6
with G. P. Hughes beat A. Rado and V. Taroni 6–1, 6–4, 9–7

Semi-final v. Czechoslovakia at Eastbourne, 17, 19, 20 June
beat R. Menzel 6–1, 6–4, 6–3
beat L. Hecht 6–2, 6–2, 6–2
with G. P. Hughes beat Menzel and F. Marsalek 6–3, 6–4, 6–4

Final v. Australia at Wimbledon, 13–15 July
beat V. B. McGrath 6–4, 7–5, 6–3
with G. P. Hughes beat D. P. Turnbull and A. K. Quist 7–5, 6–4, 3–6, 6–3

Inter-Zone Final
v. United States at Paris, 21–23 July
beat W. L. Allison 6–1, 7–5, 6–4
beat H. Vines 1–6, 6–0, 4–6, 7–5, 7–6 (retd)
with G. P. Hughes lost to G. M. Lott and J. Van Ryn 6–8, 4–6, 1–6

Challenge Round
v. France at Paris, 28–30 July
beat H. Cochet 8–10, 6–4, 8–6, 3–6, 6–1
beat A. Merlin 4–6, 8–6, 6–2, 7–5

1934
Challenge Round
v. United States at Wimbledon, 28, 30, 31 July
beat S. B. Wood 6–1, 4–6, 5–7, 6–0, 6–3
beat F. X. Shields 6–4, 4–6, 6–2, 15–13

1935
Challenge Round
v. United States at Wimbledon, 27, 29, 30 July
beat J. D. Budge 6–0, 6–8, 6–3, 6–4
beat W. L. Allison 4–6, 6–4, 7–5, 6–3

1936
Challenge Round
v. Australia at Wimbledon, 25, 27, 28 July
beat A. K. Quist 6–1, 4–6, 7–5, 6–2
beat J. H. Crawford 6–2, 6–3, 6–3

Overall Record
Total ties: 20
Total matches: 52
Singles: won 34; lost 4
Doubles: won 11; lost 3

The Championships, Wimbledon

1929, 24 June–6 July
Singles: 1. beat C. Bocciardo (Italy) 7–5, 2–6, 6–4, 3–6, 9–7
             2. beat N. Dicks (GB) 3–6, 6–2, 6–2, 6–4
             3. lost to J. Olliff (GB) 4–6, 2–6, 6–2, 3–6
Doubles: (F. H. D. Wilde) first round (retd.)
Mixed: did not enter

1930, 23 June–5 July
Singles: 1. beat B. Hillyard (GB) 6–3, 6–4, 6–2
             2. beat O. Wright (GB) 6–1, 6–2, 6–3
             3. beat U. L. de Morpurgo (Italy) 10–8, 4–6, 6–1, 6–2
             4. lost to J. C. Gregory (GB) 6–3, 7–9, 1–6, 6–3, 1–6

Doubles: (F. H. D. Wilde) first round
Mixed: (Miss M. Heeley) first round

1931, 22 June – 4 July
Singles: 1. beat J. Cummins (GB) 6–1, 6–3, 6–3
      2. beat I. Aoki (Japan) 7–5, 6–2, 6–3
      3. beat A. Gentien (France) 6–2, 6–3, 8–6
      4. beat G. von Cramm (Germany) 7–5, 6–2, 6–4
      Q. beat J. Van Ryn (USA) 6–4, 8–6, 7–5
      S. lost to S. B. Wood (USA) 6–4, 2–6, 4–6, 2–6
Doubles: (G. P. Hughes) semi-final
Mixed: (Miss M. Heeley) semi-final

1932, 20 June–2 July
Singles: 1. beat G. O. Jameson (GB) 6–3, 6–2, 6–4
      2. beat H. F. David (GB) 6–4, 6–3, 5–7, 6–1
      3. beat J. Van Ryn (USA) 6–3, 6–4, 6–0
      4. beat W. L. Allison (USA) 6–4, 6–1, 4–6, 6–2
      Q. lost to J. H. Crawford (Australia) 5–7, 6–8, 6–2, 6–8
Doubles: (G. P. Hughes) final
Mixed: did not enter

1933, 26 June–8 July
Singles: 1. beat A. Lacroix (Belgium) 6–3, 6–3, 6–2
      2. lost to N. G. Farquharson (SA) 5–7, 1–6, 6–3, 6–4, 4–6
Doubles: (G. P. Hughes) quarter-final
Mixed: did not enter

1934, 25 June–7 July
Singles: 1. beat C. R. D. Tuckey (GB) 6–2, 6–2, 5–7, 6–0
      2. beat R. N. Williams (USA) 6–2, 6–2, 6–0
      3. beat R. Menzel (Czechoslovakia) 0–6, 6–3, 5–7, 6–4, 6–2
      4. beat A. K. Quist (Australia) 6–2, 6–3, 6–4
      Q. beat G. M. Lott (USA) 6–4, 2–6, 7–5 10–8
      S. beat S. B. Wood (USA) 6–3, 3–6, 7–5, 5–7, 6–3
      F. beat J. H. Crawford (Australia) 6–3, 6–0, 7–5
Doubles: (G. P. Hughes) second round
Mixed: did not enter

1935, 24 June–6 July
Singles: 1. beat M. Rainville (Canada) 6–1, 6–1, 6–3
      2. beat W. Hines (USA) 6–1, 7–5, 6–3
      3. beat J. Van Ryn (USA) 4–6, 6–1, 6–3, 10–8
      4. beat J. Pallada (Yugoslavia) 6–2, 6–2, 0–6, 6–2
      Q. beat R. Menzel (Czechoslovakia) 9–7, 6–1, 6–1
      S. beat J. H. Crawford (Australia) 6–2, 3–6, 6–4, 6–4
      F. beat G. von Cramm (Germany) 6–2, 6–4, 6–4
Doubles: did not enter
Mixed: (Miss D. E. Round) winner

1936, 22 June–4 July
Singles: 1. beat G. D. Stratford (USA) 6–4, 6–3, 6–1
        2. beat K. Chartikavanji (Siam) 6–3, 6–2, 6–2
        3. beat J. Van Ryn (USA) 6–3, 6–2, 6–0
        4. beat C. E. Malfroy (NZ) 6–2, 6–2, 6–4
        Q. beat B. M. Grant (USA) 6–4, 6–3, 6–1
        S. beat J. D. Budge (USA) 5–7, 6–4, 6–3, 6–4
        F. beat G. von Cramm (Germany) 6–1, 6–1, 6–0
Doubles: did not enter
Mixed: (Miss D. E. Round) winner

United States Championships

1930

Forest Hills, New York, 6, 8–13 September
Singles: 1. a bye
        2. beat S. Onda 6–4, 2–6, 6–2, 4–6, 6–4
        3. beat E. Jacobs (USA) 6–2, 6–3, 6–3
        4. lost to J. Van Ryn (USA) 6–4, 3–6, 4–6, 1–6
Longwood CC, Boston, 25–30 August

Doubles: (J. S. Olliff) quarter-final
Mixed: (Miss R. Oexman) second round

1931

Forest Hills, New York, 5–12 September
Singles: 1. beat J. Seligson 6–4, 7–5, 4–6, 6–0
        2. beat E. G. Tarangioli 6–3, 6–2, 10–8
        3. beat H. L. Bowman (USA) 6–3, 7–5, 6–2
        4. beat C. B. Sutter (USA) 4–6, 6–4, 6–3, 6–3
        Q. beat F. Bowden (USA) 6–2, 6–3, 6–4
        S. lost to H. E. Vines (USA) 6–4, 6–3, 4–6, 4–6, 3–6

Longwood CC, Boston, 24–29 August
Doubles: (G. P. Hughes) third round
Mixed: (Miss P. E. Mudford) second round

1932

Forest Hills, New York, 3–10 September
Singles: 1. a bye
        2. beat J. Lang (USA) 6–4, 6–2, 4–6, 6–0

        3. beat R. N. Williams (USA) 6–0, 6–2, 6–1
        4. lost to S. B. Wood (USA) 6–3, 6–4, 0–6, 0–6, 5–7

Longwood, CC, Boston, 22–27 August
Doubles: (H. W. Austin) quarter-final
Mixed: (Miss S. Palfrey) winner

1933

Forest Hills, New York, 2–9 September
Singles: 1. beat E. W. Burns (USA) 6–1, 6–1, 6–2
           2. beat R. Bryan (USA) 3–6, 6–3, 6–0, 6–3
           3. beat M. Hecht (Czechoslovakia) 6–1, 6–4, 6–4
           4. beat K. Gladhill (USA) 6–2, 4–6, 1–6, 6–3, 6–3
           Q. beat A. K. Quist (Australia) 6–4, 6–4, 6–0
           S. beat L. R. Stoefen (USA) 6–3, 6–2, 6–2
           F. beat J. H. Crawford (Australia) 6–3, 11–13, 4–6, 6–0, 6–1

Longwood CC, Boston, 21–26 August
Doubles: (F. D. H. Wilde) quarter-final
Mixed: (Miss D. E. Round) semi-final

1934

Forest Hills, New York, 1–8 September
Singles: 1. beat C. H. Schweikhardt (USA) 6–0, 6–1, 6–3
           2. beat M. Buxby (USA) 6–3, 6–1, 6–4
           3. beat J. Talbot (USA) 6–3, 6–1, 6–4
           4. beat E. W. Feibleman (USA) 6–2, 6–1, 6–2
           Q. beat C. Sutter (USA) 6–3, 6–0, 6–2
           S. beat V. G. Kirby (SA) 6–2, 2–6, 6–4, 6–2
           F. beat W. L. Allison (USA) 6–4, 6–3, 3–6, 1–6, 8–6

Germantown, Philadelphia, 20–25 August
Doubles: (F. H. D. Wilde) second round
Mixed: (Miss B. Nuthall) semi-final

1935

Forest Hills, New York, 29 August–6 September
Singles: 1. a bye
           2. beat A. S. Fowler (USA) 6–3, 6–2, 6–1
           3. beat L. Hartmann (USA) 6–4, 6–3, 7–5
           4. beat F. A. Parker (USA) 6–4, 6–2, 6–0
           Q. beat F. X. Shields (USA) 6–4, 4–6, 8–6, 6–0
           S. lost to W. L. Allison (USA) 5–7, 3–6, 3–6

Doubles: did not enter
Mixed: did not enter

1936

Forest Hills, New York, 3–12 September

Singles: 1. beat A. L. Jarvis (USA) 6–0, 6–0, 6–2
2. beat E. Sutter (USA) 8–6, 6–2, 6–1
3. beat D. N. Jones (USA) 6–3, 6–1, 4–6, 6–0
4. beat C. G. Mako (USA) 6–0, 6–3, 6–2
Q. beat H. M. Culley (USA) 6–3, 6–2, 6–1
S. beat B. M. Grant (USA) 6–4, 3–6, 7–5, 6–2
F. beat J. D. Budge (USA) 2–6, 6–2, 8–6, 1–6, 10–8

Doubles: did not enter
Mixed: did not enter

French Championships, Paris

1931, 17–31 May

Singles: 1. beat L. Gerand (France) w.o.
2. beat P. Goldschmidt (France) 6–0, 6–3, 6–3
3. beat M. Bernard (France) 6–4, 6–1, 6–4
4. lost to G. de Stefani (Italy) 3–6, 4–6, 7–5, 5–7

Doubles: (G. P. Hughes) semi-final
Mixed: (Miss M. Heeley) quarter-final

1932, 22 May–5 June

Singles: 1. a bye
2. beat A. Coutanson (France) 6–2, 6–3, 6–3
3. beat A. Gentien (France) 14–12, 4–6, 6–2, 6–2
4. beat F. Matejka (Austria) 6–2, 6–4, 6–4
Q. lost to R. Menzel (Czechoslovakia) 6–2, 1–6, 6–1, 3–6, 5–7

Doubles: (J. S. Olliff) semi-final
Mixed: (Miss B. Nuthall) winner

1933, 21 May–4 June

Singles: 1. a bye
2. beat R. Billandot (France) 6–1, 6–1, 6–2
3. beat J. Rimet (France) 6–3, 6–3, 6–3
4. beat R. Malacek (Czechoslovakia) 6–0, 4–6, 7–5, 6–3
Q. lost to J. Satoh (Japan) 6–1, 5–7, 4–6, 6–3, 2–6

Doubles: (G. P. Hughes) winner
Mixed: (Miss B. Nuthall) final

1934, 20 May–3 June

Singles: 1. a bye

    2. beat J. Augustin (France) 6–4, 6–1, 6–1
    3. beat F. Merlin (France) 6–2, 6–3, 6–4
    4. beat H. C. Hopman (Australia) 6–2, 6–3, 6–3
    Q. lost to G. de Stefani (Italy) 2–6, 6–1, 7–9, 2–6

Doubles: (G. P. Hughes) third round
Mixed: did not enter

1935, 19 May–2 June
Singles: 1. a bye
    2. beat V. Landau (Monaco) 3–6, 6–4, 6–3, 6–2
    3. beat E. Maier (Spain) 6–2, 6–4, 6–2
    4. beat D. P. Turnbull (Australia) 6–3, 6–3; 6–3
    Q. beat C. Boussus (France) 6–1, 6–0, 6–4
    S. beat J. H. Crawford (Australia) 6–3, 8–6, 6–3
    F. beat G. von Cramm (Germany) 6–3, 3–6, 6–1, 6–3

Doubles: (C. R. D. Tuckey) semi-final
Mixed: did not enter

1936, 19 May–1 June
Singles: 1. a bye
    2. beat R. George (France) 7–5, 8–6, 9–7
    3. beat F. Terrier (France) 6–0, 6–4, 6–4
    4. beat A. Martin Legeay (France) 6–2, 6–3, 0–6, 6–3
    Q. beat E. Maneff (Switzerland) 9–7, 6–3, 4–6, 6–3
    S. C. Boussus (France) 6–4, 7–5, 5–7, 6–2
    F. lost to G. von Cramm 0–6, 6–2, 2–6, 6–2, 0–6

Doubles: (H. W. Austin) semi-final
Mixed: did not enter

Australian Championships

1934, at Sydney, 18–27 January
Singles: 1. beat L. O. S. Poidevin (Australia) 6–3, 6–2, 2–6, 6–2
    2. beat J. Rodgers (Australia) 6–0, 8–6, 6–3
    Q. beat H. C. Hopman (Australia) 6–3, 6–4, 6–3
    S. beat V. B. McGrath (Australia) 2–6, 5–7, 6–4, 6–4, 6–1
    F. beat J. H. Crawford (Australia) 6–3, 7–5, 6–1

Doubles: (G. P. Hughes) winner

1935, at Melbourne, 3–12 January
Singles: 1. beat J. Mahony (Australia) 6–3, 6–4, 6–2
    2. beat R. Malcolm (SA) 6–2, 6–3, 6–0
    Q. beat G. de Stefani (Italy) 6–0, 6–0, 6–0
    S. beat V. B. McGrath (Australia) 6–2, 6–3, 6–1

F. lost to J. H. Crawford (Australia) 6–3, 4–6, 4–6, 4–6
Doubles: (G. P. Hughes) final
Mixed: (Miss D. E. Round) quarter-final